SYBASE

REPLICATION SERVER

An Administrator's Guide

JOHN KIRKWOOD

and

GARRY ARKLE

Sybase Replication Server: An Administrator's Guide

By John Kirkwood and Garry Arkle

ISBN: 0 9537155 0 7

First published 1999 by

Kirkwood Associates Limited
19 Ruskin Way
Wokingham
RG41 3BP

Produced in the United Kingdom by

The Short Run Book Company Ltd
St Stephen's House, Arthur Road
Windsor, Berkshire SL4 1RY

Preface

This book describes Sybase Replication Server for those involved in setting up and administering the Replication Server. It covers the architecture of the replication environment, the Replication Server architecture, how to define the required replication and how to troubleshoot the Replication Server if there is a problem.

The book is in three parts: architecture, replication definition and maintenance and monitoring and troubleshooting. Chapters 1 and 2 describe the architecture of Sybase Replication Server; how Sybase implements replication and how the internals Replication Server components process the messages. Chapters 3 – 10 describe how to set up and maintain the replication system; discussing publishing, subscribing, functions and function strings and overall replication aspects such as Warm Standby. Chapters 11 – 16 describe the more interesting aspects of installation, monitoring and troubleshooting the Replication Server.

This administration guide is intended to be applicable to all levels of expertise. The beginner will gain an understanding of how Replication Server works and be able to build and maintain the replication system. The expert will find the internals chapter informative and I would be surprised if you do not learn something from the configuration and troubleshooting chapters.

If you are new to using Replication Server start from the administration chapters 3 – 10 and then tackle the architecture and troubleshooting chapters in any order. As a separate study you may find the installation chapter 13 useful before you get too involved. If you have already set up a Replication Server, you will probably gain more by sampling the first two chapters on the architecture and then skipping to the troubleshooting chapters 11 – 16. The bulk of the administration chapters 3 – 10 will be worth a visit but I would expect that they will be most useful as reference material.

That's about it. I hope that you gain something from the material. It represents many years of experience with the product for both Garry and myself. I hope that you find it a good read as it is not easy writing about boring subjects and we have tried to keep it as readable as possible. I hope that you find it so.

Thank You

John Kirkwood and Garry Arkle

Contents

1

Architecture

Introduction

Before we get into a detailed treatment of Sybase Replication it is useful to define the type of data distribution and the approach to replication that we are dealing with. This chapter looks at data distribution in general and the architecture that suits replication best. We then look at the various approaches to replication and drill down further on this to define the Sybase approach and architecture.

The Sybase Replication Server supports replicated data across multiple databases, maintaining the replicate copies in an asynchronous manner. The replication of the primary data changes preserves the source transaction, ensuring the integrity and consistency of the replicated data. Sybase replication allows the schema of the replicated data to be different to the primary data: as part of this facility you may also alter the execution of the primary database command at each replicate site. Sybase also supports the replication of procedure execution, which can be a factor in reducing the network activity.

Data Distribution

Why distribute data at all? Why not just hold it all centrally and provide enough connectivity to allow everyone to login? It certainly makes security easier and can simplify the backup and recovery options.

The principal reason for data distribution is that the current communication technologies are not as fast as we need to support a high performance central configuration. Or, if they are, they are prohibitively expensive and we need to adopt a cheaper solution. Another compelling reason is that computer power has tended to decentralize. The local sites have a large investment in hardware and see no reason why they should lose control of their data to a remote central resource.

Local sites may have had complete control over when they run programs and how fast these programs execute based on the mixture of work being rigorously controlled. Giving up this control to a central resource which is also running other applications, often means that the individual applications suffer a performance degradation. Because the applications are sharing the central resource there can often be a loss of autonomy over exactly when certain processes can run. Once the application and data go central there can be times when the system is no longer available, not because of a problem with the application but because another application has created a problem at tje central resource.

As it can make sense from performance, availability and reliability aspects, there is often a significant argument for locating the data close to the user in a distributed architecture. The simple introduction of the network into the architecture, especially on a Wide Area Network (WAN) basis, can significantly lower the performance and reliability of the application. Local processing does not eliminate all problems but it can remove some of them from the equation. Distribution brings problems of its own – this book is devoted to one of them: keeping multiple copies of data up-to-date. However design and implementation problems with replication are becoming easier to solve as the vendors catch up with the requirements of replicated architectures.

Another important reason for distributed data in modern architectures is the existence of legacy applications i.e. working applications which must co-exist with the new systems being developed. It is often the case that the existing systems do not fit into the new architecture and are either different hardware and software and/or they are geographically remote from the new operations area.

In summary there are several reasons for having to support a distributed architecture, most of which are business aligned. I like to summarize them as in table 1.1.

Reason	Justification
Availability/reliability	The network, especially a WAN, is often the least reliable component in most system architectures and local placement of data can remove any problems with wide area network failures or delays.
Performance	The network has tended to lag behind the other infrastructure components in increased throughput and is often the capacity bottleneck in modern architectures. Local placement of data can reduce this problem as the Local Area Networks (LAN) tend to have a higher performance profile than the WANs.
Global site autonomy	Modern business practice often requires that individual applications do not suffer because of other site failures and processing profiles. This is very difficult to ensure in a central configuration and is most easily supported by local placement of data.
Scalability	It has traditionally been difficult and often expensive to add to an existing central configuration to increase capacity. The easier approach in recent architectures has been to add more of the same in a shared environment. This does not mean that the data has to be local to the user but it does imply inherent distribution when the component level of addition is a complete hardware and software configuration. This is not often the case and so scalability is not that strong an argument for distribution but it can be a supporting one as the underlying design issues are similar to a distributed design.

Table 1.1: Reasons for a distributed architecture

Note that all of the above has discussed distribution of data and, apart from a brief mention, has not really considered the related subject of distribution of processing. Discussing processing distribution is a level of detail that is unnecessary when discussing replication. However it must not be ignored when designing the distribution as processing location will often determine or at least influence the data location.

Distribution V Replication

Concentrating on the distribution of data, let's be more precise and introduce the replication of data. What's the difference?

Distributed data is viewed as a single logical database which is partitioned into multiple fragments. These are then distributed and located at different geographical sites. Although each site is an autonomous unit with its own schema and objects, there is no duplication of data across the sites and one can view all of the data as a single logical image. The easiest way to visualize this is to consider two sites each with half of the orders table based on a geographical split. A third site has the customer table because this data is maintained centrally at the third site. This is illustrated in figure 1.1.

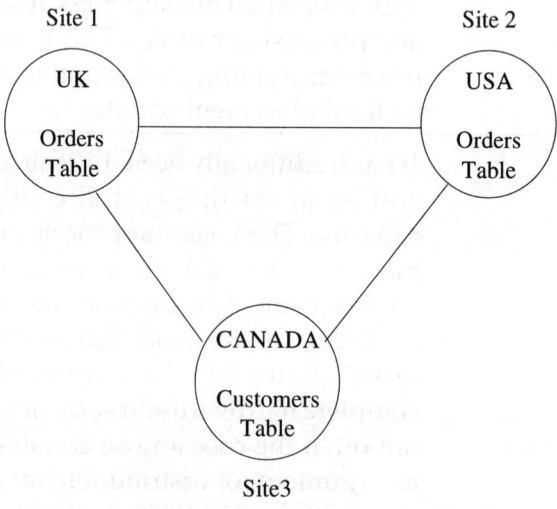

Figure 1.1 Distributed orders:customer data

Each of the two operational sites inputs and processes its own orders on the basis that orders are placed locally. However the customers are controlled by Head Office which is at another physical location. In this distributed case a command to view all UK orders with a customer name requires a distributed join between the UK and CANADA databases.

If we now consider the replication of some of this data, we allow read only copies of the data at sites which require read access to that data. In our orders:customer situation we could simply replicate the customer table from the Head Office

CANADA site to both of the operational sites in UK and USA. This is illustrated in figure 1.2.

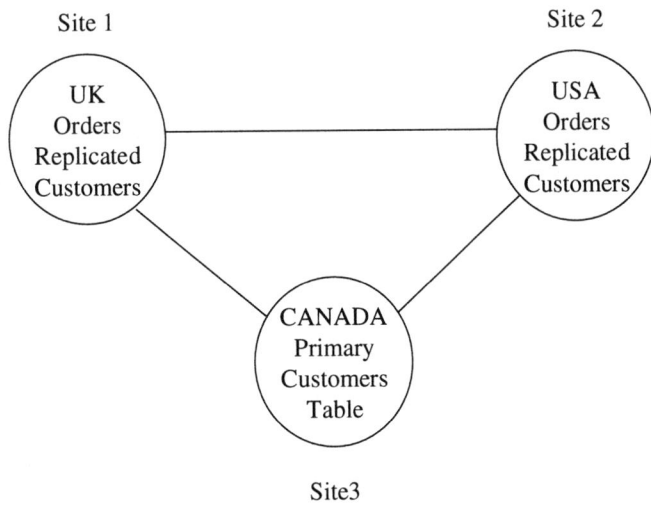

Figure 1.2: Replicated orders:customer data

Now we have local processing of the customer data to satisfy the above enquiry of all UK orders showing customer name. We clearly have an overhead in space requirements to store the multiple copies of the customer data and a problem in how timely the replicated data is.

How up-to-date the replicated data is can be an important problem and it is worthwhile taking some time to discuss the various approaches to replicated data timeliness or **latency** as it is most often called. To do this we shall look at the various methods which support data replication and see how long the latency is for each of them. There are other considerations of course and so it will not just be the latency that you should consider.

Replication Methods

Synchronous Replication

First of all let's get the **two-phase commit** approach out of the discussion. Two-phase commit is an approach which ensures that there is no latency by using an all or nothing update method. If we are updating multiple pieces of distributed data then the two-phase commit does not commit a single update until it is guaranteed that all updates can commit. This is done by synchronizing the multiple updates in a distributed transaction which coordinates the multiple commits so that they all happen at the same time. The theory is that if one of them fails to commit then all of the other updates will not commit and the complete distributed transaction will be rolled back to its beginning. In practice, of course, it is impossible to impose "same time" over a geographical distributed system and there are always occasions when the two-phase commit coordinator will be unsure of the result at one site – mainly because of time delays – and may take the wrong decision for the other sites.

In two-phase commit the sequence of events is:

- Indicate that a distributed transaction is required.

  This instructs the server (or sometimes a client) at one of the sites to take control of the distributed transaction.

- Issue the update commands to the sites.

  This requests the sites to carry out the updates independently of each other. We are in a transaction so all locks are being held and other transactions cannot see the changes.

- Ask each site to indicate when it is ready to commit.

  This lines everybody up just prior to commit – the prepare phase. If a negative reply is received, such as one site failing, all of the sites are instructed to rollback.

- Instruct the sites to commit

  If all sites are prepared to commit, the coordinator instructs them to commit.

Note the heavy reliance on all sites being available and remaining available for the duration of the transaction. Also, what does the coordinating site do if one of the participating sites simply fails to reply once the final commit instruction has been issued? Has the remote site committed or has it rolled back? How long should the coordinating site wait for a reply? How many other sites have committed?

The problems with two-phase commit are considerable and you should use it with care and only when absolutely necessary. Even then you should think about it and possibly alter the design to reduce the incidence of two-phase commit. However, if you must, there is no other advice but to be careful when you do use it. If you must have a distributed transaction and it must be all or nothing then you will have to use two-phase commit. But be aware that the performance of the two-phase commit will be less than the throughput of the individual sites or components involved in the transaction. There is an overhead to the two-phase commit processing, especially with the multiple network requests. The user will not see any updated data locally until all of the remote data has been changed and you should consider two-phase commit as a rather slow transaction. Finally with two-phase commit, you need to code something into the application. This is usually quite simple – such as **begin distributed transaction** – but it is not an application independent process. If you change the distribution of the data you may have to change your two-phase transaction.

Asynchronous replication

The type of replication that we are considering throughout the book is an asynchronous process where the processing of the primary data does not have to wait on the processing of the replicated data. The primary may commit its update irrespective of what replication has been defined. The replication is actioned asynchronously to the initial processing. In practice the processing of the primary data will have no knowledge of the existence of any replication of the data that has just changed. This has the obvious benefit that the replication configuration may be changed without any impact on the primary data processing. This asynchronous approach also means that the primary processing is not dependent on any other action in the distributed architecture and can commit even if the replication cannot be actioned because there is a problem with one of the remote sites. (There are problems with replication itself when a remote site is unavailable. We shall consider this later, but the important aspect of replication is that remote problems have no impact on the primary processing.)

The asynchronous independent approach does mean that there is always a finite latency between the primary data being changed and the change being visible at a remote site. This may be quite short if all goes well but it may be longer than you expect if there is a problem contacting a remote site. You need to make the user aware of this possible time delay in times of failure, as the data will be in multiple different states across the organization. It may not be immediately obvious that there is a problem at the local site. But if the connection is down for some time, the asynchronous replications will start to mount up and it will take some time to action all of the stored replication transactions. In this case the user at the remote site is still working against their local database but it is not being updated with replicated changes. Even when the problem is addressed it will take time to process the stored replication transactions and the user will see further delay in the changes being visible on their local database. Make sure that you raise the awareness of this so that it does not come as a surprise to the user.

If we take our simple orders:customer replication of figure 1.2 we can get into processing problems if the replication is not fast enough. Consider a new customer identified by the UK to Head Office in CANADA. This is input at CANADA immediately and under normal circumstances would be replicated to the UK and available for use quite quickly. However if the network connection fails, the replicated insert will not reach the UK. This means that the order for the new customer cannot be entered as it keeps being rejected by the business logic of the local application. So, do we send the customer information again to Head Office? Do we allow special processing to override the local business logic based on the knowledge that the customer will exist eventually? But has the customer been rejected at Head Office because of a credit check? The decisions are obviously application dependent but the questions – and they are not comprehensive – illustrate the problems that can arise from a failure to replicate in the normal expected time. You may need to determine what a delay in replication will mean and design in the appropriate application or manual adjustments to cater for this[1].

And finally, the asynchronous replication works best if the target replicated data is read only. It's not a mandatory rule of replication but you will get into horrible update problems if you allow the replicated data to be changed locally. The synchronous two-phase commit overcomes this by locking all primary and secondary data for the duration of the transaction. This is obviously not very good for concurrency but is a 100% consistent solution. The asynchronous replication takes no locks on the secondary data while the primary data is being updated. This clearly does not add to any primary update transaction concurrency problems but it does mean that up-front design decisions are required to cope with update collision problems at the secondary sites. The sites need to agree their update policy in advance – at the design stage – to avoid update collisions and potential corruption or loss of data.

Types of asynchronous replication

When using Sybase Replication Server we are dealing with asynchronous replication. I shall define the specifics later. There are several approaches to asynchronous replication all of which you can implement with Sybase. Some of them are not automatically supported and you need to develop them yourself. I categorize the asynchronous approaches as Table 1.2:

---

1 Fortunately Replication Server provides some system tables which record the last transaction replicated and committed at each Primary Database and this is a significant help in resolving this type of question.

Type	Description
File transfer	A table by table transfer at a specific point in time from one site to another.
Snapshot	A transfer of specific data, possibly from multiple tables, at a specific point in time from one site to another.
Log based	The use of a transaction log dump to restore a secondary site to a more recent state.
Transactional	The use of a separate replication service to extract the replicated data from the transaction log and apply it to the secondary sites.

Table 1.2: Types of asynchronous replication

All of these approaches are asynchronous to the original transaction and clearly have different degrees of latency between the primary data being changed and the replication being actioned at the secondary. The level of intrusion of the replication process also varies for each approach. The file transfer and snapshot extracts are best executed with **isolation level 3** locking set on the primary data to ensure that the data does not change during the extract. This imposes a significant concurrency problem at the primary as no other transaction will be able to change the data while the extract process is running. This is discussed in detail later in this section.

File Transfer Replication

I define File Transfer Replication as a full table extract to an operating system file; the transfer of this file across the network to a secondary site and the complete replacement of the secondary table with the extracted data. A typical approach to this in a Sybase environment would be:

- **bcp** the primary data to an operating system file.
- **ftp** the operating system file to the secondary server.
- **delete** the existing data from the secondary table.
- **bcp** the operating system file into the empty secondary table.

The last two steps are a little more complicated from a performance and data integrity viewpoint. Without going into the pros and cons of the various approaches to **bcp** into existing data tables, this particular scenario is dominated by the need to **delete** all of the existing data before the load. In this case you will probably drop the indexes, **delete** the data, **bcp** in and recreate the indexes. Not a normal **bcp** load approach when the data is large, but in this case there is no fear of data inconsistency as the primary table already contains consistent data and you are replacing the complete table. You could even consider **truncate table** to speed things up. As this command does not log the deletes you will need to dump the database after the **bcp** in but as you have decided to rebuild the indexes on the table, you will probably do this anyway.

So my scenario for the file transfer load is:

- Drop indexes or constraints on the target table.

- **bcp** in the data.

- Recreate the indexes or constraints.

- **dump** the database.

If the data volumes make this prohibitive – the index builds take too long – a more normal approach will be to **bcp** into a staging table.

- **bcp** into a staging table (with no indexes/constraints)

- **delete** the target data

- **insert** across from the staging table to the target table

- **truncate** the staging table (if it is in a separate database – **delete** if in the same database)

File transfer is a perfectly feasible approach for small tables which do not change frequently and a high latency can be supported by the application. It's also only really applicable when you have a reasonable batch window to do the processing as the locking will be at the table level and may reduce your throughput while it is taking place. If the table is not subject to frequent change the concurrency impact at the primary will be negligible, as very few transactions will conflict with the data extract. However at the secondary it will be prudent to ensure that nobody is accessing this table while it is being refreshed. As the load process is not transactional we want to minimize the time when the user can see incomplete data, and so it is reasonable to do this while no other transactions have access to the table.

Snapshot

This is effectively a version of file transfer as it goes through the same processing but, usually, with low data volumes. The extract process is based on a **select** command and so it can extract a fragment of the table: horizontally with a **where** clause and/or vertically with a column list. The extracted data is output to an operating system file, transferred to the secondary site and loaded into the target table. In some systems snapshot replication is supported and the system will take care of the extract:transfer:load mechanism. In Sybase you need to do this yourself.

The main problem with snapshot replication centers around the load process, as you will have to decide if existing records will be updated or deleted and inserted. It is not a simple **bcp** situation and you will have to write something yourself.

A benefit of the snapshot is that you could maintain data integrity by extending the extract to include more than one table. This is not that difficult as it is only a **select** command on the extract and you will be writing the load yourself. However this routine is most commonly used with single tables mainly because it is easier to implement. The simplest approach is illustrated in figure 1.3.

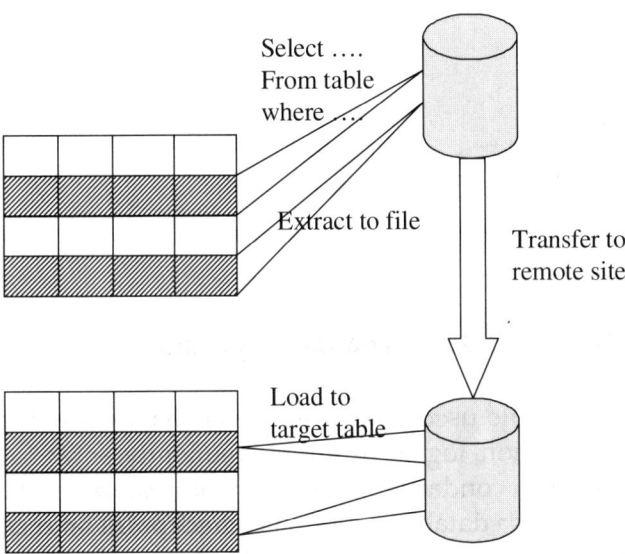

Figure 1.3: Snapshot replication

As with file transfer, snapshot has a high latency and the load process should lock the target tables to ensure that other transactions do not see an intermediate data state. You can run the snapshot frequently to reduce both the latency and the intrusion of the load process but, in general, this type of replication is most suitable to small data volumes with static data so that the volume and frequency of the replication are both low. If you write the extract so that it outputs only the data that has changed and then only replicate if there are any changes, you could run the extract frequently but only replicate on an as-needed basis. This might be quite adequate for low volume, slow changing data.

Log based

I define log based replication as using a dump of the transaction log to keep a secondary site up-to-date. This is illustrated in figure 1.4.

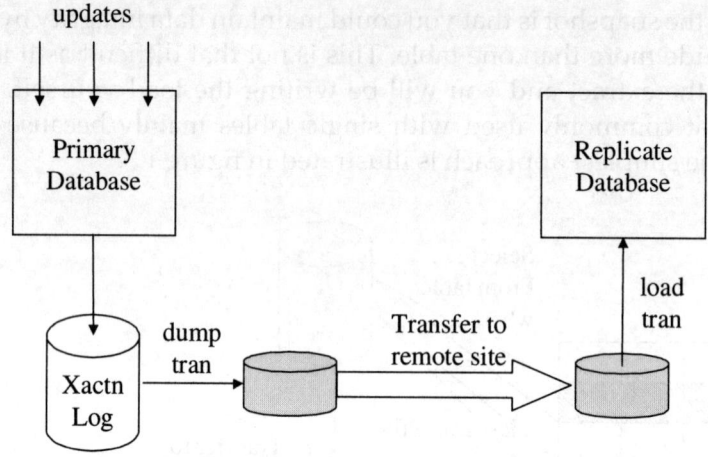

Figure 1.4: Log based dump and load replication

This is a reasonably documented and used procedure which Sybase provides some support for. The database transaction log is dumped frequently – say every 15 minutes – and transferred to the secondary site where it is restored against the secondary database. Sybase provides a database option **no checkpoint on recovery** to ensure that the restore process does not write a checkpoint to the transaction log. If it does you will not be able to reuse this transaction log to recover the primary database if there is a problem. Of course in the figure 1.4 scenario you are copying to a new version of the log as part of the file transfer and then you do not need any special database settings.

This technique is most commonly used to keep a backup site on warm standby so that it is no more out-of-date than the length of the transaction log to be restored. This has very low impact on the primary and maintains transactional integrity. However the secondary database is locked from use while the transaction log is being recovered. The impact on the secondary is considerable but as this technique is generally used for warm standby there will be little activity against the secondary.

Transactional replication

In transactional replication the transactions to be replicated are extracted from the transaction log, transferred to the secondary site and replayed against the target data. This maintains full transaction integrity and has a low impact on both primary and secondary as it is dealing with one transaction at a time. The primary transaction does not see any replication overhead on its processing and the secondary sees only record locks while the transaction is being replayed. Of course if one transaction updates 10 million records, the replication of this will have as much – if not more – of an impact on the secondary as the initial transaction had on the primary. But when the transactions are sensible i.e. short, the imposition of transactional replication is low on both primary and secondary databases. Also, the latency is low as the primary transaction may be replicated immediately it has completed. The major factor in transactional replication is often the network time involved in sending the replicated transaction from the primary to the secondary.

In some transactional implementations the extract can be defined to link tables together for replication purposes to ensure logical transaction integrity. For example defining the *orders* and *order_item* tables as linked for replication purposes will ensure that a process which adds an order and then multiple items – in more than one transaction – is treated as a single replication unit to ensure that the logical link of the tables is maintained. You can achieve this by having all of the inserts in one physical transaction but this may not be practical in the application. Unfortunately Sybase does not support this logical linking. There is no data corruption problem but there may be a data consistency problem at the secondary. If the primary processing is made up of two transactions – **insert** *orders* record and **insert** multiple *order_item* records – these will be replicated as two transactions. The correct sequence will always be maintained so the *orders* **insert** will always arrive before the *order_item* inserts. No problems so far, but consider a failure which stops replication just after the *orders* **insert** is replicated. The secondary database now has an order with no items and this may persist for some time until the replication failure is rectified. Not a showstopper – and it could just as easily happen – but something that you need to be aware of in Sybase replication.

Transactional replication is illustrated in figure 1.5.

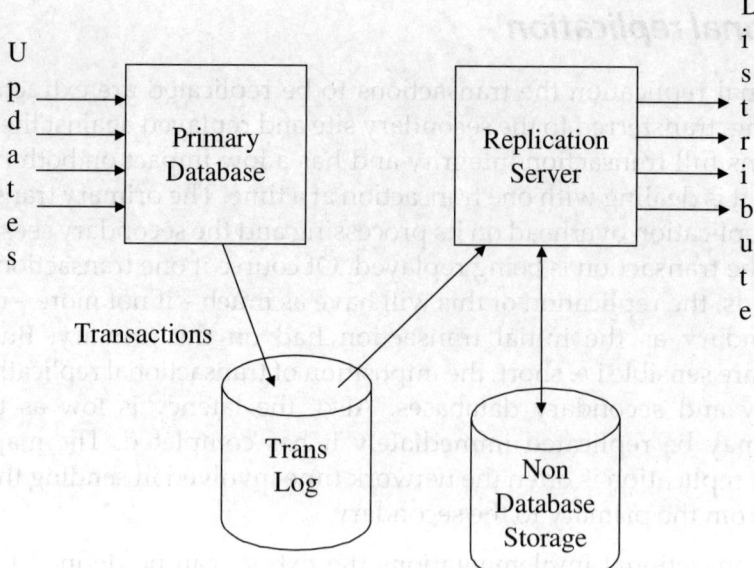

Figure 1.5: transactional replication

This is how Sybase replication works. The primary transaction log is read to extract the completed transactions which are to be replicated. These are then transmitted to the secondary database and actioned against the data. The definition of which transactions are to be replicated and to which databases they are to be applied is defined to the replication process independently of the transactions actually updating the primary data. The replication of the transaction is carried out asynchronously to the primary update. The primary update completes, writes the log records to the transaction log and releases all locks on the primary data to make it available to other transactions. The replication process is reading the transaction log independently of the primary transactions and picks up the completed transactions, moves them to a separate storage area from where they are replicated to the appropriate secondary databases. At the secondary databases the impact on other transactions is low as the transaction is replayed and any locking will be similar in extent and duration to the original transaction.

There is some latency but this depends almost totally on the network. If the network is not available, the replication process will keep trying to replicate the transaction to the secondary database until it is successful. In general transactional replication is a low impact, low latency, transactionally consistent method of replication and is the most common approach supplied by the database vendors.

Sybase Replication

Having established that transaction replication is the optimum approach let's look at how Sybase actually does it. Just before we do that, let me define the stages which must be addressed by the replication process and we will then fit the Sybase Replication Server into these stages. Replication involves five stages:

- Publish the replicated data.
- Subscribe to the replicated data.
- Extract the replicated data.
- Transform the replicated data.
- Distribute and apply the replicated data.

Before replication can take place the following must be defined.

- The data that may be replicated.

  A definition of the tables and columns that will be made available by the primary database for replication. This is called **publishing** the data. Note that being made available for replication does not mean that it has to be replicated. A secondary database must specify that it will copy the replicated data before it is physically replicated. Publishing the data is done in Sybase by defining a **replication definition** for the data and marking the data in the primary database for replication.

- The data that a secondary database will receive from the primary.

  A definition of the tables, rows and columns that will be copied to a secondary database. This data must have been defined as available for replication at a primary database. Each secondary database must define the data it will accept and each definition may be different. This is called **subscribing** to the published data. Subscribing to the published data is done in Sybase by defining **subscriptions** to the published data.

- Extract the data that is available for replication i.e. defined as published.

  A process needs to read the transaction log and move the appropriate transactions to a staging area from where they can be replicated to the subscribers. In Sybase this is carried out by the Log Transfer Manager (LTM) which reads the log, extracts all transactions for replicated data and writes them to a staging area provided by Replication Server.

- Transform the replicated data.

  If the primary and secondary data are not an exact schema match or you wish to action the replicated transaction differently than it was originally processed at the primary database, some transformation is required. This may be as simple as different data formats or as complicated as different tables which require different commands at the secondary than occurred originally at the primary. Sybase implements this with **functions**, **function strings** and **function string classes** which transform the primary transaction into a potentially different secondary transaction.

- Distribute and apply the replicated data.

  One or more processes are required to take the data extracted from the transaction log and apply the replicated transactions to the appropriate subscribers. Sybase uses internal Replication Server processes and the Replication Server system table information in the Replication Server System Database (RSSD) to carry this out.

So the basic model is a publish:subscribe model where the primary database defines the data which is published for replication and the secondary database defines which published data it will subscribe to. If data is not published then it may not be subscribed to. Data which is published does not have to have any subscriptions linked to it: in this case it will not be replicated. It is extracted from the primary transaction log – as it has been defined for replication – but it is discarded by the Replication Server processes as the data has no subscriptions. These publications and subscriptions are held in the Replication Server system tables to allow the data to be extracted from the publishers and distributed to the subscribers. The LTM extracts the transactions from the log and writes them to the staging area. Based on the publication and subscription definitions, the Replication Server processes the publication data in the staging area and distributes it to the subscribers. This is illustrated in figure 1.6.

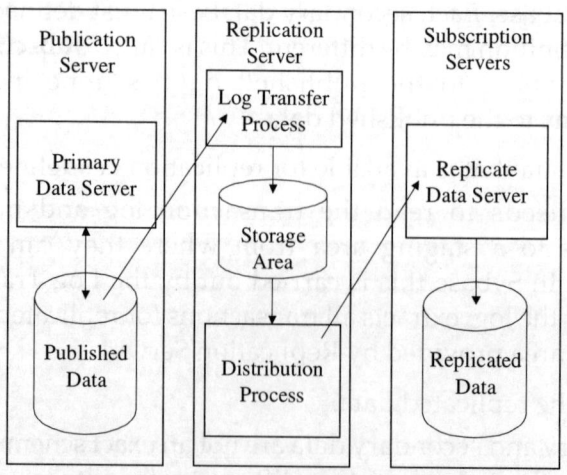

Figure 1.6: Sybase replication

Prior to or during the distribution stage, the replicated data may be transformed so that it is actioned differently at the subscriber than it was initially at the publisher. Such requirements as convert a datatype; make a single table insert into multiple table inserts; make a deletion into an update, all are possible with Sybase replication.

First a few definitions of Sybase terminology so that the descriptions are easier to follow.

Primary Data Server (PDS)

A Sybase SQL Server holding primary data which is published for replication.

Primary Database (PDB)

A database on the Primary Data Server which holds primary data that is published for replication.

Replicate Data Server (RDS)

A Sybase SQL Server holding replication data which has subscribed to published data on a Primary Data Server.

Replicate Database (RDB)

A database on the Replicate Data Server which holds replicate data produced by a subscription to published data on a Primary Data Server.

Primary Replication Server (PRS)

The Replication Server which receives data for replication from a Primary Data Server and distributes it to other Replication Servers or directly to a Replicate Database.

Replicate Replication Server (RRS)

A Replication Server which receives transactions from a Primary Replication Server and applies them to Replicate Databases.

Log Transfer Manager (LTM)

The process that reads the transaction log, extracts the transactions that contain data which is defined as published i.e. for replication, and passes these transactions to the Primary Data Server.

Stable Device (SD)

The stable device is non-database storage managed by a Replication Server which holds the data to be replicated.

Replication Server System Database (RSSD)

A Sybase SQL Server database which contains the system catalog information for a Replication Server.

In general I shall not use the abbreviations as often the descriptions do not read very well when they are littered with lots of mnemonics. The exceptions to this will be the LTM and the RSSD as these are quite accepted mnemonics.

Mapping these Sybase components to our generic replication phases we have:

Publishing

The definition of which data is available for replication. Sybase implements this with a **replication definition** which defines the data and/or stored procedures to be replicated. This replication definition is defined at the Primary Replication Server and is stored on the RSSD. The replication definition for a table defines the columns that are to be made available for replication; the columns that comprise the primary key; the location of the primary copy of the table and the columns that may be used by a subscriber to limit the rows that will be replicated. The replication definition for a procedure defines the procedure and its parameters in a similar way to the table and its columns: the parameters that may be replicated; the location of the procedure and the parameters that may be used to limit the executions of the procedure. Sybase also requires the table/procedure in the primary database to be marked for replication so that the records written to the log can indicate that the data is to be replicated. Publishing data for replication is dealt with in chapter 5.

Subscribing

The definition of which published data will be replicated to a specific Replicate Database. Sybase implements this with a **define** or **create subscription** command. The difference between these commands is based on how the Primary Database and Replicate Database data is synchronized before replication begins. The subscription to replicated data defines the replication definition that the subscription will use, the Replicate Database to receive the data and any **where** clause restrictions to apply to the replicated data. The subscription is defined at the Replicate Replication Server which manages the Replicate Database and is stored in the RSSD. Subscribing to data is dealt with in chapter 6.

Extraction

The process which extracts the replication data from the transaction log. Sybase implements this with the LTM. The LTM reads the transaction log; extracts transactions containing objects – tables or procedures – marked for replication and passes them to the Primary Replication Server. LTM processing is dealt with in chapter 2.

Transformation   The process which transforms the extracted replication data into the required format of the subscriber. Sybase implements this with **function classes, functions** and **function strings**. A Primary Database command, such as **insert/update/delete**, is passed to the Replication Server as a function consisting of the function name and a set of parameters. The Replicate Replication Server uses its function strings to convert the function back to the original command. By altering the function strings or defining new function strings, you can transform the original command into a different structure or even into multiple new commands. These are dealt with in chapters 8 and 9.

Distribution   The process which stores the extracted data from the publishers and distributes it to the subscribers. Sybase implements this as Replication Server tasks which use the RSSD to identify the processing requirements and the Stable Device to store the data. The Replication Server processing threads are dealt with in chapter 2.

Synchronization   The initialization process which synchronizes the primary and secondary databases before replication starts so that both data sources are consistent before replication begins. Sybase can implement this automatically or you can handle it manually with a bulk extract and load process. The approaches to this are dealt with in chapter 6.

The simplest configuration we can have for Sybase replication is shown in figure 1.7.

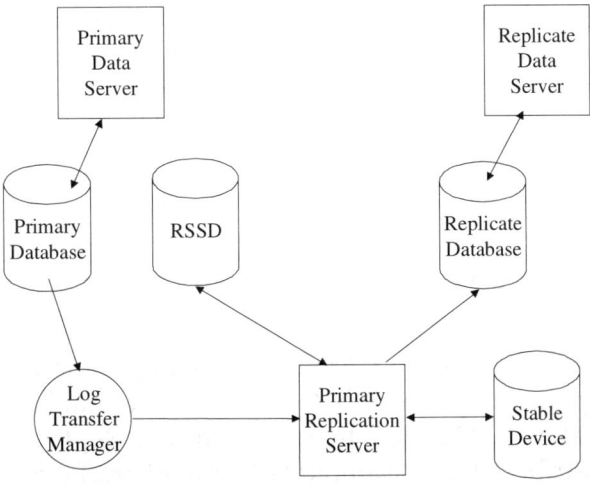

Figure 1.7: Sybase replication

The RSSD contains the publications and subscriptions that define the replication requirement. Note that this is located on the Primary Data Server as the only requirement is that it needs to reside on a SQL Server. However be careful of the RSSD location as it is frequently updated by the Replication Server and network activity can be quite high. The Replication Server itself is an Open Server application and so it cannot provide a home for the RSSD.

The LTM reads the Primary Database transaction log to extract transactions that contain objects marked for replication and forwards these to the Primary Replication Server. The LTM is an Open Server application and you need one for each Primary Database. So one Primary Replication Server can process the replication requirements for multiple Primary Databases but each Primary Database requires a separate LTM process.

The instructions on how to process this replication data are held in the replication system tables of the RSSD. A transaction executed in the Primary Database is replicated in the following steps:

- The transaction is logged in the transaction log by the data server.

- The LTM reads the log and forwards transactions for replicated tables and procedures to the Primary Replication Server. Each transaction in the log is marked for replication on the basis that it contains commands against a table or procedure which is marked for replication in the Primary Database.

- The Primary Replication Server checks the RSSD to see if there are any subscriptions for the data. If not the transaction is discarded. If subscriptions exist the transaction is forwarded to the relevant Replicate Replication Servers or applied directly to a connected Replicate Database.

- On receipt of the transaction, the Replicate Replication Server stores it in a queue on the Stable Device. The Replicate Replication Server then checks its RSSD and forwards the transaction to other Replication Servers in a route or applies the transactions directly to a connected Replicate Database.

The data involved in each replication transaction is stored on the Stable Device of the Primary Replication Server. There is one Stable Device for each Primary Replication Server and the data is held in the Stable Device until the transaction is committed on all Replicate Databases which have subscribed to it or until it is moved to a Replicate Replication Server.

In the simple scenario of figure 1.7 the Primary Replication Server distributes the transactions by applying them directly to the Replicate Databases. This is not such a great idea across a slow WAN when there are multiple Replicate Databases to which the data is being distributed, as the amount of network traffic could be high. It is quite common to have a Replicate Replication Server at the subscribing end to provide a single target for the Primary Replication Server. The Replicate Replication Server then cascades the replication transaction to any number of local Replicate Databases. This is illustrated in figure 1.8.

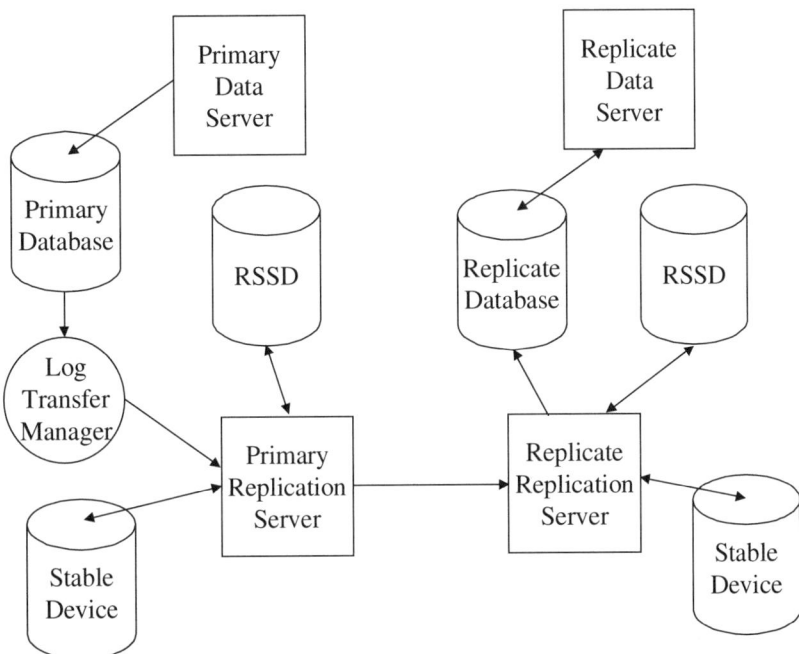

Figure 1.8: Replication with a Replicate Replication Server

In this scenario the Replicate Replication Server has its own RSSD and Stable Device. There is no need for an LTM as there are no Primary Databases connected to the Replicate Replication Server. Note that a Replication Server may function as both a Primary Replication Server and a Replicate Replication Server as it may have both Primary Databases and Replicate Databases connected to it.

The Replication Server coordinates the replication activities of the local data servers and exchanges replication data with the other Replication Servers in the replication domain. A Replication Server has two principal roles in the replication architecture:

- Receive Primary Database transactions and forward them to subscribers.

- Receive replication transactions from other Replication Servers and apply then to Replicate Databases or forward them to other Replication Servers in a route.

When a configuration has multiple Replication Servers, one of them is classified as the ID Server and is used to register all of the other Replication Servers and databases used. The ID Server must be the first Replication Server installed in the configuration.

Figure 1.9 shows four Replication Servers at three sites. Each Replication Server is considered a distinct site even though it may be on the same machine as another Replication Server.

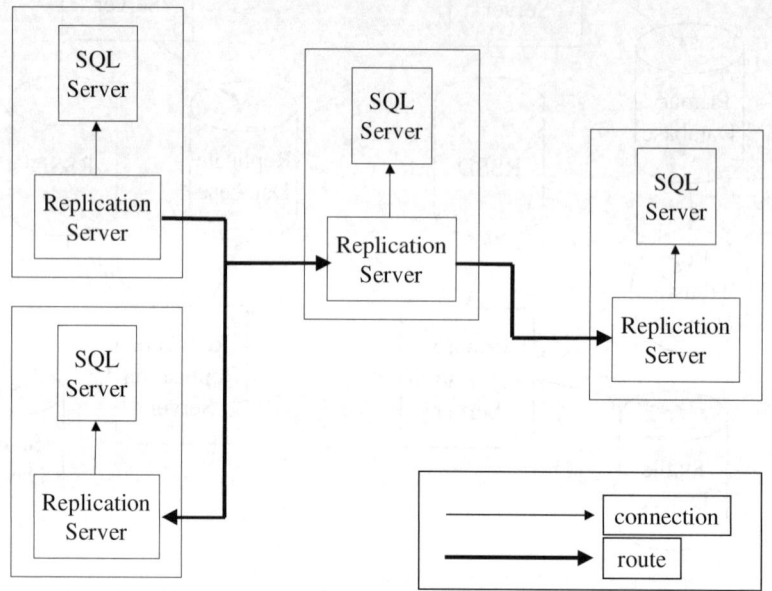

Figure 1.9: Connections and Routes

So in figure 1.9 there may be three machines but there are always four Replication Servers. Each Primary Database or Replicate Database has a **connection** to a Replication Server. Connections may be across a WAN, LAN or locally on the same machine. In general a connection will not be used across a WAN simply from a performance viewpoint. Connections are discussed in Chapter 4. In the WAN configuration the Replication Servers are usually linked together by **routes**. Routes establish the replication path between Replication Servers and all Replication Servers linked together by routes comprise a **Replication Domain**. Routes between two Replication Servers are called **direct routes** and routes which cascade across multiple Replication Servers are called **indirect routes**. Routes are one directional and if you need to replicate both ways between two Replication Servers you must define a route in each direction. Figure 1.9 has three direct routes and one indirect route. Routes are discussed in Chapter 3.

2

Internal Architecture

Introduction

This chapter describes the internal architecture of the Replication Server, taking each major component in turn and showing how they operate and interact with each other. The components covered are:

- Log Transfer Manager (LTM)

  The LTM extracts the transactions from the Primary Database transaction log and writes them to the inbound stable queue.

- Stable Queue Manager (SQM)

Each queue has an SQM which manages the **insert/delete** activity against the queue and prevents duplicate messages being written to the queue.

- Stable Queue Transaction Manager (SQT)

  Each inbound queue has an SQT which forwards the transactions on the inbound queue in commit sequence to the appropriate Replication Server services.

- Distributor (DIST)

  The DIST receives transactions from the SQT and matches them with the RSSD replication definitions and subscriptions to allow the message to be applied to the required destination databases.

- Data Server Interface (DSI)

  The DSI manages the writing of transactions directly to Replicate Databases managed by the local Replication Server.

- Replication Server Interface (RSI)

  The RSI manages the passing of transactions to other Replication Servers in a route.

Replication Server Processing

The Replication Server is a multi-threaded Open Server which receives and forwards replication transactions, holding them in inbound and outbound stable queues. The Replication Server reads the RSSD to determine how to process and distribute the transactions. This is illustrated in figure 2.1.

The LTM places transactions in inbound queues. All queues are managed by a Stable Queue Manager (SQM) and a Stable Queue Transaction Manager (SQT). These prevent duplicates being written to the inbound queue and present the transactions in commit sequence to the distributor (DIST) thread which uses the RSSD to determine how to process the transactions and where to send them. The DIST thread places the transactions on outbound queues with one queue per destination. The outbound queues are managed by the Data Server Interface (DSI) if being written by the local Replication Server to a Replicate Database or the Replication Server Interface (RSI) if being sent to another Replication Server in a route.

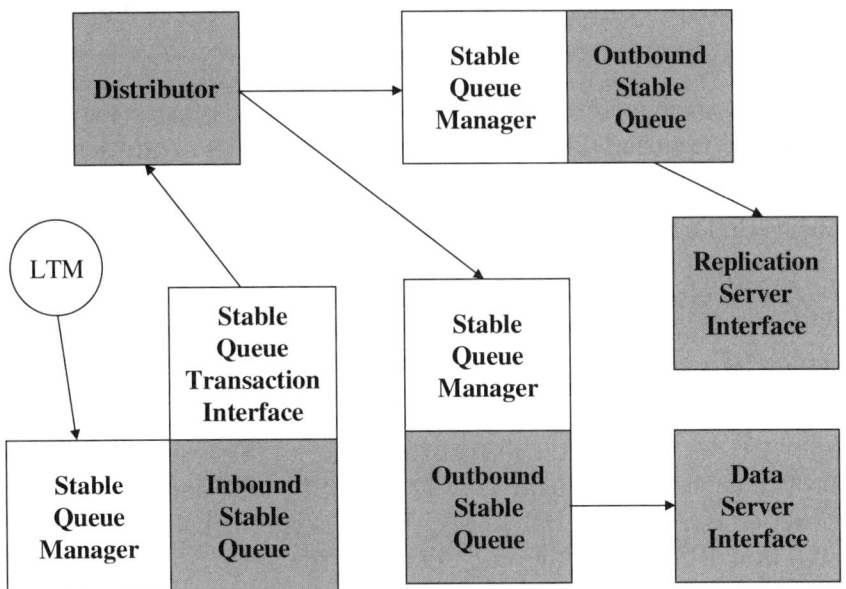

Figure 2.1: Replication Server Threads and Queues

There are three types of stable queue:

- Inbound queue.

  This holds transactions from an LTM.

- Outbound queue.

  This holds transactions to be replicated to a Replicate Database. Outbound queues are further divided into Data Server Interface (DSI) queues and Replication Server Interface (RSI) queues. A DSI queue holds transactions to be applied directly to a Replicate Database; an RSI queue holds transactions to be sent across a route to a Replicate Replication Server.

- Subscription materialization queue.

  This holds data related to a subscription being materialized or dropped.

Each queue is controlled by a Stable Queue Manager (SQM) which is responsible for inserts and deletes on the stable queue. Each queue has another manager process, the Stable Queue Transaction Interface (SQT), which is responsible for ensuring that the incoming transactions are replicated in commit sequence. The SQT is the process that recognizes a transaction rollback and discards the records for that transaction from the queue.

The distribution of the replication transaction is handled by the Distribution Thread (DIST) which uses three other components to carry out the distribution.

- Subscription Resolution Engine (SRE)

  The SRE matches the transaction records to subscriptions, attaching a destination database ID to each qualifying record. If no subscriptions exist for the record the SRE tells the Distributor to discard the record.

- Transaction Delivery Service (TD)

  The TD service packages the transaction records for distribution to the Primary Databases or other Replication Servers.

- Message Delivery Service (MD)

  Using the destination database ID the MD service determines the optimum routing of the transaction records and places the transaction records in the appropriate outbound queue i.e. a DSI or RSI queue depending on whether the destination is a database or a Replication Server. The DSI/RSI then forwards the transaction from its outbound queue to the target database or Replication Server.

Log Transfer Manager (LTM)

The LTM is an Operating System application which processes the database log records and passes those which have to be replicated to the Replication Server. Each table or procedure in the Primary Database which has been enabled for replication has the *sysstats* column in *sysobjects* set to –32768 and this column is written to the header of each transaction log record to enable the LTM to easily identify those log records which have to be replicated. The LTM sits between the Primary Data Server and the Replication Server and pulls records from the transaction log, converts them to Log Transfer Language (LTL) and pushes them to the Replication Server. The conversion to LTL is carried out to give the LTM a generic appearance so that it is not Sybase SQL Server, i.e. Transact-SQL, specific but may be adapted for other versions of SQL. The use of LTL has no relevance to the functionality of the LTM or the Replication Server as far as this book is concerned: it is simply a transport mechanism to move the transaction log records to the Replication Server.

Replication (or Secondary) Truncation Point

To ensure that records are not deleted from the transaction log before they have been replicated, the LTM maintains a replication truncation point[1] on the log which prevents the **dump tran** command from removing log records which have been written to the log after the replication truncation point. This functions in conjunction with the primary truncation point which is maintained by the **checkpoint** to point to the oldest active transaction on the log, after which no log records can be deleted. Consider the log shown in figure 2.2.

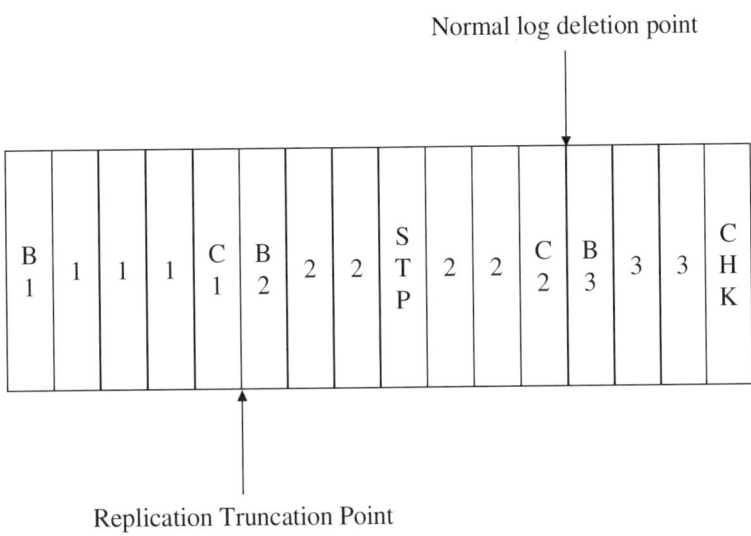

Figure 2.2: Truncation points on the log

The oldest open transaction is transaction 3. With no replication a **dump tran** would remove transactions 1 and 2 as they committed before this transaction. However with the LTM replication truncation point, the **dump tran** is able to delete transaction 1 only as it is the only transaction which has committed before the replication truncation point.

If replication is going slowly and you have a high activity on the Primary Database then this can give lots of bother as the log will not be cleared quickly because of replication delays and will be increasing as commands are actioned against the Primary Database. Be prepared to have to increase the size of the transaction log when you have replication enabled.

---

[1] The replication truncation point is also referred to as the secondary truncation point. However my preference is replication truncation point simply because I find that it is used more often.

You can view the position of the truncation points on the log from the *syslogshold* table in **master**.

select * from master..syslogshold

dbid	reserved starttime name	spid	page	xactid	masterxactid
7	0	41	1567872	0x0017ec800004	0x001516510000
	Jan 20 19994:57PM				
	$ins				
13	0	41	1381969	0x001516510000	0x000000000000
	Jan 20 19994:57PM				
	$user_transaction				
15	0	0	175849	0x000000000000	0x000000000000
	Jan 20 19994:55PM				
	$replication_truncation_point				

If either of the truncation point page numbers is the same as the first page of the log:

select first from sysindexes where id = 8/* syslogs*/

first
___
175849

then **dump tran** will not be able to delete any records from the log as a truncation point is at the beginning of the log. If several iterations of these commands do not show any movement in the replication truncation point but the Replication Server is moving data, it is most likely that the LTM has got confused and needs a restart[2]. This is discussed in more detail in the troubleshooting section.

The current replication truncation point is maintained in the DBINFO structure of the Primary Database and the current scan point - i.e. where the LTM is currently reading – is maintained in the RSSD table *rs_locater*. When the LTM logs into the Primary Database to read the log it uses the *rs_locater* value as its start point. If the LTM gets confused about the validity of this start point use the **rs_zeroltm** command to zero this value and point the LTM to the beginning of the log. This is also discussed in detail in the troubleshooting section.

___

[2] Do not be shy in restarting the LTM or the Replication Server. In most occasions one of these will clear the problem. You have still got to determine why it happened from the error logs, but it gets things moving again.

When the Primary Database has lots of replication activity, the replication truncation point will move forwards through the log as the LTM processes transactions to the Replication Server. Once a transaction has been completely read by the LTM and passed to the Replication Server stable queue, the LTM moves the replication truncation point forward. This is illustrated in figure 2.3

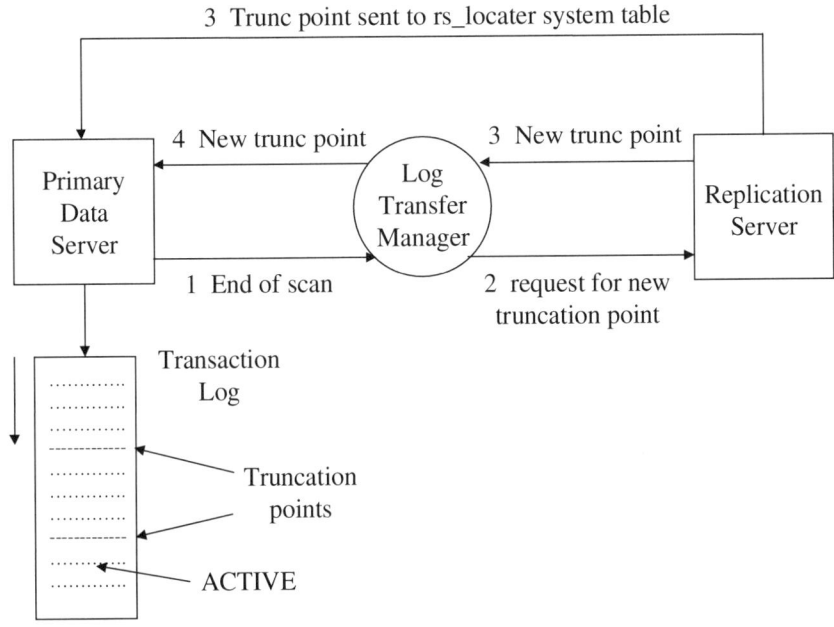

Figure 2.3: Truncation Point Processing

Once the LTM has completed its read of the transaction log it requests a new truncation point from the Replication Server. This is returned to the Primary Data Server which writes it to the database log and also records the truncation position in the *rs_locater* table in the Primary Database. Writing a truncation point involves:

- The LTM requests a new truncation point from the Primary Replication Server.

- The Primary Replication Server updates the truncation point in the *rs_locater* system table and returns the new truncation point to the LTM.

- The LTM executes the **dbcc settrunc** command on the Primary Data Server to set the truncation point.

This is fine when there is activity on the log but the LTM must still move the replication truncation point regularly when there is no replication activity on the

Primary Database. If this does not happen, the log may fill up as the **dump tran** would be unable to delete any closed transactions. Regular movement of the truncation point when there is no activity is achieved by the use of the configuration parameters: *scan_retry* and *batch_sz*.

The *scan_retry* configuration parameter defines the maximum sleep time of the log scan thread. When the *scan_retry* is reached without any new log activity, the Primary Data Server sends an end of scan message to the LTM which causes a truncation point to be written to the log. The maximum time that the LTM log scan thread will sleep for is 2*scan_retry. When the log scan thread processes all outstanding log records before the *scan_retry* limit is reached, it goes to sleep and the remaining time from its current scan is added to its *scan_retry* sleep time up to a maximum of 2*scan_retry.

When the LTM is processing transactions the *batch_sz* configuration parameter defines the maximum number of log records read by the LTM before writing a truncation point. When the PDS reaches the *batch_sz* limit it sends an end of scan message to the LTM which causes a truncation point to be written to the log. These parameters are defined with the **rs_config** command.

LTM Processing

The LTM consists of two threads: Log Scan Service Thread and Log Transfer Service Thread. The Log Scan Service Thread reads the log, extracts transactions from the log and converts them to LTL. The Log Transfer Service Thread sends the LTL to the inbound queue of the Replication Server. The Log Scan Service Thread uses the **dbcc logtransfer** command to read the log and create the LTL.

You can log into the LTM but there is very little that you can do: the most common command that you will issue will be **shutdown**. I have run a few others – such as **scan** – but this is not a server to spend much time in. Most of the time in the LTM will be to solve a problem. I know of six commands supported in the LTM.

shutdown	**scan**	**recover_stat**
trace	**suspend**	**resume**

The LTM is created during the **rs_init** process and has a RUNSERVER file and errorlog as any other server. These live in $SYBASE/repserver/install and the RUNSERVER file contains the ltm command:

```
#! /bin/sh
DSLISTEN=LTM_LNPRD1_SALES_DB; export DSLISTEN
SYBASE=$SYBASE/repserver; export SYBASE
```

```
$SYBASE/ebf7712/bin/ltm -S$DSLISTEN \
-C$SYBASE/install/$DSLISTEN.cfg -W \
-E$SYBASE/install/$DSLISTEN.log > $SYBASE/install/$DSLISTEN.stderr
2>&1&
```

To stop the LTM, log in as **"sa"** and issue the **shutdown** command. To start the LTM, go to the $SYBASE/repserver/install directory and run the RUNSERVER file. The default file names are *RUN_ltm_name* and *ltm_name.log*.

Allocation of memory by the LTM can be a little strange as it assumes that the largest transaction that it has processed is the amount of memory that it needs. So, if you have a very large transaction being replicated, the LTM will have allocated memory to process this and will retain this memory even although the subsequent transactions are smaller. If you see LTM memory usage as a problem simply restart the LTM and it should free memory – as long as the large transaction is not still being processed.

Stable Queue Manager

The SQM controls the reading, writing and deleting of records on all queues in the stable storage device. There will be one queue per LTM and one queue per DSI/RSI, each of them with its own SQM thread. The SQM also detects duplicate transactions and prevents them being written to the queue. The SQM is a management thread only and calls the **dAIO** library service to carry out all I/O operations. You can see all of the threads and library services with an **admin who** command:

admin who

Spid	Name	State	Info
	DSI EXEC	Down	101614(1) LNPRD1_SALES_DB
	DSI	Down	101614 LNPRD1_SALES_DB
22	DIST	Active	101614 LNPRD1_SALES_DB
27	SQT	Awaiting Wakeup	101614:1DIST LNPRD1_SALES_DB
16	SQM	Awaiting Message	101614:1 LNPRD1_SALES_DB
15	SQM	Awaiting Message	101614:0 LNPRD1_SALES_DB
	LTM USER	Down	LNPRD1_SALES_DB
33	DSI EXEC	Awaiting Command	101589(1) NYPRD1_MKT_DB

18	DSI	Awaiting Command	101589 NYPRD1_MKT_DB
23	DIST	Active	101589 NYPRD1_MKT_DB
28	SQT	Awaiting Wakeup	101589:1DIST NYPRD1_MKT_DB
12	SQM	Awaiting Message	101589:1 NYPRD1_MKT_DB
11	SQM	Awaiting Message	101589:0 NYPRD1_MKT_DB
51	LTM USER	Awaiting Command	NYPRD1_MKT_DB
21	dSUB	Active	
6	dCM	Awaiting Message	
8	dAIO	Awaiting Message	
26	dREC	Active	dREC
58	USER	Active	sa
5	dALARM	Awaiting Wakeup	

The queue space is allocated from the partition in units of 1M called **segments**. Each segment is divided into **blocks** of 16K which is the unit of I/O. You can see the segment usage with an **admin who, sqm** command:

admin who, sqm

Spid	State		Info		Duplicates
	Writes	Reads	Bytes	B Writes	B Filled
	B Reads		B Cache		Save_Int:Seg
		First Seg.Block		Last Seg.Block	
	Next Read		Readers		Truncs
9	Awaiting Message	100512:0	LNRSSD_MKT.lnrssd_mkt		0
	0	0	0	0	0
	0		0		240:0
		0.1		0.0	
	0.1.0		1		1
10	Awaiting Message	100512:1	LNRSSD_MKT.lnrssd_mkt		80
	104442	104748	34712951	16321	28
	16366		16262		0:2773
		2773.46		2773.46	
	2773.47.0		1		1

This shows the progress of the queue with the following columns being important:

First Seg.block	This shows the first undeleted segment and block number in the queue. The difference between *First Seg.Block* and *Last Seg.Block* provides the amount of data in M bytes that remains in the queue for processing.
Last Seg.block	This shows the last segment and block written to the queue.
Next read	This shows the next segment, block, and row to be read from the queue.
Save Int.Seg	The save interval for the queue which determines how long a delete from the queue will be delayed. This is specified in minutes using the **rs_config** command. The column also shows the segment associated with the save interval i.e. the next segment to be deleted. The difference between this and the *Last Seg.block* value gives the size of the queue in M bytes. This feature provides redundancy in the event of replication system failure. The save interval feature lets the sending Replication Server re-create all messages saved during the save interval.
Duplicates	This gives a running total of the number of duplicates detected since the queue thread was started. This is particularly important for the inbound queue which must detect and ignore duplicates. In a recovery situation the LTM may re-read log records which are already on the inbound queue. These are detected by the LTM and recorded in the *duplicates* column of this output.

Queue Space Management

The space available for all queues is defined with the **add partition** command.

add partition logical_name

on 'physical_name' with size size_mbytes

[starting at vstart]

The *starting at vstart* is not a normal clause to use.

add partition LN_SPACE_1

      on '/dev/PRS1_LN/LN_SPACE_1' with size 2000

This space is not database space and therefore may be increased and decreased with a bit more freedom than devices in SQL Server. Monitoring of the used partition space is done with the **admin disk_space** command.

admin disk_space

Partition Logical State	Part.Id	Total Segs	Used Segs
/dev/LNPRD_1/QUEUE_02			
QUEUE_02	102	2040	602
ON-LINE//			
/dev/LNPRD_1 /QUEUE_01			
QUEUE_01	103	2040	0
ON-LINE//			

If you are running short of queue space at a critical point in your processing and there is no obvious problem, you can simply add another partition to the queue space to provide more disk space. Once the peak period is over, or you have identified and corrected the problem, you can remove the additional disk space with the **drop partition** command.

drop partition LN_SPACE_1

Allocation of space to the dropped partition is stopped immediately and, when the current used space in the partition has been freed, the partition is dropped. This can be extremely useful at times of abnormal replication activity.

Information on a partition is held in *rs_diskpartitions*:

select * from rs_diskpartitions

name logical_name status allocation_map vstart	id	num_segs	allocated_segs
/dev/LNPRD1/LN_SPACE_1			
LN_SPACE_1	103	2040	327
1			

0xffffffffffffffffffffffffffffffdeaf7ffffffa7bdf5ffffffffffffffffffffffffffffffffffc27f7eb74d020000000000
0000000000000000000000000000000000000000000000000000000000000000000000000000000000
0000000000000000000000000000000000000000000000000000000000000000000000000000000000
0000000000000000000000000000000000000000000000000000000000000000000000000000000000
0000000000000000000000000000000000000000000000000000000000000000000000000000000000

0000000000000000000000000000000000000000000000000000000000000000000000000000000000
00000000000000000000000000

0

/dev/LNPRD1/ LN_SPACE_1

| LN_SPACE_1 | 102 | 2040 | 295 |

1

0xffffdffffffffffffffffffffffffffffffffffffffffffffffffffffffffffffffffffffffff0000000000000000000000000000000
0000000000000000000000000000000000000000000000000000000000000000000000000000000000
0000000000000000000000000000000000000000000000000000000000000000000000000000000000
0000000000000000000000000000000000000000000000000000000000000000000000000000000000
0000000000000000000000000000000000000000000000000000000000000000000000000000000000
0000000000000000000000000000000000000000000000000000000000000000000000000000000000
00000000000000000000000000

0

and on the segments in *rs_segments*:

select * from rs_segments

partition_id version	q_number flags	q_type	partition_offset	logical_seg	used_flag
101	100787	1	0	94	1
344	0				
101	0	0	1	0	0
367	0				
101	100791	0	2	0	1
277	0				
101	0	0	3	0	0
380	0				
101	100790	1	4	841	1
156	0				

Each message has a fixed length header plus variable length data. The header overhead is 380 bytes for an inbound queue and 200 bytes for an outbound queue. In addition to the fixed overhead, each column in the message has a 30 byte overhead.

Transactions are deleted from the queue by the SQM when they have been acknowledged as delivered to their destination. These deletions are not immediate but will wait until the end of a segment i.e. until a 1M boundary or until the save interval has expired. The messages are deleted when the recipient acknowledges delivery i.e. when the DSI thread has successfully applied the transaction to the

Replicate Database. You can specify a *save_interval* in minutes which will retain the message until the save interval has expired. The save interval is defined with the **rs_configure** command, held in the *rs_queues* table and displayed with the **admin who, sqm** command. This is discussed in more detail in chapter 4 on connections.

SQM Duplicate Detection

A major role of the SQM is detecting duplicates from the LTM i.e. messages which are already in the inbound queue, and ignoring them. In normal operation duplicate messages should not occur but, if the Primary Database is recovered to a previous point or the LTM is instructed to read from the beginning of the log, there is the possibility that the records read from the log will already have been processed by the LTM. The SQM must detect these duplicates and ignore them.

The duplicate detection is based on an "origin queue id (oqid)" value which is assigned to each log record passed from the LTM to the SQM. The oqid is made up as table 2.1:

Bytes	Description
1-2	The database generation id used to ensure a unique oqid during a reload of a transaction log. Shown by the **admin get_generation** command.
3-8	The transaction log page timestamp.
9-14	The rowid of the current row. (4 byte page number and 2 byte row offset number)
15-20	The rowid of the **begin tran** record for the oldest open transaction.
21-28	The date and time of the **begin tran** record for the oldest open transaction.
29-30	Used by the LTM to rollback orphan transactions i.e. those with no **commit** or **rollback tran** record.
31-32	Unused

Table 2.1: Format of the oqid

Apart from the database genid these values are generated from the log record information. So if the database genid stays the same, the SQM can analyse the oqid to see if the record has already been received. The last received oqid is held in memory and the SQM can simply test to see if the oqid being received from the LTM is less than or equal to the last received value. If it is then the message has already been received and the SQM ignores it. The SQM keeps a running total of duplicates detected for each inbound queue which you can see in the **admin who, sqm** output.

This is particularly important when you reload a database or make the LTM read from the beginning of the log, as the SQM will have a stored last received oqid value greater than many of the records currently on the transaction log. If you wish the transactions on the log to be replayed against the Replicate Database then the generated oqid must be forced to be greater than the last received value currently held by the SQM. This is done by increasing the database genid before allowing the LTM to read the log. As the genid is the first bytes of the oqid, all generated oqids will now be greater than the value held by the SQM and none of the log transactions will be ignored as duplicates. The database genid is increased with the **dbcc settrunc** command. This is issued in the appropriate Primary Database.

First you determine the current genid value using the **admin get_generation** command in the Replication Server:

> **admin get_generation, server_name, database_name**

> **admin get_generation LNPRD1, SALES_DB**

Current generation number for LNPRD1,SALES_DB is 1.

and then you can increase it with the **dbcc settrunc** command in the Primary Database:

> **dbcc settrunc('ltm', 'gen_id', value)**

Do not panic when you see values in the *duplicate* column of the **admin who, sqm** output under normal operation. The deletion of records from the inbound queue is not dynamic but is deferred until the SQM hits a segment boundary i.e. each 1M or until the *save_interval* has expired. Therefore a restart of the Replication Server or the LTM may naturally detect duplicates as logically deleted messages are read until the first "active" message is detected.

Stable Queue Transaction Manager

The SQT ensures that queues are accessed in a transactional manner so that clients are passed the queue messages in transaction sequence. The SQT consists of four queues:

Open queue

This holds the transaction records until the **commit** or **rollback** is read from the LTM. In this queue the transaction records are held in **begin tran** sequence. Once the **commit** or **rollback** is received for the transaction, all records for the transaction are moved to the 'closed' queue.

Closed queue

This holds the transaction records for completed transactions i.e. those for which the **commit** or **rollback** has been read from the LTM. Transactions in the closed queue are held in **commit tran** sequence. Records are read from this queue by a DIST or DSI thread. Once all records for a transaction have been read from this queue the transaction is moved to the 'read' queue.

Read queue

This holds all transactions which have been completely read from the closed queue. Once the recipient of the transaction has acknowledged the receipt of the transaction, a delete request is issued and the transaction is removed from this queue.

Truncation queue

This contains the **begin tran** record for all transactions in the queue. When the **begin tran** is first placed in the open queue it is also placed in the truncation queue. The truncation queue is used to determine which records may be deleted from the queue. Delete requests are made by logical qid (LQID) which is a unique reference applied to every record in the queue. The delete request will specify a range of LQIDs to delete. Unfortunately this may not be possible as the LQID range may include a transaction which has not yet been fully processed. The truncation queue is able to assist in making this decision of what may or may not be deleted.

Consider the following queue situation in figure 2.4.

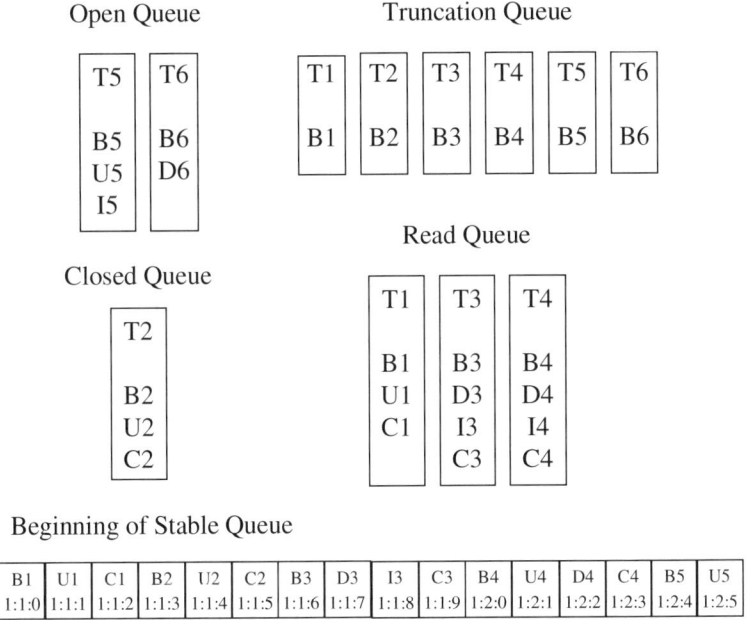

Figure 2.4: Transactions in a Queue

A delete request is received for the transactions in the read queue i.e. LQID range of 1:1:0 to 1:2:3. This cannot be actioned as there is a transaction (T2) which has not yet been fully read out. Once T2 has been fully read and placed in the read queue the delete may be actioned.

SQT Cache Size

The cache available to the SQT is defined by the configuration parameter *sqt_max_cache_size*. This is set with **rs_config** and has a default value of 131,072 bytes.

rs_config 'sqt_max_cache_size', 262144

Each inbound queue and each DSI thread uses the *sqt_max_cache_size* of memory. So if we have an *sqt_max_cache_size* of 1M and a Replication Server configuration of two Primary Databases and 6 Replicate Databases, we will require the a total memory of 12M as shown in table 2.2. Each Primary Database has both an inbound and outbound queue and each Replicate Database has one outbound queue.

Database	Number of queues	Sqt cache
RSSD	2	2M
PDB1	2	2M
PDB2	2	2M
RDB1	1	1M
RDB2	1	1M
RDB3	1	1M
RDB4	1	1M
RDB5	1	1M
RDB6	1	1M

Table 2.2: Memory requirements for SQT

If the SQT fills the cache for a queue, the SQT stops reading transactions from the queue. If the closed or read queues have transactions in them, then the SQT simply waits until these have been processed in which case space in the cache will become free. If the closed and read queues are empty the transaction which has the largest number of records is flushed to disk to free space. Neither of these situations is desirable, so check the errorlog to see if there are any messages concerning the SQT cache. Another way to determine if the SQT cache is too small is from the **admin who, sqt** command.

admin who, sqt

Spid	State		Info		Closed
	Read	*Open*	*Trunc*	*Removed*	*Full*
	SQM Blocked First Trans		*Parsed*	*SQM Reader*	
	Change Oqids	*Detect Orphans*			
54	Awaiting Wakeup		101393:1DIST LNPRD1_L.PROD_DB		0
	0	*1*	*1*	*0*	*0*
1 st:O,cmds:2,qid:7178:6:6			*0*	*0*	
	0		*0*		
55	Awaiting Wakeup		101472:1DIST LNPRD1.MKT_DB		0
	0	*0*	*0*	*0*	*0*

```
          1                        0              0
     0                   0
 56   Awaiting Wakeup    101296:1DIST NYPRD1.SALES_DB              0
     0              0            0         0            0
          1                        0              0
     0                   0
 57   Awaiting Wakeup    100514:1DIST LNPRD1.SALES_DB              0
     0              0            0         0            0
          1                        0              0
     0                   0
```

The *removed* column will show any transactions which have been flushed to disk to free space. Do not panic over an occasional cache full situation, but frequent occurrences mean that you will have to increase the *sqt_max_cache_size* parameter.

This configuration parameter is closely linked with the *sqt_max_prs_size* parameter which determines the memory available for pre-parsing of messages. The default for *sqt_max_prs_size* is 257K bytes and if you increase *sqt_max_cache_size* you should ensure that the *sqt_max_prs_size* is equal or greater than *sqt_max_cache_size*.

Replication Server memory

The Replication Server memory is controlled by the *memory_max* configuration parameter which defaults to 3M. At start-up 66% of this is allocated to memory segment pools which have fixed block sizes of 256 bytes, 1K, 4K, 16K and 64K. The Replication Server memory is divided into these 5 equal segment pools. For example if we leave *memory_max* at the default of 3M, then Replication Server will allocate 66% of this (2,076,162 bytes) to be split between the five segment pools i.e. 415,232 bytes each. The appropriate number of segments are then allocated to each of the pools. This is illustrated in figure 2.5.

	Total Memory (3M)				

Memory Pool	256 Byte	1K	4K	16K	64K
Memory Size	415232	415232	415232	415232	415232
Total Segments	1622	405	101	25	6

Figure 2.5: Memory segment allocation

When Replication Server requests a segment of a specific size it is allocated from the appropriate segment pool. If there are no available segments in the pool, the pool is expanded from the reserved memory (the remaining 34% left at start-up). If there is no free reserved memory an error is written to the log. If this becomes frequent, you need to seriously consider increasing the memory available to the Replication Server. The **admin statistics, mem** command shows the current allocation of memory to Replication Server:

admin statistics, mem

Segment_Size	Number_of_Segments	Number_Allocated
256	10813	3585
1024	2703	2703
4096	675	125
16384	168	82
65520	42	42
65520	21	21
65520	21	11
1024	1351	1351
16384	84	4
1024	1351	1351

Distributor Thread

The DIST is the thread which matches the replication definition with the subscriptions and forwards the Primary Database transactions to the appropriate Replicate Databases. To do this the DIST thread reads the inbound queue in commit sequence and calls three library services to process the transaction.

- Subscription Resolution Engine (SRE) to determine where the transaction should be sent i.e. to match the replication definition and the subscriptions.

- Transaction Delivery (TD) to package the transaction.

- Message Delivery (MD) to deliver the transaction if a route is involved.

The DIST thread is started when the Replication Server is started, independently of the LTM or the DSI, and is resumed with the **resume distributor** command if it is down.

resume distributor server_name.db_name

There is one DIST thread per inbound queue.

Subscription Resolution Engine (SRE)

The SRE uses the RSSD to match the table to a replication definition and the replication definition to its subscriptions, to determine where the transaction should be applied. If there are no subscriptions for a replication definition the transaction will be ignored. If there is no replication definition for the table, a warning is written to the error log and the transaction is ignored. The **admin who, dist** command gives totals of the number of commands processed and ignored.

admin who, dist

Spid	State		Info		PrimarySite
	Type	*Status*	*PendingCmds*	*SqtBlocked*	
	Duplicates	TransProcessed	CmdsProcessed	MaintUserCmds	NoRepdefCmds
	CmdsIgnored		*CmdMarkers*		
44	Active		100582 LNPRD1.SALES_DB		100582
	P	*Normal*	*0*	*1*	
	0	5562	1567536	0	0
	0		*0*		

45	Active		101472 LNPRD1.MKT_DB			101472
	P	Normal	0		1	
	0	234	586		0	0
	0		0			
46	Active		101296 NYPRD1.SALES_DB			101296
	P	Normal	0		1	
	0	4616	173115		0	0
	0		0			

A copy of the transaction is created for each output queue and the SRE adds a destination database id to each row.

Transaction Delivery (TD)

The TD service packages the messages which have to be delivered, ensuring increasing uniqueness of the oqid and calls MD to deliver the messages. The oqid generated by the LTM is unique but is based on the date and time the record was written to the transaction log. As the transactions are now being delivered in commit sequence this order may be compromised and the duplicate detection of the outbound SQM may fail. To avoid this, TD creates an increasing counter per transaction to reestablish the sequence of the transaction records. The counter is reset for each **begin tran** received by TD.

Consider the example in figure 2.6.

LTM generated oqid		TD generated oqid	
LTM oqid	Transaction	TD origin oqid	Transaction
1	BEGIN 1	6-1	BEGIN 2
2	INSERT 1	6-2	INSERT 2
3	BEGIN 2	6-3	UPDATE 2
4	INSERT 2	6-4	COMMIT 2
5	UPDATE 2	8-1	BEGIN 1
6	COMMIT 2	8-2	INSERT 1
7	INSERT 1	8-3	INSERT 1
8	COMMIT 1	8-4	COMMIT 1

Figure 2.6: TD Generated oqid

In figure 2.6 we have two transactions with transaction 2 committing before transaction 1. To maintain the oqid sequence TD allocates a new oqid for each transaction taking the original **commit tran** oqid as the base number.

Message Delivery (MD)

The MD service is called by each RSI to route the messages to their destination Replication Servers. MD will try to group messages to different destinations if they can be reached across the same route. Consider a replication architecture as shown in figure 2.7.

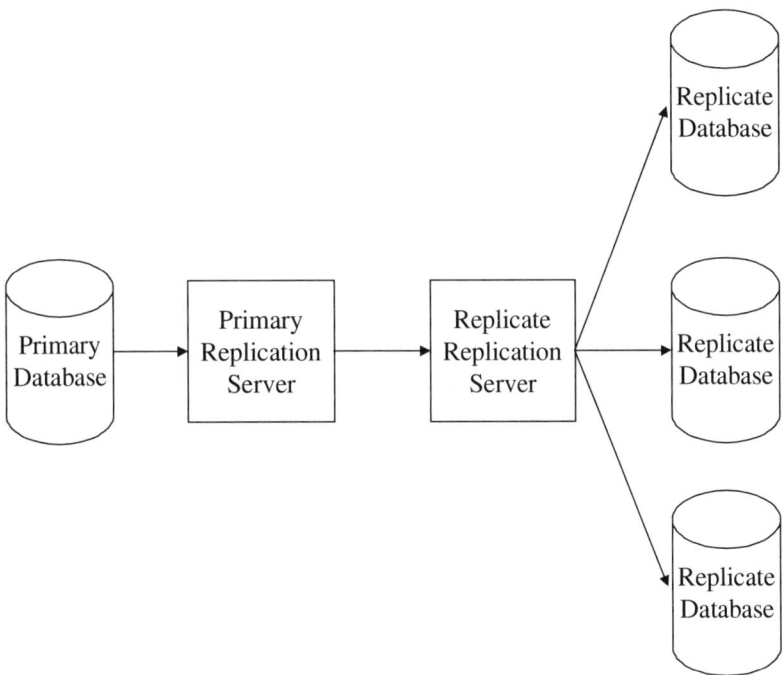

Figure 2.7: Message delivery to multiple targets

If a message is to be applied to each Replicate Database managed by the Replicate Replication Server, then MD will send only one copy of the message to the Replicate Replication Server which will then create three copies, one for each Replicate Database.

Data Service Interface

The DSI reads commands from the SQT closed queue and applies them directly to a Replicate Database. The DSI thread provides the error mapping processing which translates the SQL Server errors into Replication Server errors and actions them according to the error class definitions.

The DSI is notified by the SQT when the closed queue has a complete transaction. The DSI then checks that the transaction is not a duplicate or that there are no "lost" transactions and applies the transaction to the Replicate Database.

The DSI thread checks for duplicates as an extra check on the LTM duplicate handling mainly to ensure that duplicates do not occur in a recovery situation. The DSI holds a memory copy of the *rs_lastcommit* table to check the closed queue *oqid*. The *rs_lastcommit* table[3] resides on the Replicate Database and holds information on the last committed transaction at the Replicate Database. If the incoming *oqid* is less than the *rs_lastcommit oqid*, the transaction is rejected as a duplicate. The DSI also holds a copy of the *rs_exceptslast oqid* which is the latest *oqid* sent to the exception log, just in case the last transaction processed was skipped and written to the exception log instead of being applied to the Replicate Database. So the incoming *oqid* is tested against the larger of the *rs_lastcommit* and *rs_exceptslast oqid* for duplicate detection

When the DSI is started the *oqid* values of the last transaction committed or skipped as an exception are reconstructed from the *rs_lastcommit* and the *rs_exceptslast* tables. Any transactions in the queue with an *origin_qid* less than the larger of these two values is assumed to be a duplicate. The DSI ignores any such transaction and prints a warning message that transactions may have been lost. Pay attention to these 'detecting loss' messages in the error log. If you have dropped a connection to a database but there are records in the *rs_exceptslast* system table, the **drop connection** command does not remove these. When you resume the connection the *rs_exceptslast* table is examined to calculate the last *oqid* sent to the database and the resumed connection may start from the last *oqid* written to the exceptions table. Keep the exceptions tables empty with regular investigation and deletion with **rs_delexception** if necessary.

The DSI attempts to group transactions to a Replicate Database to reduce the log contention at the Replicate Database. In general, if the closed queue contains transactions from the same origin, user and password[4] they will be grouped together for application at the Replicate Database. When several transactions are grouped, the *oqid* of the grouped transaction is taken as the *oqid* of the last **begin tran** transaction in the group. The limits on grouping are defined with the parameters *dsi_xact_group_size* and *dsi_cmd_batch_size*.

---

[3] This is an extremely useful table and a regular **select origin, origin_time, dest_commit_time from rs_lastcommit** will show you how up-to-date replication is from each source database.

[4] The constraints are a bit stricter – such as no DDL, a 64K size limit and a hard coded limit of 20 transactions.

Once the DSI has applied the transaction to the Replicate Database and received an acknowledgement from the Replicate Database, the DSI sends the update of the *rs_lastcommit* table.

Replication Service Interface

The RSI sends messages across routes to distributed Replication Servers. The RSI consists of two services: the RSI Receiver thread which calls MD to write the message to the appropriate queue and the RSI Sender thread which sends the messages from the outbound queue and forwards them to the Replicate Replication Server.

RSI Receiver Thread

The RSI Receiver thread manages the RSI outbound queue, calling MD to populate the queue.

RSI Sender Thread

For each direct route Replication Server starts an RSI Sender thread which is the thread displayed by the **admin who** command The RSI Sender thread has the configuration parameters shown in table 2.3.

Parameter	Description
rsi_batch_size	Number of bytes processed before requesting a truncation point.
rsi_fadeout_time	Number of seconds of inactivity before the connection is faded out.
rsi_packet_size	Number of bytes in a packet (fixed at 2K in 11.0.3).
rsi_synch_interval	Number of seconds before RSI attempts to synchronize outbound queues

Table 2.3: RSI Configuration Parameters

The RSI Sender thread reads messages from the outbound queue and forwards them to the Replicate Replication Server. The RSI Sender thread handles message deletion from the queue and the moving of the truncation point. When the total number of bytes sent to the Replicate Replication Server is greater than the *rsi_batch_size* parameter, the RSI Sender thread requests a new truncation point from the Replicate Replication Server. This truncation point is maintained by the RSI Sender thread using the **rsi_get_trunc** and **rsi_set_trunc** commands. The use of these is similar to the transaction log replication truncation point commands for inbound queues. The location of the truncation point is held in the *rs_locater* table.

Once the truncation point is received, the RSI Sender thread calls the SQM for the RSI queue to delete the messages forwarded to the Replicate Replication Server. When a message has been delivered MD will pass the *lqid* to the RSI Sender thread for deletion from the queue. As messages are delivered in commit sequence, not *lqid* sequence, this message may not be the first in the queue and therefore cannot be physically deleted. This is similar to message deletion for the inbound queue.

3

Routes

Introduction

If you have only one Replication Server in your architecture then you do not need to define **routes**. With only one Replication Server the databases are linked directly to the Replication Server with **connections**. Database connections are covered in chapter 4. However if you decide to have multiple Replication Servers to minimise the network traffic, then the Replication Servers are linked together over routes which you need to define. To allow a Primary Replication Server to replicate transactions to a Replicate Replication Server you need to define a route between them. Also, the routes are uni-directional which means that you need to define two routes if the replication is both ways between two Replication Servers: RS1 to RS2 and RS2 to RS1. You also need to define a route from the Replicate Replication Server to the Primary

Replication Server if the Replicate Database supports request functions as these need to execute the real function in the Primary Database.

In this chapter I shall assume that replication is one way as this allows me to continue to use the terms Primary Replication Server and Replicate Replication Server without any ambiguity or further qualification.

If you have decided to have more than one Replication Server in the architecture you will have to create routes for:

- Replication Servers which manage primary data must have routes defined to all Replication Servers that manage the subscriptions to that data.

- Replication Servers where request functions originate require a route to the Primary Database Replication Server.

- Replication Servers that change class scope function strings or error mappings require routes to all Replication Servers that use the function string or error class.

- Replication Servers that function as Intermediate Replication Servers require routes to the destination Replication Server in the indirect route.

Defining Routes

Routes may be **direct** or **indirect**.

A **direct** route is simply a route between two Replication Servers.

An **indirect** route uses an Intermediate Replication Server (IRS) as a staging Replication Server to forward transactions from the Primary Replication Server to one or more Replicate Replication Servers.

In theory there may be any number of Intermediate Replication Servers in a hierarchical configuration. In practice the more Intermediate Replication Servers that you have in a replication path, the longer the replication latency will be.

Direct route

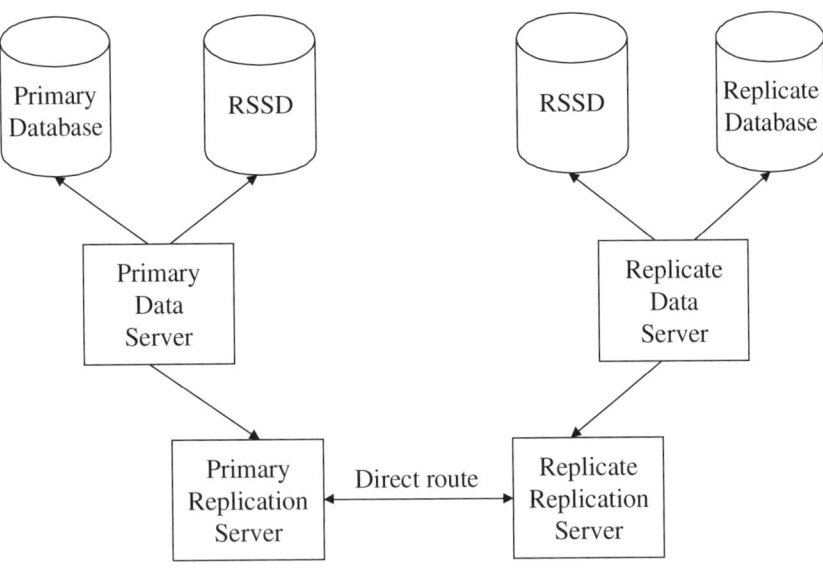

Figure 3.1: Direct route between two Replication Servers

A direct route connects two Replication Servers as shown in figure 3.1 and is defined with the **create route** command at the Primary Replication Server.

create route to dest_rep_server_name

[set username [to] user_name]

[set password [to] pass_word]

[set rsi_batch_size [to] 'value']

[set route_param to 'value']

[set security_param to 'value']

where

username	The login name used to login to the destination Replication Server and to the RSSD to register the route in the system tables.
password	The associated password for the login name.

rsi_batch_size   The number of bytes sent before requesting a truncation point.

route_param   A route parameter as described later in the **configure route** section.

security_param   A security parameter for the route as defined in table 3.1. Only the *use_security_services* parameter is implemented in the initial release of 11.5.

parameter	description
msg_confidentiality	Indicates whether Replication Server sends and receives encrypted data. If set to "required" outgoing data is encrypted. If set to "not required" Replication Server accepts incoming data that is encrypted or not encrypted.
msg_integrity	Indicates whether data is checked for tampering.
msg_origin_check	Indicates whether the source of data should be verified.
msg_replay_detection	Indicates whether data should be checked to make sure it has not been read or intercepted.
msg_sequence_check	Indicates whether data should be checked for interception.
mutual_auth	Requires the remote server to provide proof of identify before a connection is established.
security_mechanism	The name of the third-party security mechanism enabled for the pathway.
unified_login	Indicates how Replication Server seeks to log in to remote data servers and accept incoming logins. required: always seeks to log in to remote server with a credential. not_required: always seeks to log in to remote server with a password.
use_security_services	Tells Replication Server whether to use security services. If *use_security_services* is "off" no security features take effect. This parameter can only be set by the **sp_configure** command.

Table 3.1: Parameters affecting network based security

The default user name is *rep_server_name_rsi* with password *rep_server_name_rsi_ps*. This is created by the **rs_init** process to allow Replication Servers which originate routes to log into the other Replication Servers. If you use another user name and password, make sure that you create them before you issue the **create route** command.

Wait for the route to become active before you create another route. The **create route** holds locks on the system tables while they are being materialized, so this runs as a single threaded command anyway. You can check this with the **rs_helproute** system procedure which displays the route status.

rs_helproute [rep_server_name]

rs_helproute LNPRD_PS1

route	status
LNPRD_RS1————————> NYPRD_IRS1	Active

route	status
LNPRD_RS1———————— (Next Site: NYPRD_IRS1) ————————> TKOPRD_RS1	Active

route	status
TKOPRD_RS1 ————————> LNPRD_RS1	Active

The status values are:

- Being created.
- Active.
- Being dropped.
- Being dropped with nowait.

Creating or dropping a route creates or drops the subscriptions to the system tables in the RSSD. If these subscriptions do not appear or disappear during a materialization or dematerialization then the Replication Server is probably having trouble executing the **create** or **drop route** command. You should investigate what is going on if there is a delay: it might only be a network problem but check the error logs anyway.

The **create route** command creates subscriptions to the RSSD system tables which causes the Replicate Replication Server to subscribe to the Primary Replication Server system tables. These system table subscriptions have to be materialized and this can take some minutes for which you simply have to wait. Creating a direct route creates an RSI outbound stable queue at the Primary Replication Server for the destination Replicate Replication Server and starts the RSI thread to log onto the destination Replicate Replication Server.

Before you create a direct route you should set up and check the following:

- The Primary Replication Server has a login account at the Replicate Replication Server.

  The Primary Replication Server needs a login account to log into the Replicate Replication Server. This is defined in the **create route** command but needs to be active at the Replicate Replication Server before you issue the **create route**.

- The LTM of the RSSD is running.

  The Replicate Replication Server subscribes to the RSSD system tables at the Primary Replication Server and so the LTM has to be running to replicate the system table changes.

- The Replicate Replication Server is defined in the *interfaces* file of the Primary Replication Server.

  The Primary Replication Server logs onto the Replicate Replication Server so it needs to know where it is.

- The destination Replication Server is running.

  Sounds a bit naïve, but it can easily catch you out.

create route to RRSLN02

set username sa

set password fred01

The **create route** command is processed as figure 3.2.

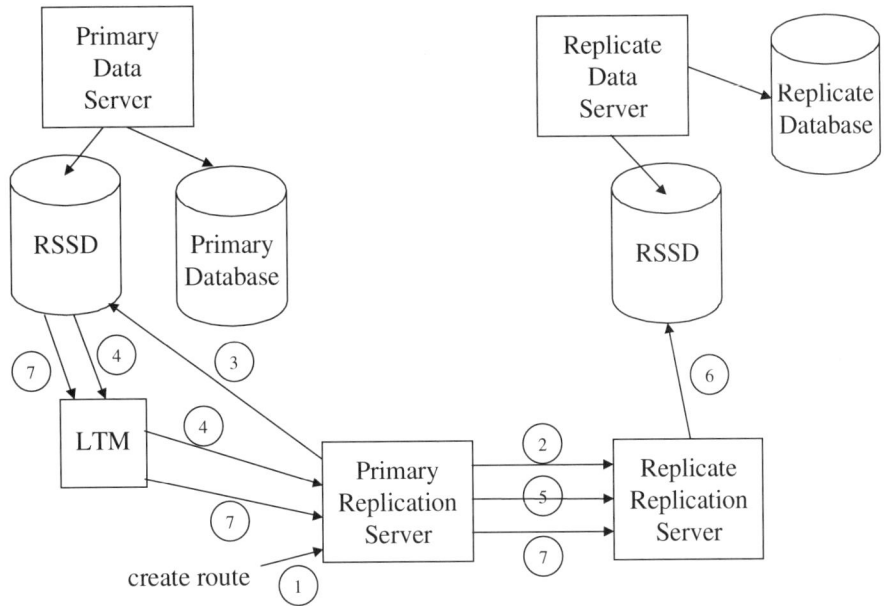

Figure 3.2: Create route processing

1. The **create route** is issued at the Primary Replication Server.

2. The Primary Replication Server logs into the Replicate Replication Server to verify the username and password.

3. The Primary Replication Server executes the **rs_marker** procedure in the RSSD to coordinate the **create route** with any other RSSD changes.

4. The LTM then reads the RSSD transaction log and forwards the transactions to the Primary Replication Server.

5. The Primary Replication Server processes the outbound queue and sends the transactions to the Replicate Replication Server.

6. On receipt of the replicated transactions the Replicate Replication Server starts subscribing to and materializing the system tables.

7. Once the materialization is complete the **create route** is complete.

This is an automatic atomic materialization the details of which are discussed in chapter 6. The most important aspect of the atomic materialization is that it is carried out as a single transaction and holds a lock on the source system tables.

Indirect route

If you have a lot of network traffic and it helps to distribute the Stable Device queues, it may be advisable to create an indirect route between the Primary Replication Server and the Replicate Replication Server via one or more Intermediate Replication Servers as shown in figure 3.3.

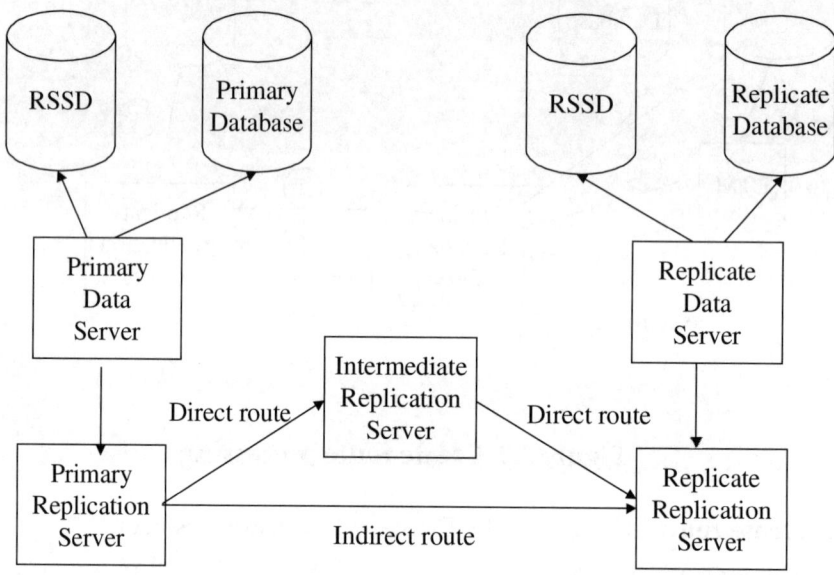

Figure 3.3: Indirect route between two Replication Servers

The indirect route is defined using the **create route** command with an extra clause **set next site**.

    create route to replication_rep_server_name

    set next site [to] int_rep_server_name

To create the indirect route you must first of all create the required direct routes. In figure 3.3, the direct routes between the Primary Replication Server and Intermediate Replication Server and between the Intermediate Replication Server and Replicate Replication Server must be created before the indirect route PRS - IRS - RRS is defined. The sequence of direct route definition is also important as described below.

PRS to IRS

create route to IRS_name

set username sa

set password january

IRS to RRS

create route to RRS_name

set username sa

set password january

Indirect route from PRS to RRS

create route to RRS_name

set next site thru IRS_name

In general the use of an Intermediate Replication Server adds to the replication latency and you need to check any network traffic savings against any increases in replication latency.

However, using indirect routes can help to distribute the stable queue usage throughout the Replication Servers. For direct routes the Primary Replication Server will have an outbound stable queue for each direct route and each of these will be managed by an RSI thread. For indirect routes it is the corresponding direct routes between the Replication Servers in the hierarchy which require outbound stable queues and RSI threads. Although the number of stable queues are not reduced they get distributed to other Replicate Replication Servers.

Consider the direct routes of figure 3.4.

This requires 6 stable queues and 6 RSI threads in the Primary Replication Server: all of the stable queues are on the Primary Replication Server.

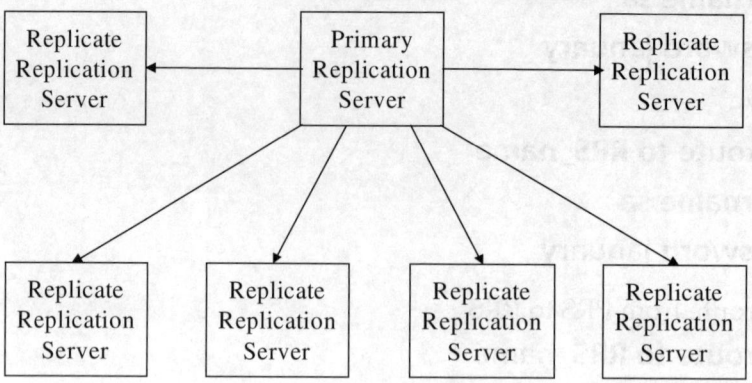

Figure 3.4: Direct routes

If we distribute this with 2 Intermediate Replication Servers as figure 3.5.

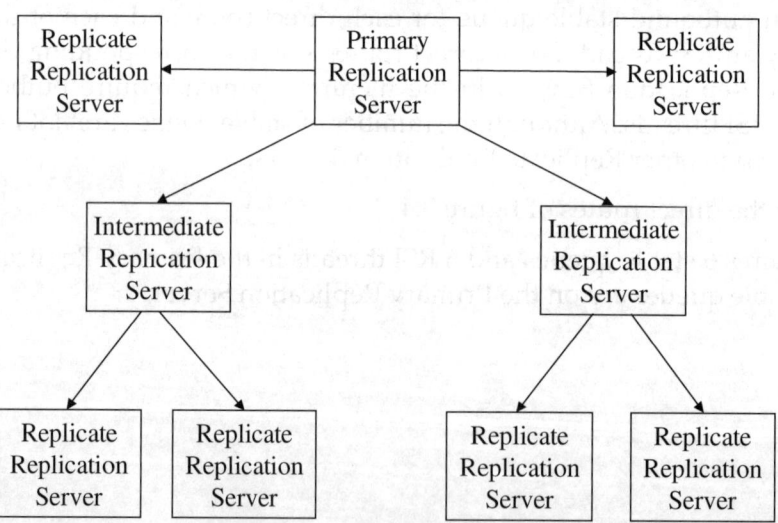

Figure 3.5: Intermediate Replication Servers

We now have 3 Replication Servers each of which has 2 stable queues and 2 RSI threads. So we have not reduced the number of outbound queues but we have distributed them in the architecture and reduced the loading on each Replication Server.

However be careful to ensure that the indirect routes always diverge. You cannot reassemble several direct routes back to one Replication Server.

Using this hierarchical indirect routing can reduce the network traffic. Consider the simple indirection of figure 3.6.

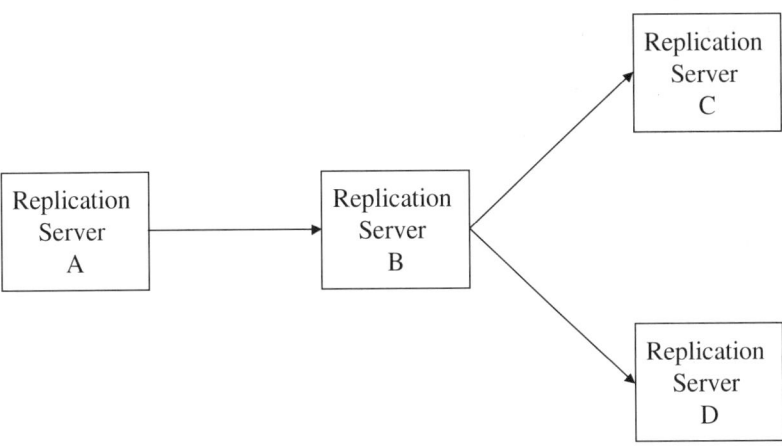

Figure 3.6: Indirect routes

If B, C, D all have the same subscriptions to A then a change at A can be sent once to B which will propagate it to C and D. This does not really reduce the total network traffic but it does reduce the output from A, which might be significant. For example A-B may be WAN traffic and B-C/D may be LAN traffic and it is normally advisable to reduce the WAN traffic as much as possible.

However the bottom line is that the more indirection i.e. Replication Servers in the hierarchy, the more times the messages have to be queued and the slower the replication becomes. Test any indirection before you go into production.

Configuring a direct route

Direct routes have a series of parameters which may be configured with the **configure route** command.

configure route to rep_server_name

set {save_interval to 'value' |

rsi_batch_size to 'value' |

rsi_fadeout_time to 'value' |

rsi_packet_size to 'value' |

rsi_sync_interval to 'value'}

set security_param [to] 'value'

set security_services [to] 'default'

where

save_interval	This specifies the number of minutes that the Replication Server saves messages after a successful delivery to the destination Replication Server. The default is 0.
rsi_batch_size	This specifies the number of bytes sent to another Replication Server before a truncation point is requested. The default is 262,144 bytes. Range is 1024 to 262,144.
rsi_fadeout_time	This specifies the number of seconds of idle time before Replication Server closes the connection to a destination Replication Server. The default is -1, which specifies that Replication Server will not close the connection.
rsi_packet_size	This specifies the network packet size in bytes. The default is 2048. Range is 1024 to 8192.
rsi_sync_interval	This specifies the number of seconds between RSI synchronization inquiry messages. These messages synchronize the RSI outbound queue with destination Replication Servers. The default is 60 seconds and the value must be greater than 0.
security_param	Specifies a security parameter as table 3.1.

set security_services to 'default'

> Sets all of the network-based security parameters to "not required".

The only one that you should need to alter is the *save_interval* as this can help to recover from a queue failure. The others should be left as the default values initially until you experience performance problems. In fact the Sybase 11.5 documentation actually recommends that you leave the others at their default values for optimum performance.

Suspending and resuming a route

Routes are suspended with **suspend route** and resumed with **resume route**.

suspend route to RRS_name

resume route to RRS_name

The replication over the route is carried out from the Primary Replication Server outbound queue to the Replicate Replication Server inbound queue. When the route is suspended the transactions simply stack up in the Primary Replication Server outbound queue until the route is resumed. If you need to suspend a route for whatever reason, remember that replication is still working and the Primary Replication Server outbound queue may fill up quite quickly. You cannot suspend an indirect route, only direct routes between two Replication Servers. **Resume route** simply resumes a suspended route and starts sending transactions in the RSI queue to the Replication Server.

Dropping a route

A route may be dropped using the **drop route** command. This command is entered at the Primary Replication Server for the route.

drop route to RRS_name

[with nowait]

The **drop route** command drops the system table subscription information at the Replicate Replication Server and Primary Replication Server and flushes the outbound queue at the Primary Replication Server.

The **with nowait** clause is the error situation when the route is dropped even if the Primary Replication Server cannot contact the Replicate Replication Server. When you do this the Replicate Replication Server will not know of the action and cannot do the necessary clean up processing on the system table subscriptions. You will need to use **sysadmin purge_route_at_replicate** to remove system table subscriptions at the replicate site. This command is entered at the Replicate Replication Server for the route.

sysadmin purge_route_at_replicate, rep_server_name

Before dropping a route, you must drop all subscriptions at the destination Replication Server for the route and also drop any indirect routes that use the direct route. Consider the indirect routing of figure 3.7.

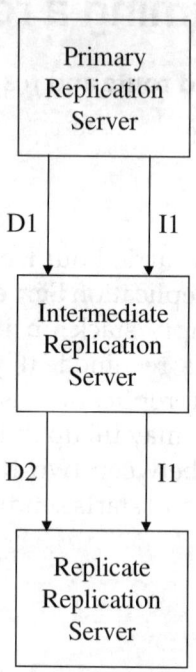

Figure 3.7: Dropping indirect routes

Before you drop route D2, you must drop all subscriptions at the Replicate Replication Server for replication definitions at both the Intermediate Replication Server and the Primary Replication Server and then you must drop the indirect route at I1.

The processing involved in dropping a route is shown in figure 3.8.

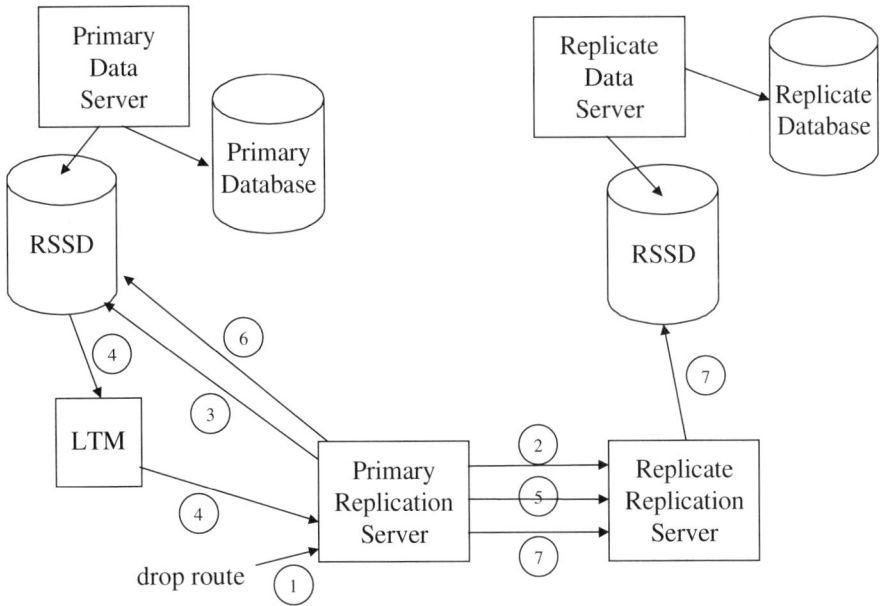

Figure 3.8: Dropping a route

1. The **drop route** command is entered at the Primary Replication Server.

2. The Primary Replication Server logs into the Replicate Replication Server to verify the user name and password.

3. The Primary Replication Server executes the **rs_marker** procedure in its RSSD to action the **drop route**.

4. The LTM extracts the **drop route** transaction from the RSSD log and sends it to the Primary Replication Server inbound queue.

5. The Primary Replication Server replicates the **drop route** command to the Replicate Replication Server.

6. The Primary Replication Server deletes the information for the system table *rs_routes* in its RSSD and deletes the outbound queue if it is a direct route.

7. The Replicate Replication Server receives the **drop route** transaction and deletes the Primary Replication Server locater from *rs_locater*.

Altering a route

A route may be changed using the **alter route** command.

> **alter route to RRS_name**
> **{set next site [to] IRS_name |**
> **set username [to] user_name set password [to] pass_word |**
> **set password [to] pass_word |**
> **set route_param [to] 'value' |**
> **set security_param [to] 'value' |**
> **set security_services [to] 'default'}**

This allows you to change the RSI user name and/or password. More interestingly it allows you to change a direct route into an indirect route and/or to change the current Intermediate Replication Server. But make sure that when you alter the Intermediate Replication Server in an indirect route that the new Intermediate Replication Server has a route already defined to the target Replication Server. The usage of the clauses is quite specific:

set next site   Use when changing a direct route into an indirect route or when changing the intermediate route of an indirect route.

set username user_name set password pass_word

Use when changing an indirect route to a direct route as the login to the destination Replication Server will now be required.

set password pass_word

Use when changing the password for a direct route. In this case you must suspend the route before making the change.

route_param   A route parameter as described in the **configure route** section earlier.

security_param   Specifies a security parameter as table 3.1.

set security_services to 'default'

Sets all of the network based security parameters to "not required".

alter route to RRS_name

set next site thru IRS_name

set user name sa set password january

As with any Replication Server change, when you alter a route you should ensure that no replication activity is taking place.

- Quiesce the Replication Server.

  sysadmin quiesce_force_rsi

- Stop the log transaction traffic by suspending the LTM.

  suspend log transfer from {server.db_name | all}

This ensures that you do not send transactions to the wrong Replicate Replication Server while you are altering the route.

- Suspend the route using the **suspend route** command.

  suspend route to replication_rep_server_name

- Create any new destination routes first, before you add a new indirection.

- Alter the route.

- Resume the route using the **resume route** command.

  resume route to replication_rep_server_name

- Resume log transfer using the **resume log transfer** command.

  resume log transfer to {server.db_name | all}

Note that this allows the LTM to reconnect to the Replication Server but does not always restart the LTM. Always check that the LTM has restarted properly after you resume log transfer.

Viewing Route Information

The **rs_helproute** displays information on the routes.

  rs_helproute [rep_server_name]

  rs_helproute LNPRD_RS1

route	status
LNPRD_RS1————————> NYPRD_IRS1	Active

route	status
LNPRD_RS1———————— (Next Site: NYPRD_IRS1) ————————> TKOPRD_RS1	Active

route	status
TKOPRD_RS1 ————————> LNPRD_RS1	Active

The status values are:

- Being created.
- Active.
- Being dropped.
- Being dropped with nowait.

System tables

rs_routes

One row for each route.

  select * from rs_routes

dest_rsid	through_rsid	source_rsid	status	suspended	src_version
16777317	16777317	16777319	2	0	
16777318	16777318	16777317	2	0	

The **rs_helproute** system procedure is quite adequate for routes.

Troubleshooting

Without trying to pre-empt the troubleshooting section, the **create route** will not always work and you should always check the error logs and system tables after a **create route** to make sure that everything looks OK.

Each component in the replication of the **create route** can go wrong and you should check them in turn.

- No entries in the RSSD of the Primary Replication Server.

    The first step of inserting entries into the RSSD by the Primary Replication Server has failed. These inserts are carried out by the RSSD primary user so check that the user_id and password are correct. Next most obvious reason for the failure is that the RSSD log is full and all processes are suspended.

- No entries in the Stable Device of the Primary Replication Server.

    The LTM extracts the RSSD inserts and writes them to the Stable Device of the Primary Replication Server. Only two real possibilities here for failure: the LTM is not running or the LTM cannot connect to the Primary Replication Server.

- No entries in the Stable Device of the Replicate Replication Server.

    The Primary Replication Server distributes the **create route** to the destination Replication Server. If the system table inserts are still in the outbound queue of the Primary Replication Server Stable Device then the connection to the Replicate Replication Server has not been successful. The most obvious cause is a failure to login but also check that the route is defined correctly.

- No entries in the RSSD of the Replicate Replication Server.

    The **create route** inserts have reached the Stable Device of the Replicate Replication Server but have not been written to the RSSD of the Replicate Replication Server. Similar to the first step at the Primary Replication Server, check the login id and password or a full transaction log.

4

Connections

Introduction

Connections are used by Replication Server to interact with a database. Every database which is managed directly by a Replication Server must have a connection defined. Connections are defined using the initialization routine **rs_init** or with the **create connection** command. A normal approach will be to use **rs_init** for the initial definition of the connection and **create connection** if the connection has been dropped at any time and needs to be recreated. Initial definition of the connection by **rs_init** is important as it initializes the objects and permissions required for replication to take place. If the database has already been defined to a Replication Server with **rs_init** these objects will already exist and so **create connection** should be used. A typical database connection scenario is shown in figure 4.1.

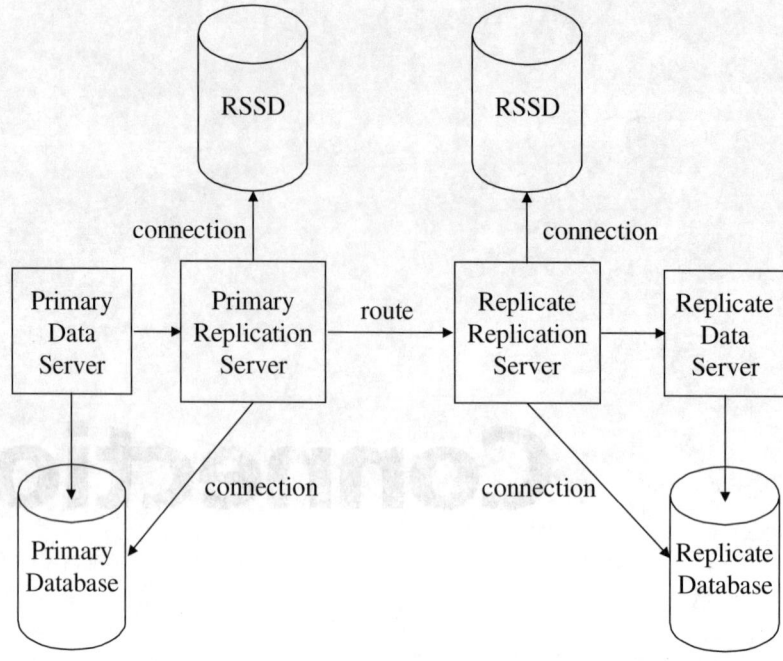

Figure 4.1: Typical database connections

Creating connections with rs_init

The **rs_init** program is used to initialize replication and its components. The **rs_init** program resides in the $SYBASE/repserver/install directory and you should be logged in as *sybase* to run this program.

After the first two initial screens asking you what you want to initialize you are presented with the Replication Server configuration screen:

CONFIGURE REPLICATION SYSTEM

1. **Install a new Replication Server**
2. **Add a database to the replication system**
3. **Upgrade an existing Replication Server**

4. **Downgrade RSSD for an existing Replication Server**
5. **Upgrade an existing database in the replication system**
6. **Enable password encryption for a Replication Server**
7. **Enable password encryption for an LTM**
8. **Alter a Replication Server configuration file password**
9. **Alter a password in an LTM configuration file**

Choosing 2 (Adding a database) presents the add database screen:

ADD DATABASE TO REPLICATION SYSTEM

1. **Replication Server Information**   **Incomplete**
2. **Database Information**   **Incomplete**

You need to complete both of these before continuing. Choosing 1 (Replication Server information) simply requests the name of the Replication Server and, as a sub-menu, the administrator's password to allow **rs_init** to log into the Replication Server.

REPLICATION SERVER NAME

1. **Replication Server Name:**

Choosing 2 (Database information) from the add database screen displays the database information screen.

DATABASE INFORMATION

1. **SQL Server name:**
2. **SA user: sa**
3. **SA password:**
4. **Database name:**
5. **Will the database require an LTM: no**
6. **Maintenance user:**
7. **Maintenance password:**
8. **DBO user:**

9. **DBO password:**

10. **Is this a Physical Connection for Existing Logical Connection: no**

Once you have completed all of the entries, the **rs_init** program will log into the database and establish the connection information. This process is covered in more detail in the installation chapter 13.

When **rs_init** is used to define the connection for the first time it carries out some installation processes which are not done by the **create connection** command.

Primary Database

For a Primary Database i.e. a database which requires an LTM **rs_init** carries out the following:

- Loads the **rs_install_primary.sql** script.

  This script lives in $SYBASE/repserver/scripts and carries out the following:

  - Creates the *rs_lastcommit* table.
  - Creates the *rs_threads* table.
  - Creates the **rs_update_lastcommit** and **rs_get_lastcommit** procedures.
  - Creates the **rs_update_threads** and **rs_initialize_threads** procedures.
  - Creates the **rs_marker** procedure.
  - Creates the **rs_check_repl_stat** procedure.
  - Executes **dbcc settrunc('ltm', 'valid')** to allow the LTM to read transactions from the log.
  - Executes **sp_setreplicate rs_marker, true** (although it should be **sp_setrepproc** of course!!!).

- Creates the config, errorlog and RUNSERVER files for the LTM. The default names are *ltm_name.cfg*; *ltm_name.log* and *RUN_ltm_name*.

- Creates the database connection.

- Starts the LTM.

Replicate Database

For a Replicate Database i.e. a database which does not require an LTM **rs_init** carries out the following:

- Loads the **rs_install_replicate.sql** script.

This script lives in $SYBASE/repserver/scripts and carries out the following:

- Creates the *rs_lastcommit* and the *rs_threads* tables.
- Creates the **rs_update_lastcommit** and **rs_get_lastcommit** procedures.
- Creates the **rs_update_threads**, **rs_initialize_threads** and **rs_get_thread_seq** procedures.
- Drops the **rs_marker** procedure if it exists.
- Creates the database connection.

In addition to the installation processes above, another crucial difference between **rs_init** and **create connection** is that **rs_init** creates the users required by the Replication Server and the LTM for the connection.

When a connection is created with **rs_init** the users shown in table 4.1 are defined:

Location	User	Purpose
Primary Database	Maintenance user	To allow the maintenance user to apply transactions to the database.
	ltm user	To allow the LTM to read the transaction log and to update the replication truncation point. My normal approach for this user (*ltm*) is aliased to the dbo in the target database.
Replicate Database	Maintenance user	To allow the maintenance user to apply transactions to the database.
LTM	*sa* user	To allow the administrator to execute the few commands supported by the LTM: such as **shutdown**, **scan**

Table 4.1: Users required for a database connection

The permissions granted by **rs_init** are:

```
grant all on rs_lastcommit to maint_user

grant execute on rs_update_lastcommit to maint_user
grant execute on rs_get_lastcommit to maint_user
```

grant execute on rs_check_repl_stat to maint_user

grant select on rs_threads to public

grant execute on rs_initialize_threads to public

grant execute on rs_update_threads to public

An additional permission is required on **rs_update_lastcommit** when "request" functions are being used. Request functions are executed at the Replicate Database which makes an **rpc** to the Primary Database to execute the procedure at the Primary Database so that it will be replicated to the Replicate Database. This means that the originating user has to update the *rs_lastcommit* table and must be able to execute **rs_update_lastcommit**. The **rs_init** routine grants execute to public to facilitate this.

grant execute on rs_update_lastcommit to public

You may want to be a little less open here, and grant execute only to those users who can execute this type of procedure.

Creating connections with the create connection command

Create the connection

A connection to a database is defined with the **create connection** command. This command is executed at the Replication Server which manages the database and requires *sa* permission.

create connection to server_name.db_name

set error class [to] error_class_name

set function string class [to] function_string_class_name

set username [to] user_name

[set password [to] pass_word]

[set database_param [to] 'value']

[set security_param [to] 'value']

[with {log transfer on, dsi_suspended}]

[as active for logical_ds_name.logical_db_name |
as standby for logical_ds_name.logical_db_name
[use dump marker]]

where

error class	The name of an error class to handle errors on the database connection. The default error class is *rs_sqlserver_error_class*.
function string class	The name of a function string class to use for operations on the database. The default function string class is *rs_sqlserver_function_class*.
set username/password	This defines the maintenance user username and password used by the Replication Server to log into the database and execute the required operations. Make sure that you have defined the login at the database and granted the user the required permissions on tables and procedures for the Replication Server commands to be performed.
database_param	A database connection parameter as defined in the **configure connection** section below.
security_param	A security parameter for the route as defined in table 4.2. Only the *use_security_services* parameter is implemented in the initial release of 11.5.
log transfer on	This indicates that the connection is to a Primary Database which has an LTM reading log transactions and passing them to the Replication Server. If you omit this clause for the database connection, the LTM will not be able to pass log transactions to the Replication Server.
dsi_suspended	This creates the connection with the DSI thread suspended. This is a useful option to allow you to bulk materialize the Replicate Database but still have the LTM extracting transactions from the Primary Database log. You can resume the connection when the Replicate Database is ready with the **resume connection** command and transactions in the DSI queue will be applied to the Replicate Database.

as active/standby for   These define the location of the active and standby
                               databases.

use dump marker   This specifies the approach to materializing the standby
                               database. Warm Standby is discussed in detail in
                               Chapter 10.

parameter	description
msg_confidentiality	Indicates whether Replication Server sends and receives encrypted data. If set to "required," outgoing data is encrypted. If set to "not required," Replication Server accepts incoming data that is encrypted or not encrypted.
msg_integrity	Indicates whether data is checked for tampering.
msg_origin_check	Indicates whether the source of data should be verified.
msg_replay_detection	Indicates whether data should be checked to make sure it has not been read or intercepted.
msg_sequence_check	Indicates whether data should be checked for interception.
mutual_auth	Requires remote server to provide proof of identify before a connection is established.
security_mechanism	The name of the third-party security mechanism enabled for the pathway.
unified_login	Indicates how Replication Server seeks to log in to remote data servers and accepts incoming logins. required: always seeks to log in to remote server with a credential. not_required: always seeks to log in to remote server with a password.
use_security_services	Tells Replication Server whether to use security services. If *use_security_services* is "off," no security features take effect. This Parameter can only be set by the **sp_configure** procedure.

Table 4.2: Parameters affecting network based security

The **create connection** updates the system tables in the local RSSD and these updates are replicated to all Replication Servers in the replication domain i.e. all Replication Servers which have a route originating at the Replication Server where the connection is defined.

> **create connection to LNPRDSRV_1.sales_db**
>
> **set error class rs_sqlserver_error_class**
>
> **set function string class rs_sqlserver_function_class**
>
> **set username rsmnt_user**
>
> **set password rsmnt_user_pw**
>
> **with dsi_suspended**

Configuring the connection

In general the default configuration of a connection is sufficient. If you find that replication problems are occurring because of connection configuration, you can configure connection parameters with the **configure connection** command. This is executed at the Replication Server which manages the database connection and requires *sa* permission.

> **configure connection to server_name.db_name {**
>
> **set function string class [to] function_class_name |**
>
> **set error class [to] error_class_name |**
>
> **set password [to] p_word |**
>
> **set log transfer [to] {on|off} |**
>
> **set database_param [to] 'value' |**
>
> **set security_param [to] 'value' |**
>
> **set security_services [to] 'default' }**

where

database_param	This may set the configuration parameters described in table 4.3.
security_param	A security parameter for the route as defined in table 4.2. Only the *use_security_services* parameter is implemented in the initial release of 11.5.

set security_services to 'default'

This resets all of the network-based security features for the connection to "not required".

Parameter	Description
batch	The default of "on" specifies that Replication Server may send multiple commands to the data server as a single command batch. When batch is set to off, commands are sent to the data server one at a time.
batch_begin	The default of "on" specifies that a **begin transaction** can be sent in the same batch as other commands.
command_retry	This specifies the number of times to retry a transaction that fails due to data server errors. The default is 3.
db_packet_size	This specifies the maximum network packet size. The default is 512 bytes.
dsi_charset_convert	This specifies Replication Server character set conversion. on – converts from the Primary Replication Server character set to the Replicate Replication Server character set. Any invalid conversion causes an error. This is the default. allow – converts when the datatypes are compatible but writes any unconverted values to the Replicate Database without causing an error.
	off – no conversion is done. During materialization "off" is actioned as "allow" i.e. conversion is applied but incompatible datatypes are written to the Replicate Database as unconverted data.
dsi_cmd_batch_size	This specifies the number of bytes that fit into a command batch. The default is 8192 bytes.
dsi_cmd_separator	This specifies the character that separates commands in a command batch. The default is a newline (\n) character.
dsi_exec_request_proc	The default of "on" allows request functions at the primary Replication Server DSI.

dsi_fadeout_time	This specifies the number of seconds of idle time before Replication Server closes a connection to a data server. The default is 600 seconds. If set to −1 the connection is not closed.
dsi_keep_triggers	The default of "on" specifies that triggers will fire in the Replicate Database. For standby databases the default is "off".
dsi_large_xact_size	This specifies the number of commands allowed in a transaction before the transaction is considered to be large. The default value is 100 and the minimum value is 4. This parameter is used to control the use of parallel DSI threads for applying transactions to a replicate data server.
dsi_max_cmds_to_log	This specifies the number of commands to write into the exceptions log for a failed transaction. The default of −1 writes all commands to the exceptions log.
dsi_max_text_to_log	This specifies the number of bytes to write to the exceptions log for each **rs_writetext** function in a failed transaction. The default of -1 writes all text and image columns to the exceptions log.
dsi_num_large_xact_threads	This specifies the number of parallel DSI threads to be reserved for use with large transactions. The default value is 0. The maximum value is one less than the value of *dsi_num_threads*.
dsi_num_threads	This specifies the number of parallel DSI threads to be used. The default value is 1 and the maximum value is 20. This parameter controls the use of parallel DSI threads for applying transactions to a replicate data server.
dsi_replication	The default of "off" specifies that transactions executed by the maintenance user are not replicated. When set to "off" the DSI executes the **set replication off** command in the SQL Server database when it connects, to prevent SQL Server adding replication information to log records for transactions executed by the DSI. In warm standby this is set to "on" for the active database and "off" for the standby database.

dsi_serialization_method	This specifies the method used to maintain serial consistency between parallel DSI threads. The values are:
	wait_for_commit – The default which waits for all updates of a transaction to complete before applying the next transaction.
	isolation_level_3 – This applies **set transaction isolation level 3** which takes table locks to ensure consistency.
	single_transaction_per_origin – This serializes transactions from the same origin database, effectively allowing parallelism only across Primary Database sources.
	none – This does not prevent concurrent access to the same data and will normally result in an increase in deadlocking.
	This parameter controls the use of parallel DSI threads for applying transactions to a replicate data server.
dsi_sql_data_style	This formats the datatypes to be compatible with DB2, Lotus Notes, SQL Anywhere or SQL Remote. To configure the connection to support Transact-SQL instead, set this parameter to any other value other than the ones used for the above ("db2", "notes", "watcom", "sqlremote"). The default is "" i.e. ASE. When you are configuring a connection to DB2 specify the name of the NetGateway using the *server_name* parameter in the main clause. When you are configuring a connection to Lotus Notes, Watcom SQL, or any other ODBC data source, specify the connection as replication_driver_name.odbc_data_source_name.
dsi_sqt_max_cache_size	This specifies the maximum SQT cache size for the database connection. The default of 0 indicates that the current setting of the *sqt_max_cache_size* parameter is used as the maximum cache size for the connection. The *sqt_max_cache_size* parameter is set with the **rs_configure** stored procedure. This parameter controls the use of parallel DSI threads for applying transactions to a replicate data server.

dsi_xact_group_size	This specifies the number of bytes, including stable queue overhead, that can fit into one grouped transaction. The default is 65,536 bytes. The value -1 means no grouping.
dump_load	This specifies whether a coordinated dump is performed. The default is "off."
parallel_dsi	This provides a fast method for configuring parallel DSI. off (the default) sets the parallel DSI parameters to their defaults on sets the parallel DSI parameters as: *dsi_num_threads* to 5 *dsi_num_large_xact_threads* to 2 *dsi_serialization_method* to "*wait_for_commit*" *dsi_sqt_max_cache_size* to 1MB
save_interval	This specifies the number of minutes that Replication Server saves transactions after they have been applied on the Replicate Database. The default is 0.

Table 4.3: Connection configuration parameters

To alter the configuration of a connection, first suspend the connection then change the configuration parameter and resume the connection.

suspend connection to LNPRDSRV_1.mkt_db

configure connection to LNPRDSRV_1.mkt_db

set save_interval 240

resume connection to LNPRDSRV_1.mkt_db

The majority of the configuration parameter settings are displayed with the **admin who, dsi** command.

admin who, dsi

Spid	State		Info				
	Maintenance User		*Xact_retry_times*		*Batch*	*Cmd_batch_size*	
	Xact_group_size	Dump_load	Max_cmds_to_log	Xacts_read	Xacts_ignored		
	Xacts_skipped	*Xacts_succeeded*	*Xacts_failed*	*Xacts_retried*			
	Current Origin DB						
	Current Origin QID						
	Subscription Name						
	Sub Command						
	Current Secondary QID						
	Cmds_read	*Cmds_parsed_by_sqt*	*IgnoringStatus*				
	Xacts_Sec_ignored	GroupingStatus					
	TriggerStatus	*ReplStatus*					
	NumThreads	NumLargeThreads	LargeThreshold	CacheSize			
	Serialization						

30	Awaiting Command		100702 NYPRD_SRV1.sales_db				
	mnt_usr		*3*		*on*	*8192*	
	65536	off	-1	4531	23		
	0	*5448*	*0*	*0*			
	100514						

0x000000012b9d0b0a001ac6130008ffffffff000000008d0700e00e240000000000000001

	NULL						
	NULL						
	NULL						
	819968	*5272*	*Applying*				
	0	on					
	on	*on*					
	1	0	100	0			
	wait_for_commit						

The save_interval is displayed with the **admin who, sqm** command.

admin who, sqm

Spid	State		Info		Duplicates
	Writes	*Reads*	*Bytes*	*B Writes*	*B Filled*
	B Reads		**B Cache**		**Save_Int:Seg**
	First Seg.Block	*Last Seg.Block*			
	Next Read	**Readers**		**Truncs**	
9	**Awaiting Message**		100512:0 LNRSSD_MKT.lnrssd_mkt		0
	0	*0*	*0*	*0*	*0*
	0		0		240:0
	0.1	*0.0*			
	0.1.0	1		1	
10	**Awaiting Message**		100512:1 LNRSSD_MKT.lnrssd_mkt		80
	104442	*104748*	*34712951*	*16321*	*28*
	16366		16262		0:2773
	2773.46	*2773.46*			
	2773.47.0	1		1	

Suspending a connection

A connection is suspended with the **suspend connection** command. This is executed at the Replication Server which manages the connection and requires *sa* permission.

suspend connection to server_name.db_name
[with nowait]

where

with nowait   This suspends the connection immediately without trying to complete the current transaction. In normal operation the **suspend connection** tries to complete the current transaction. If you are having serious problems with the connection this may simply cause the suspend command to hang. In practice this can be a simple way to check if the connection is actually talking to the database. If you are having trouble getting transactions to the Replicate Database, suspend the connection and, if it hangs, the trouble is between the Replication Server and the Replicate Database.

suspend connection to LNPRD1.mkt_db

When the connection is suspended the transactions are held in the DSI queue. If you keep the connection suspended for any length of time, keep an eye on the size of the DSI queue as you do not want to run out of partition space. If the stable device gets close to full you can add another partition until you resume the connection.

Resuming a connection

A suspended connection is resumed with the **resume connection** command. This is executed at the Replication Server which manages the connection and requires *sa* permission.

resume connection to server_name.db_name

[skip transaction | execute transaction]

where

skip transaction	This is used to skip the first transaction in the DSI queue and write it to the exceptions log. This is extremely useful when the connection has dropped out because of an error with a transaction and you cannot resolve the error but need to get the replication moving again. In this case you can resume the connection and skip the first transaction in the queue to allow replication to restart. You can then investigate the transaction from the exceptions log and resolve the problem.
Execute transaction	When you resume a connection, the default action is to ignore the first transaction if it is a system transaction i.e. a transaction which does not have a **begin tran** and **commit tran**. If this is the transaction which has failed you may wish to apply it – after you have corrected the reason for the failure. This clause will override the default action and apply the first transaction in the queue if it is a system transaction.

resume connection to NYPRD.sales_db skip transaction

Exception log

The system procedure **rs_helpexception** displays information on the exception logs.

rs_helpexception [trans_id [, v]]

where   v   includes the text of the transaction

rs_helpexception

Summary of Logged Transactions on 'LNPRD_RS1'

Total # of Logged Transactions = 1

Xact ID	Org Site	Org User	Org Date	Dest Site	# Recs/Xact
101	LNPRD_1.mkt_db	sa	Dec 29 1998	NYPRD_1.mkt_db	3

rs_helpexception 101

Detailed Summary of Logged # 101 on 'LNPRD_RS1'

Origin Site	Origin User	Org. Commit Date	#Cmds in Xact
LNPRD_1.mkt_db	sa	Dec 29 1998 2:31	3

Dest. Site	Dest. User	Date Logged
NYPRD_1.mktdb	rsmnt_user	Dec 29 1998 2:35

This transaction was skipped due to a 'resume connection' command with the 'skip transaction' option.

The system procedure **rs_delexception** lists the records in the exceptions log tables and also allows you to delete them.

rs_delexception [xact_id]

rs_delexception

Summary of Logged Transactions on 'PRS1_MKT

Xact ID	Org Site	Org User	Org Date	Dest Site	#Recs/Xact
101	PRDLN.mkt_db	sa	Dec 29 1998	PRDNY.mkt_db	3

To delete a specific logged xact., type 'rs_delexception {Xact ID}'

The exceptions log consists of three tables:

rs_exceptshdr	Header information about the origin and destination sites and information on why the error was logged.
rs_exceptcmd	Command information to retrieve the text of the command from the *rs_systext* system table.
rs_exceptslast	Queue ids and times about the last transaction written into the exception tables.

select * from rs_exceptshdr

sys_trans_id

rs_trans_id		
app_trans_name	**orig_siteid**	
orig_site	*orig_db*	
orig_time	orig_user	error_siteid
error_site	*error_db*	
log_time	ds_error	
ds_errmsg		
error_src_line error_proc	error_output_line	
log_reason	*trans_status*	*retry_status* *app_usr*
app_pwd		

0x010f432f00000067

*0x0000000136851d9300095046494f44593153545535f544d00000000000000000000000000000000
0000000000000000000000000000000000000000000000000000000000000000000000000000000000
0000000000000000000000000000000000000000000000000000000000000000000000000000000000
0000000000*

_user_transaction	100943	
PLN_SRV1	*SALES_DB*	
Mar 26 1998 5:42PM	support_dbo	100944
PLN_SRV2	*SALES_DB*	
Mar 27 1998 9:09AM	1205	
0	0	
S	*0*	*2* *rsmnt_tm*
NULL		

select * from rs_exceptscmd

sys_trans_id cmd_type	src_cmd_line cmd_id	output_cmd_index
0x010f432f00000067	1	0
S	0x010f432f2000006f	
0x010f432f00000067	1	1
L	0x010f432f20000070	
0x010f432f00000067	8	0
S	0x010f432f20000071	
0x010f432f00000067	8	1
L	0x010f432f20000072	
0x010f432f00000067	8	2
L	0x010f432f20000073	

select * from rs_systext

prsid textval	parentid	texttype	sequence
0	0x0000000008000002	O	1
execute rs_update_lastcommit @origin = ?rs_origin!sys?,			
@origin_qid = ?rs_origin_qid!sys?,			
@secondary_qid = ?rs_secondary_qid!sys?,			
@origin_time = ?rs_origin_commit_time!sys?;		commit transaction	
0	0x0000000008000007	O	1
execute rs_get_lastcommit			
0	0x0000000008000008	O	1
use ?rs_destination_db!sys_raw?			
0	0x0000000008000009	O	1
execute rs_marker @rs_api = ?rs_api!param?			
0	0x000000000800000c	O	1
sp_serverinfo server_soname			

You might find something along these lines useful:

Header error information on data servers and users

```
select
rtrim(hdr.orig_site) + '.' + rtrim(hdr.orig_db) + '.' +
rtrim(hdr.orig_user),
rtrim(hdr.error_site) + '.' + rtrim(hdr.error_db),
hdr.log_time, hdr.ds_error
from rs_exceptshdr hdr
```

Command text of error transactions

```
select
rtrim(hdr.orig_site) + '.' + rtrim(hdr.orig_db) + '.' +
rtrim(hdr.orig_user),
rtrim(hdr.error_site) + '.' + rtrim(hdr.error_db),
hdr.log_time, hdr.ds_error, txt.textval
from rs_exceptshdr hdr, rs_exceptscmd cmd, rs_systext txt
where hdr.sys_trans_id = cmd.sys_trans_id
and cmd.cmd_id = txt.parentid
```

Origin database and timing information on the last logged transaction

```
select
error_database, origin, origin_time, log_time
from rs_exceptslast
```

Dropping a connection

You can remove a database connection with the **drop connection** command. This is executed at the Replication Server which manages the connection and requires *sa* permission. This command removes the database from the Replication Server. To reinitialize it use the **create connection** command.

drop connection to server_name.db_name

Before you drop a connection to a Replicate Database you must remove any subscriptions for the database. If you do not remove the subscriptions, the Replication Server will attempt to replicate data based on the subscriptions and errors will be generated because the connection does not exist. Similarly before you drop a connection to a Primary Database you must drop all replication definitions for the database. Again you will generate errors if you have replication definitions but no connection.

drop connection to LNPRD_1.sales_db

The **drop connection** removes all RSSD system table entries for all Replication Servers in the replication domain but does not remove any data from the databases.

If you wish to recreate the connection with the same name you may need to issue the **sysadmin dropdb** command.

sysadmin dropdb, server_name, db_name

sysadmin dropdb, LNPRDSRV_1, mkt_db

This is necessary only in failure situations when the **drop connection** has not been registered in the ID server and so the ID server still knows about the original database.

Altering a connection

The attributes of a connection may be altered with the **alter connection** command. This is executed at the Replication Server which manages the connection and requires *sa* permission.

alter connection to server_name.db_name

{set error class [to] error_class_name |

set function string class [to] function_string_class_name |

set password [to] pass_word |

set log transfer [to] {on|off} |

set database_param to 'value' |

set security_param [to] 'value' |

set security_services [to] 'default'}

where

log transfer on | off   This enables or disables log transfer i.e. the ability for the LTM to extract transactions from the database log. Before you can disable this feature you must drop any replication definitions for the database.

database_param   This alters database configuration parameters for the connection as defined in the **configure connection** section in table 4.3.

security_param   A security parameter for the connection as defined in table 4.2. Only the *use_security_services* parameter is implemented in the initial release of 11.5.

set security_services to 'default'

    This resets all of the network-based security features for the connection to "not required".

Before you alter a connection you must suspend it:

suspend connection to PRDLN_1.sales_db

alter connection to PRDLN_1.sales_db

set error class to jk_error_class

resume connection to PRDLN_1.sales_db

Displaying Connection Information

Details of the connected databases are provided by the **rs_helpdb** system procedure. This is executed in the RSSD of the Replication Server.

rs_helpdb [server_name, db_name]

rs_helpdb

dsname	dbname	dbid
controlling_prs	errorclass	
funcclass		
status		
PRDLN_1	lnrs1_rssd	100787
LNRS1_PRD	rs_sqlserver_error_class	
rs_sqlserver_function_class		
Log Transfer is ON, Distribution is ON		
PRDLN_1	SALES_DB	100790
LNRS1_PRD	rs_sqlserver_error_class	
rs_sqlserver_function_class		
Log Transfer is ON, Distribution is ON		
PRDNY_1	SALES_DB	100791
LNRS1_PRD	rs_sqlserver_error_class	
rs_sqlserver_function_class		
Log Transfer is ON, Distribution is ON		

The current status of the connections from the Replication Server may be seen with the **admin show_connections** command which is issued from the Replication Server.

admin show_connections

Server	User			
	Database	State	Owner	Spid
LNPRS_PRD	rssdprm			
	lnprs_rssd	free		
LNPRD1	rsmnt_user			
	SALES_DB	already_faded_out	DSI EXEC	71
LNPRD2	rsmnt_user			
	SALES_DB	idle	DSI EXEC	67
NYPRD1	rsmnt_user			
	MKT_DB	already_faded_out	DSI EXEC	66

connection state	number	comments
connecting	0	in the process of connecting to a server
active	0	established connections owned and used by threads
idle	4	established connections owned but not being used
being_faded_out	0	idle connections that are being closed
already_faded_out	3	idle connections that have been closed
free	1	established connections not owned by any threads
closed	56	closed connections not owned by any threads
limbo	0	connection handles in state transition
total	64	total number of connection handlers available

Parallel DSI threads

Replication Server 11 allows the database connection to be configured with parallel DSI threads. This has all of the advantages of parallelism and will normally increase the Replication Server throughput and decrease the latency of individual transactions. However, be careful, as the commit sequence of the transactions has to be maintained and this can add to the overall Replication Server processing and may also cause deadlocking between the transactions if there are conflicting updates across the transactions. Less important, but still an added overhead, is the feature of parallel DSI threads that large transactions are processed before the commit is received. This means that a transaction which is eventually rolled back at the Primary Database may have been partially applied to the Replicate Database and will have to be rolled back by the Replication Server. So, by all means try parallel DSI threads when you think that the DSI is the bottleneck, but keep a close eye on deadlocking and increased system processing.

You will also need to consider the number of locks on the target server if you are using parallel DSI threads, especially if you adopt a *single transaction per origin* approach. With parallel threads multiple transactions are being processed concurrently and they will take out the same number of locks that they required in the primary database. In theory you will need to increase the number of locks to the sum of the number of locks in the primary servers. In practice you will get away with less than this but it must be somewhere between the largest source server number of locks and the total locks over all source servers.

Parallel DSI configuration

Parallel DSI threads are configured with the following configuration parameters:

dsi_num_threads
: This specifies the number of parallel threads to be used. The maximum is 20.

dsi_large_xact_size
: This specifies the breakpoint when a transaction is considered to be large by the Replication Server. A large transaction is processed differently to a small transaction when using parallel DSI threads. The minimum number of statements is 4, with a default of 100, before the Replication Server considers the transaction to be large.

dsi_num_large_xact_threads
: This specifies the number of DSI threads to be reserved for use with large transactions. The maximum is dsi_num_threads – 1.

dsi_sqt_max_cache_size
: This specifies the maximum SQT cache size for the connection.

dsi_serialization_method
: This specifies the method used to maintain transaction serialization.

  wait_for_commit – The default which waits for all updates of a transaction to complete before applying the next transaction.

    isolation_level_3 – This applies **set transaction isolation level 3** which takes table locks to ensure consistency.

    single_transaction_per_origin – This serializes transactions from the same origin database, effectively allowing parallelism only across Primary Database sources.

    none – This does not prevent concurrent access to the same data and will normally result in an increase in deadlocking.

parallel_dsi
: A fast method of specifying initial values for all of the parallel DSI configuration parameters.

  The default of on sets the parallel DSI parameters as:

  dsi_num_threads to 5

dsi_num_large_xact_threads to 2

dsi_serialization_method to *"wait_for_commit"*

dsi_sqt_max_cache_size to 1MB

Transaction serialization

Transaction serialization in Replication Server means that the transactions are committed at the Replicate Database in the same order that they were committed at the Primary Database. When there is only one DSI thread this is simply a case of executing the transactions in commit sequence. However with parallel DSI threads more than one transaction will be executed at the same time and, although commits may still be delivered in sequence, there is no guarantee that the order of the actual updates remains the same. When there are no update conflicts i.e. there are no updates to the same records in parallel transactions, this is not a problem. When conflicting updates are detected, the transactions involved are processed serially. Replication Server has four methods of detecting conflicting updates, set with the *dsi_serialization_method* configuration parameter.

Wait_for_commit

This is the default and causes the DSI thread to wait until one transaction is ready to commit, i.e. has processed all update commands, before committing the next transaction.

Isolation_level_3

This uses transaction isolation level 3 in the Replicate Database to enforce serialization. This is an extremely low concurrency level of locking as it uses table locks to ensure that a transaction has complete control of the data until it commits. I would not recommend this level of locking although Sybase do state that this level of serialization "should be used" if you are using triggers in the Replicate Database to enforce referential integrity because it prevents phantom records while the trigger is executing.

Single_transaction_per_origin

This method forces serialization of transactions from the same origin Primary Database. In this case parallelism can occur only when there are multiple Primary Databases managed by the Replication Server. It depends on your architecture but, in my opinion, this is the approach to take with parallel DSIs.

None

This does no update conflict detection. The assumption is that you know that there is no possibility of update conflict across the transactions either because of the nature of the processing or the "brilliant" design that you have implemented. If you get this one wrong and update conflicts occur, a deadlock will be raised in the Replication Server which your error detection should trap and retry the transaction.

Details of update conflict

Update conflicts are detected with the use of the *rs_threads* table. This contains a row for each DSI thread with the row packed to one row per page to force record level locking. The *rs_threads* table has two columns: *id* – the DSI thread id and *seq* – a sequential number generated for each transaction processed by the DSI.

When a transaction is received by a DSI thread, the DSI updates its row in *rs_threads*. This creates a "softlock" indicating that the DSI is processing a transaction. When the transaction is about to commit, the DSI thread issues a **select** on the *rs_threads* table for the transaction which should have committed prior to the current transaction. If the previous transaction is still processing, the **select** will block and the transaction will have to wait until the previous transaction has committed. If the **select** succeeds, the transaction may commit. This allows parallel transaction processing but serial commits based on the sequence number of the transaction in *rs_threads*.

If you find that update conflict is causing a large number of deadlocks, you should consider the configuration parameter settings shown in table 4.4.

Parameter	Setting
dsi_serialization_method	wait_for_commit
dsi_num_large_xact_threads	2 (For warm standby set this to number of concurrent large transactions + 1.)
dsi_num_threads	3 + dsi_num_large_xact_threads
dsi_sqt_max_cache_size	2M (see detailed calculation below)

Table 4.4: Configuration settings to reduce deadlock

The *dsi_sqt_max_cache_size* may be calculated in detail as:

$$T * (O + (S * N))$$

Where T   number of transactions to cache

$20 * (1 + dsi\_num\_threads - dsi\_num\_large\_xact\_threads)$

O   SQT cache overhead (3K)

S   SQT statement size

1K for data < 100 bytes

2K for data between 100 bytes and 300 bytes

5K for data > 300 bytes

N   number of statements modified by a transaction (application dependent)

Processing large and small transactions

As the configuration parameters suggest, the parallel DSI threads process large and small transactions differently.

Small transactions

Small transactions or groups of small transactions are submitted to the DSI executor thread only when the transaction commit is read. The DSI then submits the transactions to the Replicate Database and when an acknowledgment of successful processing is received, the DSI submits the update of the table and the commits of each small transaction.

Large transactions

Large transactions are submitted to the DSI thread and to the Replicate Database before the commit record has been read. This means that the transaction may have to be rolled back at the Replicate Database if a rollback is received instead of a commit.

5

Table Replication Definitions

Introduction

Sybase allows both data and stored procedures to be replicated. This is obviously important from a performance aspect as a large insert/update/delete command which is replicated will cause a lot of network traffic. If the command is placed in a stored procedure then only the procedure call and any parameters are replicated which is more efficient based simply on the reduced network traffic. Replication is established by defining the columns/parameters of the object which are to be replicated and marking the table/procedure for replication. The replication is defined with the **create replication definition** and **create function replication definition** commands and marking the object for replication is carried out with the **sp_setreptable** and **sp_setrepproc** system procedures. Procedure replication is covered in detail in Chapter 9.

Defining the data for replication requires two steps:

- Make the data available for replication to subscribers by defining a replication definition using the **create replication definition** command.

- Mark the data for replication in the Primary Database using the system procedure **sp_setreptable**. This step should be carried out after the **create replication definition** as marking the table for replication without a corresponding replication definition will cause the LTM to pass transactions for the table to the Replication Server. The Replication Server then has no replication definition for the transactions and it logs warning messages in the error log which may affect the Replication Server performance.

There are some simple pre-requisites for replication of data:

- The table must have a primary key.

  That's what the documentation says but the term primary key is a little misleading. It does not imply the constraint primary key or even that you need a unique index on the table. What it means is that the **create replication definition** command has a **primary key** clause which specifies the columns defining a unique identifier for the rows of the table. Interestingly this uniqueness does not need to be enforced at the primary table. However replication will fail because the default function string application of the transactions at the replicate requires the primary key columns to identify the row in the replicate table. So, no matter how you apply the uniqueness constraint, make sure that the replicated tables have a primary key.

- Prior to 11.5 the table name must be unique in the database.

  Not really a problem as it would be extremely unusual to have two tables with the same name in a live production system. Development might be more common where multiple users have **create table** authority and create the same table name. This is allowed as the table is qualified by the user name so *user_1.tab_name* and *user_2.tab_name* is quite possible. Do not let it happen in a production environment and there will be no replication problems. Create all objects as *dbo* in production and the problem cannot occur. In 11.5 the subscription may be made to the *table_owner.table_name* qualified name. This removes the table name uniqueness requirement from the replication definitions. However I would not recommend this, even in a development environment.

- You cannot replicate system tables.

  No surprise this one although occasionally it would be helpful.

- The target table in the subscription must exist.

  Sounds quite logical, but if you are replicating to an empty database it would be useful for the subscription to create the table structure - say during materialization. This does not happen, and you must define the table in all replication databases. It can be empty but it must exist.

- A connection to the Primary Database must exist at the Replication Server.

  Connections between Replication Servers and databases are defined with the **create connection** or the **rs_init** command (see chapter 4).

- The maintenance user must have access to the replicate table.

  The maintenance user applies the transactions to the replicate table and therefore must have **select**, **insert**, **update** and **delete** permissions on the replicate table.

Creating a replication definition

The definition of the data to be replicated is carried out in Sybase by the **create replication definition** command. This is not a particularly simple command, so I shall show the syntax and then build it up from the minimum information, describing each clause in turn.

The **create replication definition** command is executed at the Primary Replication Server i.e. the Replication Server which manages the primary version of the data. The replication definition is then propagated to all the other Replication Servers which have a route from the Primary Replication Server. This globally defines the replication definition and allows subscriptions to be defined at any Replicate Replication Server.

The full syntax of the **create replication definition** command is:

```
create replication definition rep_def_name
with primary at server_name.db_name
[with all tables named 'table_name' |
[with primary table named 'table_name']
[with replicate table named 'table_name']]
(col_name [as replicate_column_name] datatype [null|not null]
```

[, col_name [as replicate_column_name] datatype [null|not null]] ...)

primary key (col_name [, col_name] ...)

[searchable columns (col_name [, col_name] ...)]

[send standby [{all | replication definition} columns]]

[replicate {minimal | all} columns]

[replicate_if_changed (col_name [, col_name] ...)]

[always_replicate (col_name [, col_name] ...)]

The replication definition defines the following about the table replication to the Replication Server.

- The name of the replication definition.

  The replication definition must be unique in the replication domain as the replication definition is replicated to all Replication Servers in the domain. As replication is involved here the uniqueness of the replication definition cannot be enforced at creation time and so you always need to check that the replication has been successful and that the replication definition is registered at all Replication Servers in the domain. If it is not you will not be able to define subscriptions at that Replicate Replication Server.

- The location of the Primary Database.

  The data server and database name of the Primary Database.

- The name of the table.

  In its simplest form the name of the replication definition and the table in all schemas are the same. The syntax of the **create replication definition** command allows the replication definition name to be different to the table name. Replication Server 11.5 allows all three names to be different using the **with primary table named** and **with replicate table named** clauses. If you quote one of these clauses without the other, the assumption is that the table name which is not included is the same as the replication definition name. Prior to 11.5 if the primary and replicate table names were different you needed to handle this with a view in the replicate database or with a function string mapping. (Function strings are discussed in chapter 8.) Use single quotes for the table name in these clauses. If you need an embedded quote use two single quotes.

- The columns of the table and their datatypes.

  You cannot use user defined datatypes in a replication definition. The null/not null option may be used only for text/image datatypes and must agree with the Primary Database table definition. Be careful here. You must match the replication columns to the Primary Database table. If a replication table column does not allow nulls then you must replicate this column or the replicated insert will not work as it is missing a mandatory column. If the replicate table column allows nulls and you do not replicate the column, its inserted values will be set to null. This column list must also include all the columns quoted in the replication definition i.e. the primary key and searchable columns. In 11.5 the schemas at primary and replicate may have different column names and the **as replicate_column_name** clause identifies the replicate column of the table into which the primary column is copied. Prior to 11.5 you need to handle schema differences with customized function strings or a view in the replicate database.

If you specify multiple replication definitions against the same table, each replication definition must use the same datatypes and null/not null status for columns quoted in the replication definition.

- The columns that comprise the primary key.

A replication table must have a primary key. This is required to support the application of replication data to the Replicate Database. When using the default function strings, the Replication Server uses the primary key in the **where** clause of a **delete** and **update** statement at the Replicate Database. You cannot use *text/image* or *rs_address* type columns in the **primary key** clause.

- The searchable columns.

These are the only columns that a subscription to the replication definition may use to restrict the rows that are replicated. You cannot use *text/image* type columns in the **searchable columns** clause.

- A minimal columns feature.

For updates and deletes the default activity is to replicate all columns of the table even though they have not changed. Using the **replicate minimal columns** clause instructs the Replication Server to replicate only those columns which have changed plus the primary key columns. So, for a **delete**, only the primary key columns are replicated.

- Text/image options.

These options specify to replicate the column only when it changes or every time the record is changed. Text/image column replication is discussed later in this chapter.

- Standby mode options.

These options replicate all columns or just those listed in the warm standby clause. Warm standby is discussed separately in chapter 10. Normally in warm standby you would not define a replication definition for each table but allow the warm standby to default to replicating all rows and columns of all table which are marked for replication. If you define warm standby replication definitions – the documentation says that it is more efficient, but I have no support for this – the **send standby all columns** replicates all columns in the table to the warm standby database. The **send standby replicated columns** sends only the columns defined in the replication definition. If you have multiple replication definitions on a table then the latest replication definition defined as warm standby is the one used for warm standby. Be careful here as you can accidentally override a previous warm standby replication definition.

Datatype Considerations

There are a few rules concerning the column datatypes which are a little different from normal column definition.

- You cannot use User Defined Datatypes but must specify the base system datatype. Unfortunately Replication Server has no knowledge of the User Defined Datatypes which you may be using in the SQL Server database.

- The *numeric* datatype is quoted without any precision or scale. Replication Server processes *numeric* columns without affecting the precision or scale of the value.

- *Timestamp* columns are defined as *binary(8)*.

- If you are replicating an identity column then the maintenance user must own the table (either explicitly or as *dbo*) at the replicate database. This is necessary to allow the maintenance user to use the **identity_insert** option.

- Columns declared with the *rs_address* datatype must have a base datatype of *int* in the primary table.

Minimal Replication Definition

As a minimum the **create replication definition** defines a unique name for the replication definition, the name of the table being replicated, the location of the table and the primary key of the table. The uniqueness of the replication definition name is in the context of the replication domain which is the group of Replication Servers linked by defined routes. The replication definition is globally available in the replication domain as it is replicated to all Replication Servers linked to the Primary Replication Server by routes when the replication definition is defined.

So the replication definition:

create replication definition orders

with primary at PDS01.sales_db

primary key (order_no)

defines a replication as shown in figure 5.1.

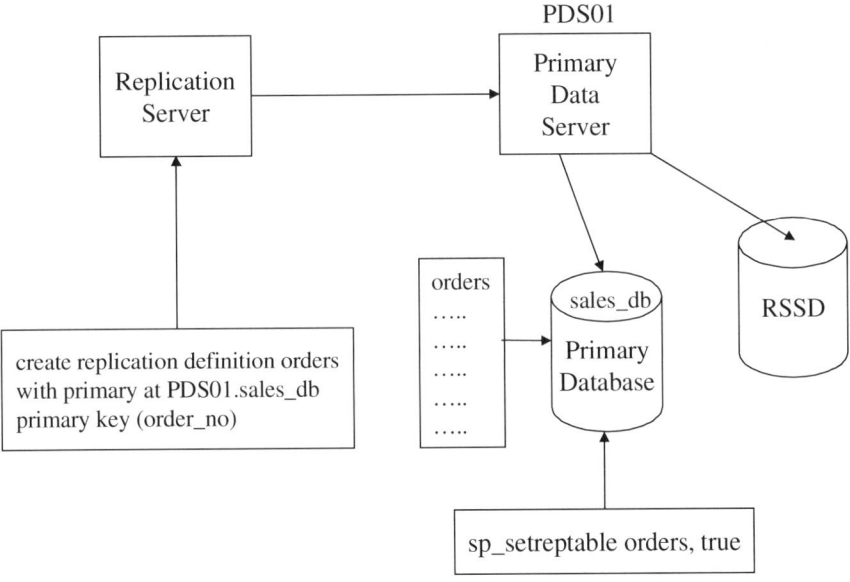

Figure 5.1: Table replication definition

This defines that all columns and all rows of the table *orders* are available for replication.

Restricting the Columns

If you want to restrict the columns that are replicated you need to include them in the column list. If you want a subscription to subscribe to a limited set of rows, you must define the searchable columns in the replication definition. Note the interesting design that the replication definition is for all of the rows in the table and it is the subscriber that restricts the rows applied to the Replicate Database.

To replicate some of the columns you quote the columns in the column list. Also, to provide the ability for a subscription to take only some of the rows, you need to expand the replication definition to define the searchable columns.

create replication definition sales

with primary at PDS01.sales_db

(order_no int, cust_no int, order_date datetime)

primary key (order_no)

searchable columns (order_no, cust_no)

This now marks only the *order_no*, *cust_no* and *order_date* as available for replication and allows subscriptions to restrict the rows that will be replicated with **where** clauses on *order_no* and *cust_no*. Columns in the searchable clause are not allowed to be null.

An accepted **create replication definition** command does not mean that the definition is correct. Any errors in schema names are resolved at run time when a subscription is made against the replication definition. Errors are written to the Replication Server error log file. Always check the error log at each stage of the replication definition - publication, subscription, function strings - and when replication starts. If you are not sure of the location of the errorlog file, you can query the Replication Server with the **admin log_name** command.

admin log_name

Log File Name

/home/programs/sybase/repserver/install/PLN1_RS.log

Different Replication Table Name

If you want to name the replication definition different from the tables, you need to use the **with all tables named**, **with primary table named** or **with replicate table named** clause. The **with primary table named** and **with replicate table named** clauses are 11.5 features.

create replication definition sales

with primary at PDS01.sales_db

with all tables named 'orders'

(order_no int, cust_no int, order_date datetime)

primary key (order_no)

searchable columns (order_no, cust_no)

This sets up the replication configuration as shown in figure 5.2.

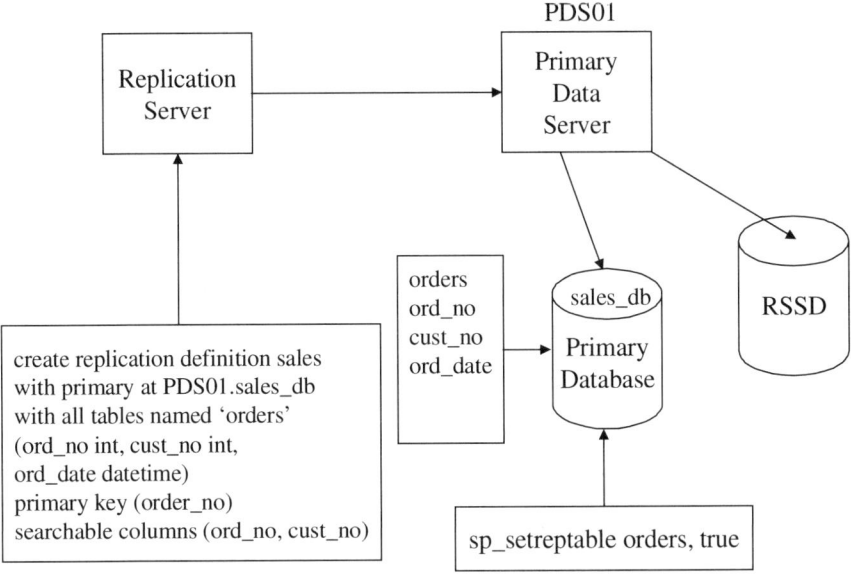

PDS01

Replication Server

Primary Data Server

orders
ord_no
cust_no
ord_date

sales_db
Primary Database

RSSD

create replication definition sales
with primary at PDS01.sales_db
with all tables named 'orders'
(ord_no int, cust_no int,
ord_date datetime)
primary key (order_no)
searchable columns (ord_no, cust_no)

sp_setreptable orders, true

Figure 5.2: Table replication definition

If you have not had any control over the table names and they are different between the Primary and Replicate Database, you need to create a view at the Replicate Database or create functions strings which map the different names (if running prior to 11.5). If you use function strings to do this, you do not need to include the with all tables named clause. Function strings are defined in chapter 8. In 11.5 additional **table named** clauses have been provided to allow the replication definition, primary table and replicate table names to be different.

```
create replication definition employee_def
with primary at PLN_SALES.emp_db
with primary table named 'employee'
with replicate table named 'personnel'
(emp_id int, emp_name varchar(32), ...)
primary key (emp_id)
searchable columns (empid, emp_name)
```

The Sybase documentation recommends for performance to quote only the columns that you need in both the column list and the searchable columns clause. In my opinion this is not a good idea as it is much better to keep replication changes to a minimum. If you are having performance problems with replication, solve them by another means – such as function replication – rather than restricting the columns in a table replication definition.

Minimal Columns

A further performance enhancement clause is the **replicate minimal columns** clause.

create replication definition sales

with primary at PDS01.sales_db

with all tables names 'orders'

(order_no int, cust_no int, order_date datetime)

primary key (order_no)

searchable columns (order_no, cust_no)

replicate minimal columns

This replicates only the columns necessary to perform **update** and **delete** at the Replicate Database. For a **delete** only the primary key is replicated. For an **update** only the primary key and the changed columns are replicated. Although this feature can reduce network usage and improve DSI throughput because it reduces the message size and consequently the queue size, it does have several usage restrictions which often make it impractical.

- It does not allow you to run **autocorrect**.

  If you accidentally have **autocorrect** on and specify **minimal columns** the **autocorrect** is ignored and the **update** and **delete** commands log an informational message. Not a disaster but it slows things down and can easily fill the error log.

- It does not allow the use of customized function strings.

  If you have used **replicate minimal columns** you cannot create non-default **rs_update** and **rs_delete** function strings. You may think that this is not a problem as you have adopted a "keep it simple" approach and have no intention of altering function strings. However you will be surprised how often the need to alter a specific function string can arise, even temporarily. The most common occasion that I have experienced is when a DSI or LTM has been down for some time and you want to start it moving again. If the delay has been long enough there may be deletes in the queue for earlier inserts. In this case the replication may action so quickly that the user does not see the inserts and data will be "lost". In this situation it is necessary to alter the **rs_delete** function string to do nothing – **select 1** – so that the user of the replicated data has time to process the inserts.

- It does not allow you to create a subscription using non-atomic or bulk materialization.

  This is the most common reason for not using this option as large amounts of data are best materialized with bulk materialization.

Recording the Replication Definition

Let's look at what happens and where things are stored when the replication definition is created. The steps carried out by the **create replication definition** are as shown in figure 5.3.

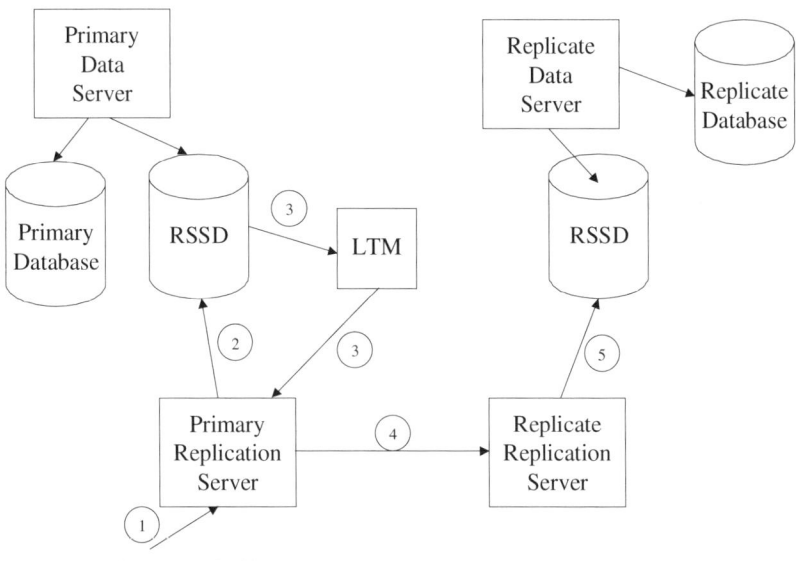

Figure 5.3: Replication definition creation steps

1. The **create replication definition** is defined at the Primary Replication Server i.e. the Replication Server which manages the primary data. Default functions and function strings for the replication definition are created at the Primary

Replication Server. The **create replication definition** command creates the default functions **rs_insert**, **rs_update**, **rs_delete**, **rs_select** and **rs_select_with_lock** for the replication definition.

2. The Primary Replication Server logs into its RSSD and updates the RSSD system tables by inserting entries into *rs_objects* and *rs_columns*.

3. The LTM reads the RSSD log and copies the system table replication definitions and default function and function string entries to the Primary Replication Server.

4. The Primary Replication Server then distributes the replication definition changes to all other Replication Servers in the replication domain i.e. those Replication Servers which have routes from the Primary Replication Server.

5. Each Replicate Replication Server inserts the replication definition changes into its replicate site RSSD.

We now have the replication definition replicated to every Replication Server in the replication domain.

Marking the table for replication

All of the above does not complete the replication setup at the Primary Database and a system procedure **sp_setreptable** has to be executed at the Primary Database to inform the LTM that transaction log records for this table have to be flagged as available for replication.

sp_setreptable [table_name [, {true|false} [, {owner_on | owner_off}]]]

where

true	switches replication on
false	switches replication off
owner_on	Uses both the owner and table name to identify the table. This allows tables with different owners to be enabled for replication. This is both a Replication Server 11.5 and an ASE 11.5 feature.
owner_off	Use the table name only to identify the table. This is the default mode and the mode prior to 11.5.

sp_setreptable orders, true

The **sp_setreptable** updates the *sysobjects.sysstats* column (to –32768) in the Primary Database to indicate that the table is available for replication. SQL Server writes the *sysstats* value to the transaction log and the LTM uses this to determine if the transaction should be replicated. Once you have issued the **sp_setreptable tab_name, true** the LTM will start to send transactions for the table to the Primary Replication Server. If you do not want this to occur then make sure that the LTM is not running. Either **shutdown** the LTM or issue a **suspend_log_transfer** command in the Replication Server. The syntax of **suspend_log_transfer** is:

suspend log transfer from server_name.db_name

If you drop and recreate the table, you must rerun **sp_setreptable**.

You can view the tables which are marked for replication or the replication status of an individual table with **sp_setreptable**.

sp_setreptable

Name

---

heartbeat

ORDERS

ORDER_ITEM

sp_setreptable ORDERS

The replication status for 'ORDERS' is currently true.

sp_setreptable marks all columns of the table for replication as if all columns were 'normal' columns. This means that a text/image column will be replicated when any column of the record changes. If you have text/image columns and do not want them to be replicated or want them to be replicated only when they change, you need to specify this explicitly with the **sp_setrepcol** system procedure (see next section). (If you are still using **sp_setreplicate** to mark a replication table then the reverse is true for text/image as **sp_setreplicate** marks text/image columns as **do_not_replicate**. Recommended usage is for **sp_setreptable**.)

Be careful of how long a **sp_setreptable** takes when you have text/image columns replicated. The inclusion of text/image columns in the table can cause **sp_setreptable** to take a very long time to execute. I'm not sure exactly what is going on but it appears to read all of the text/image pages to execute the system procedure – probably because there is no unique entry in the system tables for a text column and so it has to write something in each page to mark the text/image for replication. Be aware, this can take a very long time.

You can alter the owner status of a table marked for replication with the **sp_setrepdefmode** system procedure. This is an 11.5 feature.

    sp_setrepdefmode table_name [, {'owner_on' | 'owner_off'}]

    where

        owner_on   Specifies that both the owner and table name are required to identify the table. This enables tables with different owners to be enabled for replication. This is both a Replication Server 11.5 and an ASE 11.5 feature.

        owner_off Specifies that the table name only is required to identify the table. This is the default mode and the mode prior to 11.5.

Text/image replication

Replication of text/image columns is the same as normal column replication with the addition that you can specify that the text/image column is replicated only when it changes. As text/image columns are normally large this feature can obviously save on network traffic.

    create replication definition sales

    with primary at PDS01.sales_db

    with all tables names 'orders'

    (order_no int, cust_no int, order_date datetime, text_col text)

    primary key (order_no)

    searchable columns (order_no, cust_no)

    replicate_if_changed(text_col)

As mentioned above, the **sp_setreptable** automatically marks any text/image columns for replication. If you want to change this you need to use **sp_setrepcol**:

    sp_setrepcol table_name

    [, {col_name | null}

    [, {do_not_replicate | always_replicate | replicate_if_changed}]]

where

null	If used in place of the column name, sets the replication status of all text/image columns in the table.
do_not_replicate	Marks the column not to be replicated.
replicate_if_changed	Replicates the column only if it has changed.
always_replicate	Replicates the column when the row changes even if the text/image column is unchanged. This treats the text/image column as any other column.
	This is the default of the **create replication definition** command.

If you use **sp_setrepcol** to alter the replication status of a text/image column you must coordinate this with the status quoted in the table replication definition. This is summarized in table 5.1.

sp_setrepcol	Create replication definition
do_not_replicate	Do not include the columns in the replication definition.
replicate_if_changed	Include the columns in the replicate_if_changed clause.
always_replicate	Include the columns in the always_replicate clause.

Table 5.1: Column replication status

If you mark the text/image column as *replicate_if_changed* you need to be a little careful when the subscriptions are based on a **where** clause i.e. they restrict the rows of the replicated table that they accept.

In this case it is possible for a row to migrate into the subscription when an update is made to one of the columns used in the subscription **where** clause. When this occurs the primary data update is translated into a replicated insert. If you have any text/image columns defined as *replicate_if_changed* they will not be included in the **insert** if they were not changed by the original **update** statement. You get a warning message in the Replication Server errorlog when this occurs but it is after the event, so be careful when you mix *replicate_if_changed* text/image columns and **where** clauses in the subscriptions.

Viewing replication definition information

Existing replication definitions may be displayed with the **sp_helprep** system procedure which is run from the RSSD.

rs_helprep [rep_def_name]

The rep_def_name is wildcarded at the end by the procedure so **rs_helprep** may return several replication definitions beginning with the input string. By itself the **rs_helprep** list the current replication definitions:

rs_helprep

Rep. Def. Name Type	PRS	Primary DS.DB	Primary Table	Creation Date
def_jk table repdef	PRS1	LNPRD1.SALES_DB	jk	Dec 14 1998
def_jk1 table repdef	PRS1	LNPRD1.SALES_DB	jk1	Dec 14 1998
def_jk1prc function repdef	PRS1	LNPRD1.SALES_DB	def_jk1prc	Dec 14 1998
def_jk2prc function repdef	PRS1	LNPRD1.SALES_DB	def_jk2prc	Dec 15 1998
def_jk4 table repdef	PRS1	LNPRD1.SALES_DB	jk4	Dec 15 1998
def_jk5 table repdef	PRS1	LNPRD1.SALES_DB	jk5	Dec 15 1998

The **rs_helprep** with a replication definition name displays the detailed information on the replication definition.

rs_helprep def_jk1

Rep. Def. Name	PRS	This Site	Creation Date	Type
def_jk1	PRS1	PRS1	Dec 14 1998 5:00PM	R

PDS.DB	Primary Table	Default Rep. Table
LNPRD1.SALES_DB	jk1	jk1

Colname	Datatype	Length	Primary Col.	Searchable
a	int	4	1	0
b	char	255	0	0
c	char	255	0	0
d	char	255	0	0
e	char	255	0	0
f	char	255	0	0

Function Name	FString Class	FString Source	FString Name
rs_delete	rs_sqlserver_function_class	Class Default	rs_delete
rs_insert	rs_sqlserver_function_class	User Defined	rs_insert
rs_select	rs_sqlserver_function_class	Class Default	rs_select
rs_select_with_lock	rs_sqlserver_function_class	Class Default	rs_select_with_lock
rs_update	rs_sqlserver_function_class	Class Default	rs_update

Subscriptions known at this Site 'LNPRS1'.

Subscription Name	Replicate DS.DB	Owner	Creation Date
sub_jk1	NYPRD1.SALES_DB	sa	Dec 14 1998 5:03PM

Altering a replication definition

The **alter replication definition** command allows you to:

- Alter the replicate table name.
- Alter columns in the replicate table into which the primary column is replicated.
- Add columns to the column list.
- Add columns to the searchable columns list.
- Change minimal columns information.
- Change text/image column information.

- Change standby information.

alter replication definition rep_def_name
{ with replicate table named 'table_name' |
alter columns with col_name as replicate_col_name
[, col_name as replicate_col_name]... |
add col_name [as replicate_col_name] [datatype [null | not null]]
[, col_name [as replicate_col_name] [datatype [null | not null]]] ...|
add searchable columns col_name [, col_name] ...|
send standby [off | {all | replication definition} columns] |
replicate {minimal | all} columns |
replicate_if_changed col_name [, col_name] ... |
always_replicate col_name [, col_name] ... }

The **alter replication definition** command is executed at the Replication Server which manages the primary database. As for the **create replication definition** command the **null | not null** option applies to text/image columns only.

Altering the replicate table name

alter replication definition def_order
with replicate table named 'orders'

Altering replicate table columns

alter replication definition def_order
alter columns with ord_no as ord_id, ord_placed as ord_date

Adding a replicated column

alter replication definition orders
add total_qty float

Adding a searchable column

alter replication definition orders
add searchable columns ord_date, total_qty

When altering anything on Replication Server you should always ensure that nothing is happening to avoid changing something mid-stream. This is especially true with replication definitions as you are redefining the schema of the information being loaded from the Primary Database to the Replication Server. If you change this while existing data is being copied by the LTM you will probably get both old and new schema present in the inbound queue for the LTM. Replication Server will not like this and you will cause the processing threads to hang or to fail. If you change anything while replication is taking place do not be surprised if the LTM/DSI/RSI does not move or simply fails.

So when changing anything take the approach:

- Quiesce the Replication Server and check with **admin who, sqm** that the queues have been emptied.

- If necessary suspend the DSI/RSI connection.

- Suspend the LTM.

- Make the changes.

- Resume the DSI/RSI/LTM.

In the specific case of altering the replication definition:

- Try to stop all updates to the primary.

  This is often difficult as it requires the cooperation of the user. Update activity will cause transactions to be present on the log which may not have values for the new replication columns. The best is that the columns will be replicated with nulls; the worst is that the LTM or DSI/RSI thread will fail and you will have to "zap" or "skip" the transactions. (See the troubleshooting chapter 15.)

- Quiesce the Replication Server.

- Set replication on the table to false.

- If changing the table schema, stop the LTM.

- Alter the replication definition.

- Alter any subscriptions and function strings if necessary.

- Check the RSSDs to ensure that the changes have reached the Replicate Replication Server.

- Set replication on the table to true.

- Start the LTM.

The commands involved are:

- Quiesce the Replication Server.

admin quiesce_force_rsi or admin quiesce-check

This flushes the DSI and RSI queues until all outbound messages have been sent and an acknowledgement has been received. The effect of this is checked with:

admin health

If this does not show quiesced as TRUE, wait a little and retry the **admin quiesce_force_rsi**. If this does not quiesce the Replication Server you have a problem and need to check the errorlog to see if there are any indications of the reason. The reverse of this is probably more relevant: do not try to quiesce the Replication Server if you know that there is a problem with message delivery as the quiesce will still try to send messages. Stop activity in another manner such as **drop connection**.

- Suspend outbound connection.

suspend connection to replication_server_name

This is less important if you have quiesced the Replication Server and it may actually cause you problems as the connection may be required to replicate the changes to the other Replication Server RSSDs. In general leave the DSI/RSI connection running if you can.

The connection is resumed with:

resume connection to replication_server_name

- Set replication to false.

sp_setreptable tab_name, false

- Stop the LTM.

Log into the LTM and issue a **shutdown**. To resume the LTM run the appropriate RUNSERVER file. Check the errorlog to ensure that the LTM starts OK and then issue an:

admin who_is_down

from the Replication Server to check that all components are running.

In practice you may find that you are not out of the woods yet and I would strongly recommend that you check the inbound and outbound queues to make sure that they are still moving by inspecting the **admin who, sqm** output. The troubleshooting section discusses this in more detail but issue several of these and check that the *next read* is moving. For example:

admin who, sqm

Spid	State		Info		Duplicates
	Writes	*Reads*	*Bytes*	**B Writes**	*B Filled*
	B Reads	**B Cache**	Save_Int:Seg		
	First Seg.Block	*Last Seg.Block*			
	Next Read	**Readers**	**Truncs**		
9	**Awaiting Message**		100512:0 LNRSSD_MKT.lnrssd_mkt		0
	0	*0*	*0*	*0*	*0*
	0	0	240:0		
	0.1		*0.0*		
	0.1.0	1	1		
10	**Awaiting Message**		100512:1 LNRSSD_MKT.lnrssd_mkt		80
	104442	*104748*	*34712951*	*16321*	*28*
	16366	16262	0:2773		
	2773.46		*2773.46*		
	2773.47.0	1	1		

If the *next read* figure is not changing then either there is no activity or the LTM is stuck. Check the LTM and Replication Server errorlogs and if either is stuck, follow the steps in the troubleshooting chapter 15.

If you have altered the replication status of a text/image column, the steps are the same except that:

- You MUST stop all updates to the primary table and ensure that any updates in the system have been replicated and applied to the Replicate Databases. This is really only necessary if altering the text/image column replication status to **always replicate**, but it is very good practice and I would recommend the approach in all cases of change to text/image column replication.

- Use **sp_setrepcol** to alter the primary table replication status.

If you add a column to a replication definition using **alter replication definition** the default function strings are altered. If you have defined custom function strings these will remain unchanged and you will need to alter them yourself to get the new column recognized by the Replication Server when it applies the transaction to the Replicate Database.

Dropping a Replication Definition

If you need to remove a column from a replication definition you need to drop and recreate the replication definition. To drop a replication definition issue the **drop replication definition** command. If you have multiple replication definitions on the table, then run **sp_setreptable** only after you have dropped the last replication definition for the table. You need to drop multiple replication definitions individually, there is no drop all replication definitions for a table command.

drop replication definition rep_def_name

drop replication definition orders

Before you can do this you need to drop all subscriptions to the replication definition and then you can issue the drop command from the Primary Replication Server. Dropping a replication definition completely removes all replication definitions and function strings on all Replication Servers in the replication domain. And then do not forget to switch off replication of the Primary Database table with **sp_setreptable**.

sp_setreptable orders, false

Again you should make sure that nothing is happening to the object that you are modifying. In this case I would:

- Quiesce the Replication Server.
- Set replication on the table to false.
- Stop the LTM.
- Drop the subscriptions and replication definitions.
- Start the LTM.

System tables

The system tables involved in a replication definition are *rs_objects* and *rs_columns*.

rs_objects

One row per replication definition, the type identified by the *objtype* value (R: table, F: function).

select * from rs_objects

prsid	objname	objid	dbid
	objtype *attributes*	*ownertype*	*crdate*
	parentid	ownerid	rowtype
	phys_tablename		
	deliver_as_name		
17777439	heartbeat_100790 0x010f431f00000082		100790
	R *0*	*U*	*Feb 19 1998 5:27PM*
	0x0000000000000000 0x0000000000000000		1
	rsm_heartbeat		
17777439	rs_classes 0x0000000000000051		100787
	R *0*	*S*	*Nov 3 1997 2:30PM*
	0x0000000000000000 0x0000000000000000		0
	rs_classes		
17777439	rs_columns 0x0000000000000052		100787
	R *0*	*S*	*Nov 3 1997 2:30PM*
	0x0000000000000000 0x0000000000000000		0
	rs_columns		

rs_columns

One row for each column of a replication definition.

select * from rs_columns

| prsid | objid | colname | colnum | coltype | rowtype | status |
	length	*searchable*	*primary_col*	*fragmentation*		
17777439	0x0000000000000051	classname	1		18	
	30	*0*	*1*	*0*	*0*	*0*
17777439	0x0000000000000051	classtype	3		0	
	1	*0*	*1*	*0*	*0*	*0*
17777439	0x0000000000000051	prsid	4		8	
	4	*1*	*1*	*0*	*0*	*0*
17777439	0x0000000000000051	classid	2		1	
	8	*0*	*1*	*0*	*0*	*0*
17777439	0x0000000000000052	coltype	5		6	
	1	*0*	*0*	*0*	*0*	*0*
17777439	0x0000000000000052	length	6		6	
	1	*0*	*0*	*0*	*0*	*0*
17777439	0x0000000000000052	primary_col	8		6	
	1	*0*	*0*	*0*	*0*	*0*

These reside in the RSSD.

The **rs_helprep** system procedure is quite helpful but there are a few extras you can do, mainly to improve the clarity of the output. You may want to refine these.

Primary key columns for a replication definition

```
select c.colname from rs_columns c, rs_objects o
where c.objid = o.objid
and c.primary = 1
and o.objname = <rep_def_name>
```

Searchable columns for a replication definition

```
select c.colname from rs_columns c, rs_objects o
where c.objid = o.objid
and c.searchable = 1
and o.objname = <rep_def_name>
```

Replication definitions for a server and/or database

select o.objname from rs_objects o, rs_databases d

where d.dbid = o.dbid

and d.dsname = <server_name>

and d.dbname = <db_name>

Subscriptions to a replication definition

select o.objname, s.subname from rs_objects o, rs_subscriptions s

where o.objid = s.objid

and o.objname = <rep_def_name>

Basic troubleshooting

Without trying to pre-empt the troubleshooting section, the replication definition will not always work and you should always check the error logs and system tables after a replication definition to make sure that everything looks OK.

Each component in the replication of the replication definition can go wrong and you should check them in turn.

- No entries in the RSSD of the Primary Replication Server.

  The first step of inserting entries into the RSSD by the Primary Replication Server has failed. These inserts are carried out by the RSSD primary user so check that the user_id and password are correct. Next most obvious reason for the failure is that the RSSD log is full and all processes are suspended.

- No entries in the Stable Device of the Primary Replication Server.

  The LTM extracts the RSSD inserts and writes them to the Stable Device of the Primary Replication Server. Only two real possibilities here for failure: the LTM is not running or the LTM cannot connect to the Primary Replication Server.

- No entries in the Stable Device of the Replicate Replication Server.

  The Primary Replication Server distributes the replication definition to all other

Replication Servers in the replication domain. If the system table inserts are still in the outbound queue of the Primary Replication Server Stable Device then the connection to the Replicate Replication Server has not been successful. The most obvious cause is a failure to login but also check that the routes are defined correctly.

- No entries in the RSSD of the Replicate Replication Server.

The replication definition inserts have reached the Stable Device of the Replicate Replication Server but have not been written to the RSSD of the Replicate Replication Server. Similar to the first step at the Primary Replication Server, check the login id and password or a full transaction log.

6

Subscribing

Introduction

A subscription is the definition of which data is received from a replication definition. The subscriber can receive all or part of the replication definition i.e. the whole table or a subset of the rows. It is important to remember that the columns which are replicated are defined in the publication replication definition and the rows which are replicated are defined in the subscription definition. So all the rows of a table are available for replication based on the replication definition and the subscription determines on a case by case basis which rows of the replicated table to accept. In 11.5 the replication definitions may be grouped in a publication[1] and the subscription made to the publication. This can save some definition time and – more importantly – the publication supports **where** clauses which allows the publication to present a subset of rows to the subscription.

[1] For simplicity of presentation I shall refer to subscriptions to replication definitions throughout the chapter and mention the publication explicitly only when there is a difference that needs commented on. Apart form the obviously important point that publications are 11.5 only, there is little difference between a subscription to a replication definition and a subscription to a publication.

Each Replicate Database will have its own subscriptions defined to the Replication Server which manages the Replicate Database. The manner in which a subscription is defined - **create subscription** or **define subscription** - is determined by the way that the Primary and Replicate Database data is synchronized. This is called **materialization** by Sybase. The process of defining the subscription - I shall use the word "defining" generally and not directly related to a **define** unless obviously linked - is made up of four stages:

- Definition.

  The subscription is defined to the Replicate Replication Server and recorded at both the replicate and primary RSSDs. This is done with the **define subscription** or the **create subscription** command depending on the method of materialization.

- Materialization.

  The Replicate Database is synchronized with data from the Primary Database. This can be done automatically by the replication process or manually by bulk data loading using **bcp** or **load database**. If done automatically then the subscription is defined using the **create subscription** command; if done manually then the subscription is defined using the **define subscription** command.

- Activation.

  The actual replication is started and transactions in the Primary Database are replicated to the Replicate Databases which have subscribed to the replication definition.

- Validation.

  The materialization is checked to ensure that the Replicate Database and the Primary Database data are synchronized.

Before you define the subscription there are a few simple checks that you should make.

- Check that the threads you need are running.

  An **admin who_is_down** or an **admin who** will identify any problems. You should be looking for:

  - An LTM USER thread which is extracting transactions from the Primary Database that you expect the data from.

  - A DSI/RSI thread which is applying the data to the Replicate Database that you have defined the subscription against.

Consider figure 6.1:

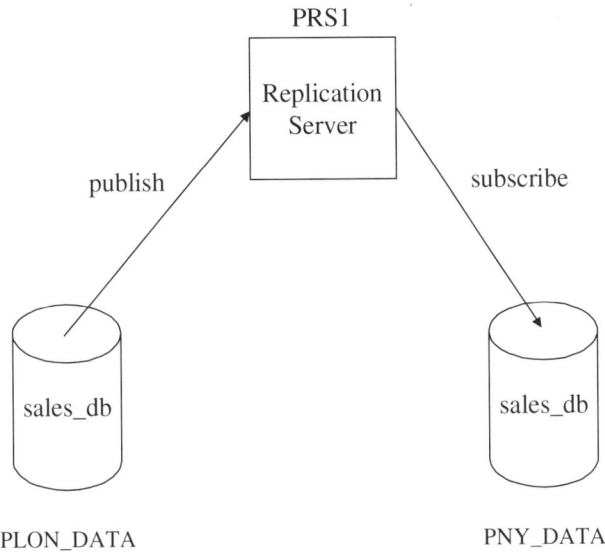

Figure 6.1: Simple subscription threads

An **admin who** at the Replication Server (PRS1) should show the following threads to support the subscription at PNY_DATA.sales_db to the replication definition at PLON_DATA.sales_db. So there are 7 threads for a Primary database: LTM, SQM, SQT and DIST for the inbound queue; SQM, DSI and DSI EXEC for the outbound queue and 3 threads for a Replicate Database: SQM, DSI and DSI EXEC for the outbound queue.

admin who

Spid	Name	State	Info
33	DSI EXEC	Awaiting Command	101589(1) PLON_DATA.sales_db
18	DSI	Awaiting Command	101589 PLON_DATA.sales_db
23	DIST	Active	101589 PLON_DATA.sales_db
28	SQT	Awaiting Wakeup	101589:1 DIST PLON_DATA.sales_db
12	SQM	Awaiting Message	101589:1 PLON_DATA.sales_db
11	SQM	Awaiting Message	101589:0 PLON_DATA.sales_db
51	LTM USER	Awaiting Command	PLON_DATA.sales_db
32	DSI EXEC	Awaiting Command	100702(1) PNY_DATA.sales_db
38	DSI	Awaiting Command	100702 PNY_DATA.sales_db
40	SQM	Awaiting Command	100702:0 PNY_DATA.sales_db

21	dSUB	Active	
6	dCM	Awaiting Message	
8	dAIO	Awaiting Message	
26	dREC	Active	dREC
58	USER	Active	sa
5	dALARM	Awaiting Wakeup	

- Check the existence and content of the replication definition you are subscribing to.

  An **rs_helprep** will provide the required information. If **replicate minimal columns** is specified you cannot materialize the data using non-atomic materialization with the **create subscription** command i.e. including the *without holdlock* clause. Non-atomic materialization requires **autocorrect** which actions the replicated transactions as a **delete** followed by an **insert**. As **replicate minimal columns** does not replicate all of the columns of an **update**, the insert phase cannot be applied properly.

- Check the required function strings exist.

  Atomic materialization with the **create subscription** command requires the **rs_select_with_lock** function string and non-atomic materialization with the **define subscription** command requires the **rs_select** function string. If you are using the default **rs_sqlserver_function_class** function string class, then the Replication Server generates the **rs_select_with_lock** and **rs_select** automatically. If you are using a customized function string class, you will need to define the appropriate function string with an input template to match the subscription **where** clause.

- Check the data server sort orders and character sets.

  An **rs_configure** will show you what is current. If the Primary and Replicate Data Server sort orders or character sets are different the subscription may not replicate the records you are expecting and any characters which cannot be recognized will be replicated as question marks. It's not going to collapse on you but it may give you some results that are difficult to understand and may cause the receiving application to fail.

- Check the user creating the subscription has the following login and permissions.

  The same login and password at the Replicate Replication Server, Primary Replication Server and the Primary Data Server if using **create subscription**.

  Select on the primary table if using **create subscription**.

Execute on the **rs_marker** stored procedure in the Primary Database.

Create object permission in the Replicate and Primary Replication Server.

Primary subscribe permission in the Primary Replication Server.

Types of materialization

Materialization can be done automatically or manually. If done manually you load the Replicate Database data with an off-line bulk process and it is your responsibility to ensure that the Replicate and Primary Database are synchronized when replication is activated. If done automatically the replication process takes the responsibility of loading the Replicate Database data and of ensuring that the loaded data is synchronized with the Primary Database data.

Manual materialization

A manual materialization is normally done by a **bcp** or a **load database**. **Load database** would be used more often when all of the database tables are defined as replicated and **bcp** would be used more often for individual tables. Any breakpoint between the two is based on volume of data. I would suggest that, if 80% of your data is in a few large tables, it is probably more convenient to use **load database**. But no real preference here: judge for yourself based on the effort required and the elapsed time of each method. The manual materialization uses the **define subscription** command.

In a manual materialization you need to ensure that the loaded Replicate Database data is fully synchronized with the Primary Database data when you activate the replication. Once publication is defined by a replication definition and **sp_setreptable** the data available for replication is extracted by the LTM and forwarded to the Stable Device of the Primary Replication Server. However, if there are no active subscriptions for that data, the transactions are simply discarded. Even if there are some subscriptions but the one that you are bulk materializing is not activated, the transactions will be discarded after they have been forwarded to the other active subscriptions. So, if you allow transactions against the Primary Database data to be replicated while you are materializing manually, you are unlikely to achieve synchronized Primary and Replicate Database data at replication activation.

Manual materialization is a reasonable technique when there is a lot of data to synchronize and automatic transactional materialization will take a long time with a significant hit on the network. In practice, the increase in network activity can make manual materialization the only option in some situations. When data volumes are high and the network is slow, automatic materialization can take so long that it affects other processes significantly and becomes so counterproductive that manual materialization is mandated. Manual materialization is mandatory for procedure replication as only the execution of the procedure is replicated, not the actual transactions themselves. As automatic materialization requires a row by row materialization, this is not possible with procedure replication.

The biggest problem with manual materialization is ensuring that the primary and replicate data remain consistent while the materialization is taking place.

The simplest approach is to stop all updates against the primary data until the materialization is complete. If you can't do this, then a **dump database** and a **load database** will cope with any active transactions via the transaction log. However if you are using **bcp** on individual tables you really need to block updates to these tables until the **bcp** is complete. Once the **bcp** out is complete you may define and activate the subscription with the outbound queue DSI thread suspended. This will allow the transactions to update the primary data while the replicate data is being created. These transactions will be replicated by Replication Server as far as the DSI outbound queue where they will wait until you resume the connection. For individual tables this is a relatively simple approach. For a higher percentage of the database being replicated I would favor the dump and load approach.

Automatic materialization

Automatic materialization is carried out by the **create subscription** command and ensures data consistency between the Primary and the Replicate Database. Automatic materialization can be done using two approaches:

Atomic
: This copies the data from the Primary to the Replicate Database as a single transaction, locking the primary data so that no updates can be carried out against it. The subscription uses the **rs_select_with_lock** function string to achieve this and guarantees data consistency.

Non-atomic
: This copies the data in a single transaction but does not lock the primary data. This means that a resolution phase is necessary at the end of the materialization to correct any inconsistencies caused by transactions updating the primary data.

Atomic materialization processes the data in a single large transaction. **With holdlock** is used in the **select** from the Primary Database table to ensure that the table remains locked as it is read. Therefore no transactions can change the selected data until the materialization is complete and the subscription is activated. This ensures transaction consistency and that the primary and replicate data is fully synchronized when the subscription is activated. However it materializes the complete data set for the subscription as one transaction and so it can have a seriously detrimental effect on the Primary Database throughput. If the data set is small, the concurrency effect is low. But for normal to large data sets, although this is a good method of materialization, it is highly intrusive.

I am not a big fan of any materialization while transactions are allowed against the Primary Database, but there can be the additional problem with atomic materialization of deadlocking on the data. As the materialization process is reading through a table, any transaction which applies multiple updates to the table has the chance of deadlocking. Not a good idea. Try to stop activity against the Primary Database while it is being materialized.

You can define the atomic materialization as **incremental** in which case the materialization is done in batches of 10 rows. This has no effect on the Primary Database but releases the locks on the Replicate Database and allows it to be accessed. However this will increase the materialization time and it is usually better to do the materialization at a quiet period and to do a complete data set in one transaction. The size of the Replicate Database log may force you to do incremental atomic materialization as a log truncation can be run frequently to keep the log small when the rows are being batched into small transactions. Another aspect in favor of incremental atomic materialization is that the Stable Device does not need to be as large because the transactions are removed from the outbound queue of the Stable Device after they are successfully applied to the Replicate Database.

I do not normally recommend incremental materialization as it allows the user to see partial results. The user can see part of the materialization before it is complete and, no matter how much you explain this, it is always better to keep the user away from the data until it is fully materialized.

Non-atomic materialization means that there is no holdlock on the Primary Database table and so changes to the primary data may be carried out. These changes are not included in the materialization to the Replicate Database table. Non-atomic materialization is processed incrementally, making the replication data more available to the user at the Replicate Database. In the non-atomic materialization, although the materialization is less intrusive as no primary transactions are blocked, it takes longer for the materialization to become valid as the materialized data is not synchronized with the primary data. Because of this non-synchronization it is recommended that **autocorrection** is set on for all non-atomic materialization - except for procedure replication.

Autocorrection applies the replicated inserts and updates as deletes followed by inserts. This means that any duplicate inserts do not cause errors as the Replicate Database record is deleted first and then the new replicated record written. This is particularly useful for non-atomic materialization as a transaction against the Primary Database table may be sent to the Replicate Database as part of the materialization and then sent again as a transaction from the Primary Database as it was extracted from the log by the LTM to be applied after materialization is complete. You can always set **autocorrection** off after the materialization is complete: replication will go faster with **autocorrection** off.

Materialization is summarized in table 6.1:

Materialization method	Description
Automatic atomic	This is the default materialization of the **create subscription** command. It copies the data from the Primary to the Replicate Database as a single transaction. This guarantees primary and secondary data consistency once the materialization is complete but it blocks any transactions against the primary data while it is executing. Atomic materialization is a useful approach for small data sets and when it can be run outside normal operating hours without any affect on the primary applications.
Automatic non-atomic	This is executed by using the **create subscription** command with the **without holdlock** clause. Non-atomic materialization does not lock the primary data and allows transactions against the primary data while the materialization is taking place. This means that the primary and secondary data may be out of synchronization at the end of the materialization. Any transactions made to the primary during non-atomic materialization will have to be replicated to the Replicate Database once the materialization is complete. This is not really the approach to use for large and/or active datasets as the correction phase can take some time.

Manual materialization	This is the manual materialization of the data using a command such as **bcp** or **load database**. This requires the subscription to be defined with the **define subscription, activate subscription** and **validate subscription** commands. This approach is most common with large datasets and must be used for procedure replication.

Table 6.1: Types of materialization

Defining a subscription for manual materialization

Manual subscription is the most efficient method of synchronizing a large amount of data. How large? Well it depends on the speed of the network as the manual materialization effectively takes the network processing out of the materialization. I know that you still have to transfer the data across the network but it will be a file transfer and not a synchronous transaction by transaction network usage. The automatic materialization puts a significant transactional load on the network. If your network is fast enough to handle it, that's fine, but if not, then manual materialization will be the answer. Also manual materialization is usually necessary when the replication data is already populated. Simple **update**/**insert** with atomic materialization may raise too many errors with existing data. The non-atomic materialization **delete**/**insert** approach can take some time, especially with lots of indexes on the table. So, when the replication table is already populated a manual materialization is often the optimum approach. And, as mentioned before, manual materialization is the only option for procedure replication as automatic materialization requires row by row transactions which procedure replication does not provide.

The characteristics of manual materialization are that you need to do each step separately. The steps are:

* Define the subscription.

  This records the subscription definition at the RSSD of both the Replicate and the Primary Replication Server using the **define subscription** command.

- Activate the subscription.

  This starts the actual replication between the Primary and the Replicate Replication Server using the **activate subscription** command. The Subscription Resolution Engine (SRE) process on the Primary Replication Server compares the log records on the Replication Server stable queue to determine if there are valid subscriptions for them.

- Validate the subscription.

  This validates that the subscription at the Primary and the Replicate Replication Server has been fully materialized and is synchronized on both servers using the **validate subscription** command.

- Check the subscription.

  This checks that the subscription has been registered at the RSSD of both the Replicate and the Primary Replication Server. You should execute **check subscription** at each stage of manual materialization to check that it has completed properly. In practice you should use **check subscription** even for automatic materialization. Although the command succeeds at the Replication Server there is still a lot of work to be done to ensure that the information reaches the RSSD. This work is done asynchronously from the submission of the command and so you should issue a **check subscription** to make sure that each stage has completed.

As you execute the **check subscription** at the definition stages, you must check the subscription status at both the Primary and Replicate Replication Server. The values that you need to achieve are defined in table 6.2.

Command	Successful completion
define	DEFINED
activate	ACTIVATED
validate	VALID

Table 6.2: Subscription status values

Define subscription

When you materialize the data manually you define the subscription with the **define subscription** command.

define subscription subscription_name

for {rep_def_name I

publication pub_name with primary at server_name.db_name}

with replicate at server_name.db_name

[where predicate_expression]

[subscribe to truncate table]

[for new articles]

where

with primary at	Defines the location of the primary data for a publication.
with replicate at	Defines the location of the replicate data.
subscribe to truncate table	Enables replication of the **truncate table** command. This option needs to be the same for all subscriptions on a replicate table.
for new articles	Refreshes the subscription by checking the subscription against the publication and creating subscriptions against any un-subscribed articles.

If the **where** clause is omitted the complete replication definition is replicated. A publication may contain a **where** clause and this is used to restrict the rows presented to subscriptions instead of the **where** clause in the subscription. When you subscribe to a publication you cannot specify a **where** clause in the subscription. This is actually advantageous as the publication **where** clause may contain the **OR** operator. (The syntax is not that great but at least it's possible.) When you subscribe to a publication, the Replication Server creates internal subscriptions for each article in the publication. These internal articles are treated as a group for all subscription commands: **activate subscription**, **validate subscription** and **create subscription**. Publications are dealt with in detail in Chapter 7.

The **where** clause restricts the data rows or the procedure executions which are replicated. This is a standard **where** clause format with the contents depending on whether it is table or function replication.

Table   **where col_name operator value**

                            [and col_name operator value] ...

Function   **where @param_name operator value**

                            [and @param_name operator value] ...

The valid operators are less than you have in a normal **where** clause. The operators allowed are shown in table 6.3.

Operator	Symbol
Equal to	=
Less than	<
Greater than	>
Less than or equal to	<=
Greater than or equal to	>=
Bitmap comparison	&

Table 6.3: Valid where clause operators

The & operator is allowed only when you have used the special *rs_address* datatype which I deal with later in the bitmap section. The only ones that you will really miss – and forget about – are **like** and **between** but it's not such a big deal.

The other major omission is that **OR** is not supported. This is more annoying as you need to define multiple subscriptions for the replication definition which mimics an **OR** as all subscriptions for a replication definition are replicated to the Replicate Database table. As mentioned earlier, you can avoid this restriction by defining the **OR** operation in a publication. Replication Server handles any possible duplication for multiple subscriptions on a replication definition and replicates only the one copy of the transaction. For example an **OR** defined as two subscriptions:

> **define subscription sub_jk_tab_area**
>
> **for def_jk_tab**
>
> **with replicate at DMKT.sales_db**
>
> **where area = 'NE'**
>
> **define subscription sub_jk_tab_ctry**
>
> **for def_jk_tab**
>
> **with replicate at DMKT.sales_db**
>
> **where country = 'UK'**

will only replicate the single insert for:

> **insert into jk_tab (pkey, area, country) values (1, 'NE', 'UK')**

Recording the subscription

If we consider the subscription:

define subscription sales_sub

for sales_rep_def

with replicate at RDSLN1.sales_db

It is recorded as shown in figure 6.2.

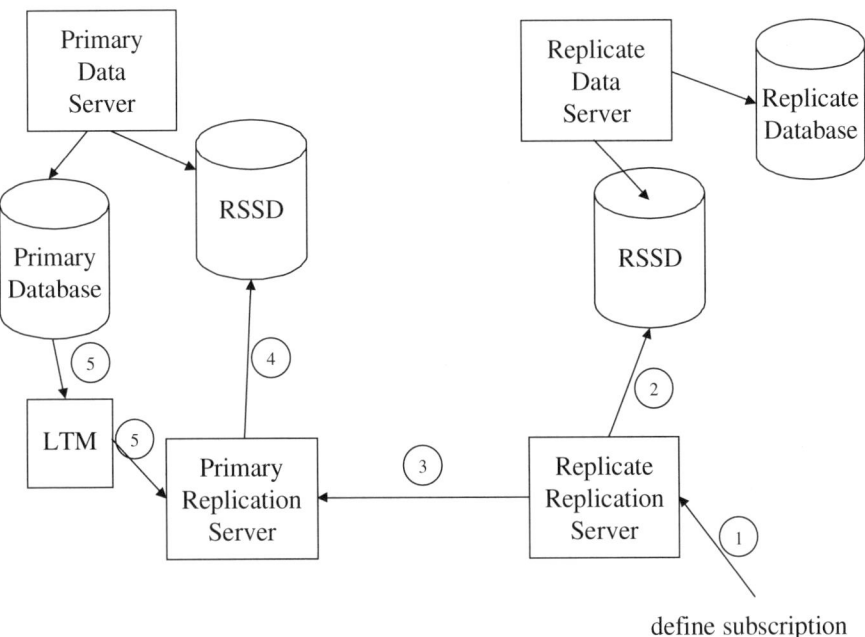

Figure 6.2: Define subscription

1. The subscription is defined at the Replicate Replication Server which manages the Replicate Database with the replicate table.

2. The Replicate Replication Server inserts the subscription into its RSSD.

3. The Replicate Replication Server sends the subscription definition to the Primary Replication Server.

4. The Primary Replication Server inserts the subscription into its RSSD. (We cannot rely on the natural replication of the system as we did with replication definitions because there may be no replication defined from the Replicate Replication Server to the Primary Replication Server.) This **define subscription**

simply records the subscription definition at the RSSD of the Replicate and Primary Replication Server but does not cause any materialization or replication to take place.

5. Any transactions at the Primary Database are sent to the Primary Replication Server by the LTM. These are simply discarded even though there is a subscription definition recorded at the RSSD because the subscription has not yet been activated.

Activate subscription

Once you have defined the subscription you activate it with the **activate subscription** command. This activates the subscription to the replication definition so that replication may start. Once the subscription is activated the replication transactions for the subscription are replicated from the Primary to the Replicate Replication Server and applied to the Replicate Database. The **activate subscription** is input at the same Replication Server as the **define subscription** command.

activate subscription sub_name

for {rep_def_name |

    publication pub_name with primary at server_name.db_name}

with replicate at server_name.db_name

[with suspension [at active replicate only]]

where

for rep_def_name	Defines the replication definition for the subscription.
for publication name	Defines the publication for the subscription.
with primary at	The location of the primary database when subscribing to a publication.
with replicate at	The location of the replicate database.
with suspension	The subscription is still activated but the data is not applied to the Replicate Database as the connection from the DSI to the Replicate Database is suspended. The transactions are stored and held in the outbound stable queue until the connection is resumed.

with suspension at active replicate only

This suspends the active database connection in a warm standby configuration. This allows you to initialize the active database without replicating the load activity. This is not really a normal approach as you would initialize the active database before defining the warm standby. It is more normal to define warm standby with the standby database connection suspended. See chapter 10 for a full treatment of warm standby.

activate subscription sales_sub

for sales_rep_def

with replicate at RRSLN1.sales_db

with suspension

Then check the subscription:

check subscription sales_sub

for sales_rep_def

with replicate at RRSLN1.sales_db

Activating the subscription tells the Primary Replication Server to start sending the replication transactions to the Replicate Replication Server for replication at the Replicate Database. Activating **with suspension** still tells the Primary Replication Server to start sending the replication transactions to the Replicate Replication Server but the Replicate Replication Server stores them in the outbound queue of its Stable Device until the connection to the Replicate Database is resumed. Activating **with suspension** can be useful if there is a time delay between unloading the primary data and populating the Replicate Database. In this case you can activate the subscription **with suspension** after the materialization data has been extracted to allow the Primary Database to be used while the Replicate Database is being populated. Any transactions made against the Primary Database will be forwarded to the Replicate Replication Server and will be played against the Replicate Database once the bulk load is complete and the connection is resumed. Make sure that the stable device is large enough to hold all the transactions in the suspended connection queue.

Recording the subscription activation

Using the above **activate subscription** command, fig 6.3 illustrates how this is recorded by the Replication Server.

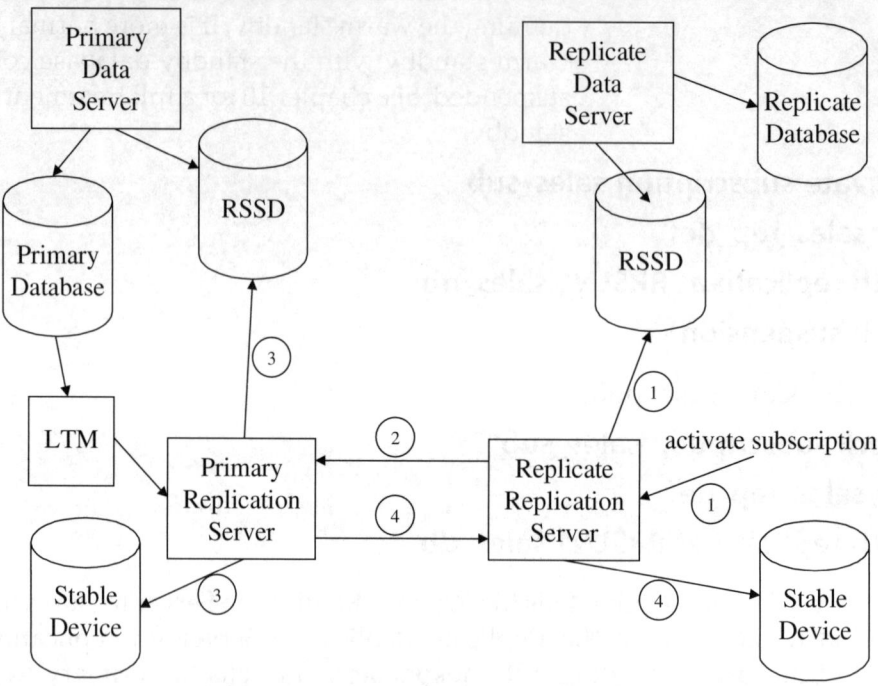

Figure 6.3: Subscription activation

1. The activate subscription is defined at the Replicate Replication Server which updates the *rs_subscriptions* table in its RSSD and, **with suspension** is specified, the connection to the Replicate Database is suspended.

2. The activation is then sent to the Primary Replication Server.

3. The Primary Replication Server updates its RSSD, changing the activation status in *rs_subscriptions* from MATERIALIZE to ACTIVE and inserts an activation marker to the Primary Database outbound queue.

4. The Primary Replication Server confirms the activation to the Replicate Replication Server which updates *rs_subscriptions* and writes an activation marker in the outbound queue of its Stable Device.

Once both Replication Servers have the subscription marked as active, the Primary Replication Server starts sending transactions to the Replicate Replication Server which stores them in the outbound queue of its Stable Device until the connection is resumed.

The connection is resumed with the **resume connection** command:

resume connection to server_name.db_name

[skip transaction|execute transaction]

where

skip transaction	Skips the first transaction in the queue, writing it to the exceptions log. This is useful when the first transaction in the queue is causing the thread to fail and the simplest answer is not to process this transaction e.g. when a duplicate insert is causing the DSI to fail.
execute transaction	This executes the first transaction in the queue when it is a system transaction i.e. a transaction without a **begin tran** and **commit tran**. The errorlog will contain a message that the DSI failure was caused by a system transaction. You need to determine whether the transaction has been applied to the replicate database and resume the connection appropriately.

resume connection to RSLN1.sales_db

When you activate a subscription for a publication, all of the underlying subscriptions to the articles of the publication are activated. If you have added new articles to a subscription, make sure that these have all been materialized before you activate the subscription for the publication.

Validate subscription

After you have activated the subscription and resumed the connection, if necessary, you need to validate the subscription using the **validate subscription** command.

validate subscription subscription_name

for {rep_def_name |

publication pub_name with primary at server_name.db_name

with replicate at server_name.db_name

Validate subscription is the final command in manual materialization. It checks that the replication and subscription functions are defined and updates the RSSD entries to VALID. The **validate subscription** command is input at the same Replication Server as the **define subscription** command.

> **validate subscription sales_sub**
>
> **for sales_rep_def**
>
> **with replicate at RRSLN1.sales_db**

Then check the subscription with:

> **check subscription sales_sub**
>
> **for sales_rep_def**
>
> **with replicate at RRSLN1.sales_db**

When you validate a subscription for a publication, all of the underlying subscriptions to the articles of the publication are validated.

Check subscription

You should check the subscription status at each stage of the manual materialization process as you need to make sure that each step has been successful before continuing. This is done with the **check subscription** command.

> **check subscription sub_name**
>
> **for {rep_def_name |**
>
> **publication pub_name with primary at server_name.db_name**
>
> **with replicate at server_name.db_name**

This is necessary because of the asynchronous nature of Sybase replication. Subscription definition commands are input at the Replicate Replication Server which inserts the information to its RSSD and then asynchronously writes to the Primary Replication Server for it to insert the information to its RSSD. It may look like the command at the Replicate Replication Server has been successful but not all of the steps may have been completed successfully.

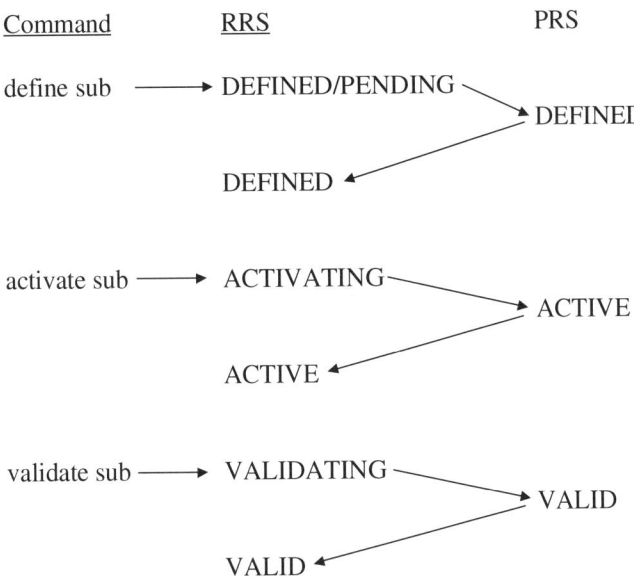

Figure 6.4: Subscription status values

So check the status of the subscription at all times and make sure that it reflects the command just completed before going on to the next stage in the subscription definition. Figure 6.4 illustrates the values that the status goes through in manual materialization.

Although the **create subscription** does this in one step i.e. define, activate and validate the **check subscription** may still be used to monitor the progress of the materialization. The status values that you see depend on where the **check subscription** command is executed. The full list of status values are given in table 6.4.

Status	Description
INVALID:	Subscription does not exist.
REMOVING:	REMOVING subscription from system tables at the Primary or Replicate.
DEMATERIALIZING:	Subscription is DEMATERIALIZING at the Primary or Replicate.
VALID:	Subscription is VALID at the Primary or Replicate.
VALIDATING:	Subscription is VALIDATING at the Replicate.

MATERIALIZED:	Subscription has been MATERIALIZED at the Replicate.
ACTIVE:	Subscription is ACTIVE at the Primary or Replicate.
ACTIVATING:	Subscription is ACTIVATING at the Primary or Replicate.
QCOMPLETE and ACTIVE:	Subscription is ACTIVE at the Replicate and Materialization Queue has been completed.
QCOMPLETE:	Materialization Queue for Subscription has been completed.
ACTIVE and not QCOMPLETE:	Subscription is ACTIVE at the Replicate, but Materialization Queue for it has not been completed.
DEFINED:	Subscription has been defined at the Primary or Replicate.
ERROR:	Subscription has experienced an unrecoverable error during Materialization or Dematerialization. Please consult the error log for more details.
PENDING:	Other subscriptions are being created or dropped for the same replication definition/database. Subscription will be processed when previous requests are completed.
RECOVERING:	Subscription has experienced a recoverable error during Materialization or Dematerialization. It will be recovered by the Subscription Daemon (dSub).

Table 6.4: Subscription status values

Defining a subscription with automatic materialization

If automatic materialization is required you define the subscription with the **create subscription** command. The **create subscription** command is entered at the Replication Server which manages the replicate database.

create subscription subscription_name

for {rep_def_name |

      publication pub_name with primary at server_name.db_name}

with replicate at server_name.dbname

[where predicate_expression]

[incrementally | without holdlock | without materialization]

[subscribe to truncate table]

[for new articles]

where

with primary at	Defines the location of the primary data for a publication.
with replicate at	Defines the location of the replicate data.
without holdlock	For non-atomic materialization, this clause materializes the data from the primary without a **holdlock** on the data. This applies the data to the Replicate Database in groups of 10 rows per transaction.
incrementally	This applies the data to the replicate in groups of 10 rows per transaction. For atomic materialization a **holdlock** is used in the **select** on the primary data.
without materialization	The data is not materialized.
subscribe to truncate table	Enables replication of the **truncate table** command. This option needs to be the same for all subscriptions on a replicate table.

for new articles   Refreshes the subscription by checking the
                            subscription against the publication and creating
                            subscriptions against any un-subscribed articles.

The same restrictions and workarounds apply to the **where** clause operators as
have already been covered for the **define subscription**. If the **where** clause is omitted
the complete replication definition is replicated. A publication may contain a **where**
clause and this is used to restrict the rows presented to subscriptions instead of the
where clause in the subscription. When you subscribe to a publication you cannot
specify a **where** clause in the subscription. This is actually advantageous as the
publication **where** clause may contain the **OR** operator. (The syntax is not that great
but at least it's possible.) When you subscribe to a publication, the Replication Server
creates internal subscriptions for each article in the publication.

The **where** clause restricts the data rows or the procedure executions which are
replicated. This is a standard **where** clause format with the contents depending on
whether it is table or function replication.

Table   **where col_name operator value**

                 [and col_name operator value] …

Function   **where @param_name operator value**

                 [and @param_name operator value] …

The valid operators are less than you have in a normal **where** clause. The operators
allowed are shown in table 6.3.

Operator	Symbol
Equal to	=
Less than	<
Greater than	>
Less than or equal to	<=
Greater than or equal to	>=
Bitmap comparison	&

Table 6.3: Valid where clause operators

The & operator is allowed only when you have used the special *rs_address* datatype
which I deal with later in the bitmap section. The only ones that you will really miss –
and forget about – are **like** and **between** but it's not such a big deal.

The other major omission is that **OR** is not supported. This is more annoying as you need to define multiple subscriptions for the replication definition which mimics an **OR** as all subscriptions for a replication definition are replicated to the Replicate Database table. As mentioned earlier, you can avoid this restriction by defining the **OR** operation in a publication.

Automatic materialization using the **create subscription** command may be defined on table replication definitions only. The **create subscription** command cannot be used on a function replication definition. This restriction applies to a publication which contains a function replication definition.

The default is atomic materialization where the data is materialized with the Primary Database data being locked to prevent maintenance of the data while the materialization is taking place. Once the data is materialized the subscription is automatically activated and validated and all blocked transactions resume against the primary data.

For small data volumes on a very fast network this is a quite feasible approach. But do not run it during the busiest time of the day as transactions against the Primary Database table will be blocked. The materialization runs against the Primary Database table **with holdlock** using the function string **rs_select_with_lock.** This blocks any transactions against data which has already been read for materialization. When using this method of atomic materialization, you need to ensure that the Stable Device is large enough to hold the materialization data in the stable queue and that the Primary Database log is large enough to hold all of the materialization transaction data.

Atomic materialization

create subscription sales_sub

for sales_rep_def

with replicate at RRSLN1.sales_db

This is recorded in the RSSDs as shown in figure 6.5.

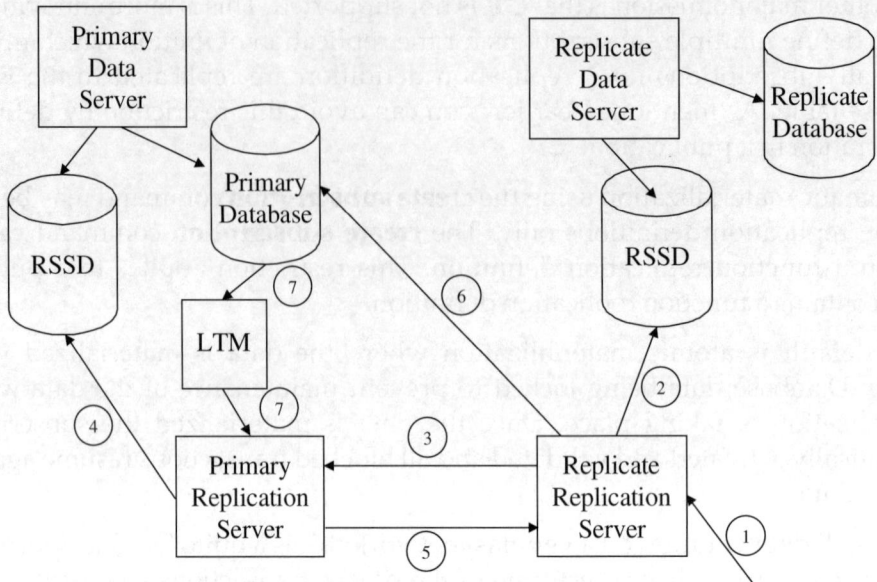

Figure 6.5: Atomic materialization

1. The **create subscription** is entered at the Replicate Replication Server.

2. The Replicate Replication Server writes the subscription to its RSSD.

3. The Replicate Replication Server sends the subscription definition to the Primary Replication Server.

4. The Primary Replication Server enters the subscription into its RSSD.

5. The Primary Replication Server then notifies the Replicate Replication Server that the subscription is defined at the Primary Replication Server.

6. The Replicate Replication Server then sends a transaction to the Primary Database to carry out the materialization and activate the subscription.

7. The Primary Replication Server sends the materialization data to the Replicate Replication Server which stores it in the Stable Device as one transaction. The LTM at the Primary Database processes the activation marker once the materialization data has been sent and forwards it to the outbound queue of the Stable Device. Once the activation marker is received the materialization data in the Replicate Replication Server Stable Device is then written to the Replicate Database as one large transaction.

The transaction sent to the Primary Database from the Replicate Replication Server consists of a **select with holdlock** of the required data based on the subscription definition and an **execute** of the **rs_marker** procedure which inserts an activation marker to the Primary Database transaction log.

For example:

begin tran

select * from sales holdlock

exec rs_marker 'activate subscription subid 0'

commit tran

where   subid is the value in *rs_subscriptions.subid*

You can see this value with the command:

select subid from rs_subscriptions

where subname = 'sub_name'

and dbid in (select dbid from rs_databases

where dbname = 'rep_db_name'

and dsname = 'rep_server_name')

Note the need for the Replicate Replication Server Stable Device to hold the full table data when you use this method. Also the Replicate Database log must be large enough to hold the transaction log data from the materialization.

In general, use this method only when the table and the Primary Database activity are small. Once the materialization data and the activation marker have been passed to the Replicate Replication Server, the transactions at the Primary Database are processed and replicated to the Replicate Replication Server. These transactions are stored in the Stable Device outbound queue until the materialization is completed at the Replicate Database. This means that the Stable Device at the Replicate Replication Server needs a bit more room for the transactions which are processed at the Primary Database while the Replicate Database is being materialized.

If you use atomic materialization for a large amount of data, keep monitoring the queues in the Stable Device with the **admin disk_space** command.

admin disk_space

Partition			
Logical	Part.Id	Total Segs	Used Segs
State			

/dev/LNPRD_1/QUEUE_02

QUEUE_02	102	2040	602

ON-LINE//

/dev/LNPRD_1 /QUEUE_01

QUEUE_01	103	2040	0

ON-LINE//

If you are running out of space you can always add another partition as this can be deleted later once the space is freed. Chapter 2 describes the defining of partitions.

Incremental atomic materialization

    create subscription sales_sub
    for sales_rep_def
    with replicate at RRSLN1.sales_db
    where sales_id > 10000
    incrementally

Incremental atomic materialization creates a transaction for every 10 inserts to the Replicate Database. This allows more concurrency at the Replicate Database but it can take a long time because of the extra network traffic. Interestingly all of the materialization data is still held in the Replicate Replication Server Stable Device until the materialization is complete and so the same size problems will occur with incremental as with a full materialization. Not really any choice - I prefer full automatic atomic materialization or manual materialization.

Non-atomic materialization

    create subscription sales_sub
    for sales_rep_def
    with replicate at RRSLN1.sales_db
    where sales_id > 10000

without holdlock

The **without holdlock** clause defines non-atomic materialization and reads the materialization data from the Primary Database without holding read locks. Therefore transactions on the Primary Database are allowed while the materialization is taking place. Unfortunately this means that the Primary Replication Server will be discarding them as there is no active subscription, and so there is no guarantee that the databases will be synchronous after the materialization. This non-atomic materialization is done incrementally in batches of 10 to minimize this problem but it will still occur. Again not really any choice in my opinion: this is not a good approach.

For all non-atomic materialization you should **set autocorrection on** to ensure that inserts and updates are processed as a **delete** followed by an **insert**. This caters for any problems associated with partial primary data transactions replicating during materialization, which may cause some primary data commands to be replicated more than once. And make sure that you **set autocorrection on** before you create the subscription as it will be ignored otherwise.

As for manual materialization using the **define subscription** command, you can monitor the subscription progress with the **check subscription** command. When this shows a status of VALID the subscription is complete.

Bitmap Subscription

Bitmap subscription allows you to replicate rows based on bit map comparisons. The approach requires you to define the column in the replication definition with the special Replication Server datatype *rs_address* and to use the bit map comparison operator (&) in the subscription **where** clause.

The most common application of this is the replication of status columns in the primary data which save space by using bit settings instead of distinct character or numeric values. For example a requirement to replicate only "single" and "married" from a table containing:

Single	1
Married	10
Divorced	100
Widowed	1000

is established in replication by defining the replication definition column as *rs_address* and then using it in the subscription as:

```
define subscription emp_single_sub
    for employee_def
    with replicate at RRSLN1.hr_db
    where status & 1
define subscription emp_married_sub
    for employee_def
    with replicate as RRSLN1.hr_db
    where status & 2
```

The *rs_address* datatype may also be used for comparison with hexadecimal values in the subscription **where** clause.

I've never used this feature in any replication but the documentation gives an important warning. Replication Server does not replicate the row if the only change to the row involves the *rs_address* columns and the row still qualifies in the subscription. For example a row which moved from "single" to "married" – with no other change – would not be replicated in the above subscriptions as the row still qualifies for replication. If the update changes the *rs_address* type column so that the replicated row must be inserted or deleted then the replication takes place.

Dropping a subscription

If you want to stop the data being replicated to the Replicate Database on a permanent basis you can drop the subscription with the **drop subscription** command. This removes the subscription in both the Replicate Replication Server and Primary Replication Server and may also remove any rows from the Replicate Database tables related to the subscription. The **drop subscription** command is entered at the Replication Server where the subscription was defined.

```
drop subscription sub_name
for {rep_def_name |
            {article article_name in pub_name |
                publication pub_name}
                with primary at server_name.db_name}
with replicate at server_name.db_name
[without purge [with suspension [at active replicate only]] |
```

[incrementally] with purge]

where

for rep_def_name	Defines the replication definition name for the subscription.
for article ... in ...	Defines the name of the article for the subscription and the publication the article is contained in.
for publication	Defines the publication for the subscription.
with primary at	Defines the location of the primary database for a publication or an article.
with replicate at	Defines the location of the replicate database.
without purge	This leaves the rows intact at the Replicate Database. In this case you will need to dematerialize the replicate data yourself – if you need to. For a table replication definition or a publication you must specify **without** or **with purge**. A subscription to a function replication definition is always dropped without purging any replicated data related to the function. In this case you do not need to quote the **without purge** clause.

without purge with suspension

The **with suspension** option leaves the Replicate Database connection suspended once the **drop subscription** has completed.

without purge with suspension at active replicate only

This is a warm standby option which suspends the DSI to the active database to allow you to delete rows at the active database after the subscription is dropped without the deletes being replicated. Warm Standby is discussed in detail in chapter 10.

with purge	The **drop subscription** removes the Replicate Database rows as long as they do not belong to another active subscription. The **incrementally** option dematerializes the data in transactions of 10 deletes at a time – similar to incremental materialization.

You may use the **check subscription** to follow the process of a **drop subscription**, especially when used with purge. When the status is INVALID at both Primary Replication Server and Replicate Replication Server, the dematerialization is complete.

```
drop subscription sales_sub
for sales_rep_def
with replicate as RRSLN1.sales_db
without purge
```

Similar to defining a subscription, the **drop subscription** is issued at the Replicate Replication Server which manages the replicate data. The Replicate Replication Server deletes the subscription from its RSSD and then sends the **drop subscription** to the Primary Replication Server which also deletes it from its RSSD.

When you drop a publication subscription **without purge** all of the subscriptions to the articles of the publication are dropped immediately. When you drop a publication subscription **with purge** the subscriptions to the articles are dropped one at a time in reverse order to how they were added to the publication.

Help on subscriptions

The **rs_helpsub** system procedure provides help on subscription information.

rs_helpsub [sub_name [, rep_def_name [, server_name, db_name]]]

With no parameters, summary information is displayed about all subscriptions. Including a parameter alters the level of detail displayed.

sub_name	Information on a specific subscription or on all subscriptions with that name i.e. for different replication definitions.
rep_def_name	Information on all subscriptions for that replication definition name.
server_name, db_name	Information on subscriptions for the replication definition name in the specific server and database.

rs_helpsub

** This site is 'LON_01' **

Subscription Name	Replicate DS.DB	Rep Def name	A/C	RRS	PRS
ny_lon_01	NY01.LON_01_RSSD	sales_rdf	0	valid	unknown
ny_lon_02	NY01.LON_01_RSSD	mkt_rdf	0	valid	unknown

Unknown simply indicates that the Replication Server has no knowledge of the subscription status at the Primary Replication Server. This is most common when there is only one Replication Server managing both Primary and Replicate Database. I have always found that you can ignore it and continue with the subscription definition.

Providing the subscription name displays the definition of the subscription.

rs_helpsub sub_jkprc

Subscription Name	Rep. Def. Name	Replicate DS.DB	A/C	RRS	PRS
sub_jkprc	def_jkprc	DLN_1.test_db	0	Valid	Valid

Owner	Creation Date
sa	Dec 14 1998

Subscription Text

define subscription sub_jkprc
for def_jkprc
with replicate at DNY1.testdb

System tables

The subscription information is stored as a row in *rs_subscriptions*.

select * from rs_subscriptions

subname	subid	type
objid	*dbid*	*pdbid*	*requestdate*
pownerid	rownerid	status	recovering
error_flag *materializing* *dematerializing*	*primary_sre* *replicate_sre*
materialization_try *method*	*generation*

rsm_heartbeat	0x010f431f80000081	2
0x010f431f00000082	100791	0	Feb 19 1998 5:27PM
0x0000000000000000 0x0000000002000001	3359	0
0	0	0	1
0	2	0x00000000

You might like to enhance these.

Databases that have subscriptions to a replication definition

```
select d.dsname, d.dbname, s.subname
from rs_repdbs d, rs_subscriptions s, rs_objects o
where d.dbid = s.dbid
and s.objid = o.objid
and o.objname = '<repdefname>'
```

Databases that have subscriptions to a primary database

```
select rd.dsname, rd.dbname
from rs_repdbs rd, rs_databases d, rs_subscriptions s, rs_objects o
where rd.dbid = s.dbid
and s.objid = o.objid
and o.dbid = d.dbid
and d.dsname = '<server_name>'
and d.dbname = '<database_name>'
```

Primary database for a subscription

```
select d.dsname, d.dbname
from rs_databases d, rs_objects o, rs_subscriptions s
where d.dbid = o.dbid
and o.objid = s.objid
and s.subname = '<subscription_name>'
```

Replication definitions and their subscriptions for a primary database

```
select d.dsname, d.dbname, o.objname, s.subname
from rs_databases d, rs_objects o, rs_subscriptions s
where d.dbid = o.dbid
and o.objid = s.objid
and d.dbname = '<database_name>'
```

Basic troubleshooting

- No entries in the RSSD of the Replicate Replication Server.

  The first step of inserting entries into the RSSD by the Replicate Replication Server has failed. These inserts are carried out by the RSSD primary user so check that the user_id and password are correct. Next most obvious reason for the failure is that the RSSD log is full and all processes are suspended.

- No entries in the Primary Replication Server.

  The Replicate Replication Server distributes the replication definition to the Primary Replication Server. The most obvious cause of a problem is a failure to login but also check that the routes are defined correctly.

- No entries in the RSSD of the Primary Replication Server.

  The replication definition inserts have reached the Stable Device of the Primary Replication Server but have not been written to the RSSD of the Primary Replication Server. Similar to the first step at the Replicate Replication Server, check the login id and password or a full transaction log.

7

Publications and Articles

Introduction

Replication Server 11.5 supports **publications** and **articles**. These allow you to collect replication definitions into a group (the publication) and then subscribe to them as this group. The publication may contain a mixture of table and function replication definitions. The publication exists as a separate object and the replication definitions are linked to the publication via the articles. A particularly useful feature of the article is that it supports the **OR** operator on multiple **where** clauses. This eliminates the need to define separate subscriptions for each clause of the **OR**.

The steps in using publications and articles are:

- Create the replication definitions.
- Create the publication.
- Create the articles linking the replication definitions and the publication.
- Validate the publication.
- Create subscriptions to the publication.

Publications

Creating the publication

The **create publication** command creates a publication for tables or stored procedures that allows the replication definitions to be subscribed to as a group. The command is entered at the Replication Server which manages the primary database.

create publication pub_name

with primary at server_name.db_name

where

with primary at   Specifies the location of the primary database.

create publication sales_pub

with primary at LNPRD_1.SALES_DB

This creates a publication to which articles may be attached to define the replication definitions which the publication contains (see **create article** later in this chapter).

The publication does not get replicated to the replicate Replication Servers until a subscription is created to the publication in the replicate Replication Server.

Checking the publication

You may issue **check publication** at any time to display the status of the publication and the number of articles that the publication contains.

> check publication pub_name
>
> with primary at server_name.db_name

Dropping the publication

You may drop the publication using the **drop publication** command. This command is entered at the Replication Server which manages the primary database.

> drop publication pub_name
>
> with primary at server_name.db_name
>
> [drop_repdef]

Dropping the publication automatically drops its articles and you can optionally drop the replication definitions for the publication if they are not part of another article and have no subscriptions. You cannot drop a publication if there are current subscriptions. You must drop all subscriptions first.

The dropped publication is not removed from the replicate Replication Server immediately but only when the subscription is updated with a **define** or **create subscription** command or when the **check publication** is issued at the replicate site.

> drop publication orders_pub
>
> with primary at PLN_MKT.SALES_DB

Validate the publication

You set the status of the publication to *valid* with the **validate publication** command. Once the publication has been marked as *valid*, subscriptions may be defined against it. This command is entered at the Replication Server which manages the primary database.

> validate publication pub_name
>
> with primary at server_name.db_name

You must validate the publication before subscriptions can be defined against it. Validating the publication verifies that the publication contains at least one article.

Viewing publication information

You may display publication information using the **rs_helppub** system procedure.

rs_helppub

[pub_name, primary_dataserver, primary_db [, article_name]]

rs_helppub displays all publications at the server or information on a particular publication/article. If you execute **rs_helppub** at a replicate server it displays information only on those publications which have subscriptions defined at the site.

rs_helppub

Publication Name	PRS	Primary DS.DB
jk1_pub	PRS_LN	PLN_MKT.SALES_DB
jk2_pub	PRS_LN	PLN_MKT.SALES_DB

Num Articles	Status	Request Date
3	Valid	Mar 23 1998 11:51AM
7	Valid	Mar 24 1998 10:41AM

Articles

Creating the article

The **create article** command creates an article for a publication which relates a replication definition to the publication. The command is entered at the Replication Server which manages the primary database.

create article article_name for pub_name

with primary at server_name.db_name

with replication definition {table_rep_def | function_rep_def}

[where {col_name | @param_name} operator value

    [and {col_name | @param_name} operator value] ...

[or where {col_name | @param_name} operator value

    [and {col_name | @param_name} operator value] ...] ...]

where

for pub_name	The name of the publication.
with primary at	The location of the Primary database.
with replication definition	The name of the table or function replication definition.
where	Optional **where** clauses to restrict the rows or parameters available from the replication definition.
operator	The valid operators are: <, >, >=, <=, =, &

The publication must contain one article before it can be validated or subscriptions can be defined against it. Any columns used in the **where** clauses must be included as *searchable* columns in the associated replication definition.

create article orders_art for orders_pub

with primary at PLN_MKT.SALES_DB

with replication definition orders_rep

create article customer_art for customer_pub

with primary at PLN_MKT.SALES_DB

with replication definition customer_rep

where locn = 'UK'

or where locn = 'US'

When you add or drop an article to/from an existing publication, the publication is invalidated and you must validate the publication and refresh the subscription (see **create subscription** later in this chapter). Fortunately existing replication continues while you do this.

Dropping the article

You may drop an article from a publication using the **drop article** command.

drop article article_name for pub_name

with primary at server_name.db_name

[drop_repdef]

The article is removed from the publication if there are no subscriptions to the article. You may optionally drop the associated replication definition if it is not part of another article and has no subscriptions.

Dropping the article invalidates the publication and you must validate it and refresh any subscriptions.

Similar to the publication, the article is not removed from the replicate Replication Server until a **create subscription** or **define subscription** is executed at the site.

Viewing article information

You may display article information using the **rs_helppub** system procedure as discussed earlier for publications.

rs_helppub

[pub_name, primary_dataserver, primary_db [, article_name]]

Subscriptions to publications

Subscriptions to publications are made identically to subscriptions to replication definitions using **create subscription** or **define/activate/validate subscription** depending on the method of materialization. One addition to the syntax is the **for new articles** clause on the **create/define subscription** commands which refreshes an existing publication when articles are added or dropped.

create subscription sub_name

for {table_rep_def | function_rep_def | publication pub_name

with primary at data_server.database}

with replicate at data_server.database

[where {column_name | @param_name} operator value

[and {column_name | @param_name} operator value]...]

[without holdlock | incrementally | without materialization]

[subscribe to truncate table]

[for new articles]

where

with primary at	Defines the location of the primary data for a publication.
with replicate at	Defines the location of the replicate data.
without holdlock	For non-atomic materialization, this clause materializes the data from the primary without a **holdlock** on the data. This applies the data to the Replicate Database in groups of 10 rows per transaction.
incrementally	This applies the data to the replicate in groups of 10 rows per transaction. For atomic materialization a **holdlock** is used in the **select** on the primary data.
without materialization	The data is not materialized.
subscribe to truncate table	Enables replication of the **truncate table** command. This option needs to be the same for all subscriptions on a replicate table.
use dump marker	Used in a warm standby configuration to assist in the synchronisation of the databases.

The syntax and use of the **create subscription** command are described fully in chapter 6.

create subscription sales_sub

for publication sales_pub

with primary at PLN_MKT.SALES_DB

with replicate at PNY_MKT.SALES_DB

The Replication Server creates a subscription for each article of the publication. When you use automatic materialization the articles are materialized one at a time in the sequence that they were defined. If you use the **without materialization** clause all of the articles are activated and validated at the same time.

define subscription customer_sub

for publication customer_pub

with primary at PLN_MKT.SALES_DB

with replicate at PNY_MKT.SALES_DB

When you **activate** and **validate** the subscription for a bulk materialization all article subscriptions are activated and validated at the same time.

When you add a new article to an existing publication or drop an existing article the subscription information is not updated immediately and you need to refresh the publication.

define subscription customer_sub

for publication customer_pub

with primary at PLN_MKT.SALES_DB

with replicate at PNY_MKT.SALES_DB

for new article

The **for new article** clause checks the subscription against the publication and creates new subscriptions for any unsubscribed articles.

Viewing subscription information for a publication

The **rs_helppubsub** displays information about publication and article subscriptions.

rs_helppubsub sub_name

   [, pub_name [, primary_server, primary_db

   [, replicate_server, replicate_db]]]

The level of detail depends on the parameters supplied.

sub_name   All publication subscriptions named sub_name.

pub_name   All publication subscriptions named sub_name for publications
                    named pub_name.

primary_server, primary_db

replicate_server, replicate_db

                    All subscriptions named sub_name for the specified publication.

rs_helppubsub jk_sub1

Subscription Name	Publication Name		
jk_sub1	jk_pub1		
Primary DS.DB	Replicate DS.DB	PRS Status	RRS Status
PLN_MKT.SALES_DB	PNY_MKT.SALES_DB	Unknown	Valid
Owner	Request Date		
sa	Mar 24 1998 11:12AM		
Subscription Name	Article Name		
jk_sub1	sales_art		
Replication Definition	PRS Status	RRS Status	
sales_rep	Unknown	Valid	
Request Date	Autocorrection		
Mar 24 1998 11:11AM	off		

rs_helppubsub jk_sub, jk_pub,
PLN_MKT, SALES_DB, PNY_MKT, SALES_DB

Subscription Name	Publication Name	Primary DS.DB	
jk_sub	jk_pub	PLN_MKT.SALES_DB	
Replicate DS.DB	PRS Status	RRS Status	Owner
PNY_MKT.SALES_DB	Unknown	Valid	mkt_dbo
Request Date	Subscription Name	Article Name	
February 25 1998	jk_sub	jk_art1	
	jk_sub	jk_art2	
	jk_sub	jk_art3	
	jk_sub	jk_art4	
	jk_sub	jk_art5	

PRS Status	RRS Status	Request Date	Replication Definition
Unknown	VALID	Feb 25, 1998	jk_rep1
Unknown	VALID	Feb 25, 1998	jk_rep2
Unknown	VALID	Feb 25, 1998	jk_rep3
Unknown	VALID	Feb 25, 1998	jk_rep4

Autocorrection	Subscribe to Truncate Table
on	off
off	on
off	off
off	off

8

System Functions

Introduction

The functions, function strings and function string classes of the Sybase Replication Server are the means by which the published data is translated into the data that is replicated to the subscriber. This may be no more than a simple one to one command translation with no alteration of the data formats, or it may be a complete transformation of the initial transaction both in what it does and in the format of the subscription data. This alteration by the system functions and function strings allows the application of the data at the Replicate Database to be different from how it was applied at the Primary Database.

The Replication Server functions are categorized as:

System functions

These are the supplied default **functions** and **function strings** which process the replicated T-SQL commands and provide support for transaction control, data manipulation and replication coordination. This chapter discusses these functions and the means to alter them.

User defined functions

Application specific functions created automatically with the **create function replication definition** command or specifically with the **create function** command. These are covered in chapter 9.

The Replication Server architecture concerning the translation of a transaction from the Primary Database to the Replicate Database is shown in figure 8.1.

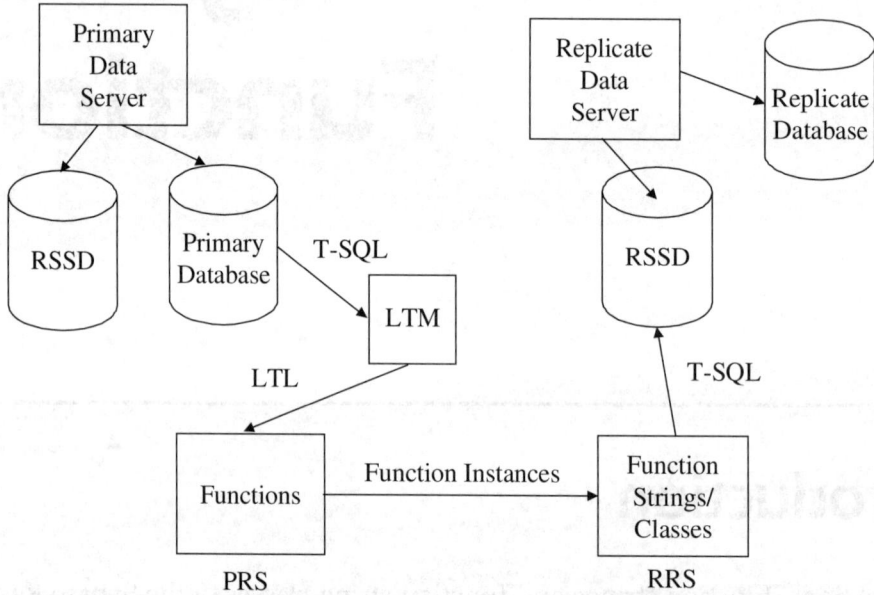

Figure 8.1: Components of transaction replication

The transactions in the Primary Database log are read by the LTM which translates the transactions into generic Log Transfer Language (LTL). The Primary Replication Server then uses the **functions** for each T-SQL command to translate the LTL into command string **function instances**. The Replicate Replication Server then uses the **function strings** to translate the command string function instances into T-SQL commands which may be applied to the Replicate Database. The function strings provide language templates which determine the execution of the function. **Function string classes** provide a classification grouping for a group of function strings.

When working with SQL Server the T-SQL defaults are provided for you:

- The LTM translates the T-SQL into LTL.

- A set of standard functions (e.g. **rs_insert, rs_delete**) is provided to translate the LTL into command strings.

- A set of standard function strings (these have the same names as the standard functions) and default function string classes *rs_sqlserver_function_class, rs_sqlserver_default_class* and *rs_db2_function_class* are provided to translate the function instances into T-SQL at the Replicate Database.

Functions and function instances

A **function** is used by the Primary Replication Server to read the input transactions from the LTM and to write **function instances** that are sent to the Replicate Replication Server for processing. There is a function for each of the actions that can be performed at the Primary Replication Server. These functions create specific function instances based on the parameters and data associated with the Primary Replication Server action. For example the function instance associated with the **rs_insert** will contain the data associated with the corresponding **insert** command. In addition to the data itself, the function instance also contains information, such as the Replicate Database and the replication definition, to allow it to be processed by the correct Replicate Replication Server. The function instances are purely transient for the specific transaction, are not stored in any RSSD table and are not available to access.

A Primary Database transaction which does:

begin tran

insert into ...

commit tran

will call three system functions at the Primary Replication Server:

rs_begin

rs_insert

rs_commit

Function scope

The system functions may be split further depending on whether they perform data manipulation or they are data independent which means that they are the same for all commands. The terms for this are **replication definition scope** if the structure depends on the schema and **function string class scope** if they are schema independent.

Replication definition scope

This includes all of the data manipulation functions:

rs_insert	rs_update	rs_delete
rs_select	rs_select_with_lock	rs_textptr_init
rs_get_text_ptr	rs_writetext	rs_datarow_for_writetext

These functions are automatically created when the replication definition is created and are replicated to all Replication Servers in the replication domain i.e. to all Replication Servers which have a route from the Primary Replication Server. The replication definition scope functions do not exist independently but only when a replication definition is defined. This is illustrated by the **rs_helpfunc** output.

rs_helpfunc

System defined Replication Definition scope functions. (excluding system defined Replication Definitions.)

Function	Rep Def Name	PRS	Rep Def Type
rs_delete	def_jk	LNDEV1_RS	R
rs_insert	def_jk	LNDEV1_RS	R
rs_select	def_jk	LNDEV1_RS	R
rs_select_with_lock	def_jk	LNDEV1_RS	R
rs_update	def_jk	LNDEV1_RS	R
rs_delete	def_jk1	LNDEV1_RS	R
rs_insert	def_jk1	LNDEV1_RS	R
rs_select	def_jk1	LNDEV1_RS	R
rs_select_with_lock	def_jk1	LNDEV1_RS	R
rs_update	def_jk1	LNDEV1_RS	R

The system functions **rs_insert**, **rs_update**, **rs_delete**, **rs_select** and **rs_select_with_lock** have been created for both the replication definitions *def_jk* and *def_jk1*. This is important as it allows the replicated action for each replication definition to be different if so desired. A system function action for a replication definition may be altered by redefining the function string action for the function with the **alter function string** command. This dependence between functions and replication definitions is emphasized when you use **rs_helpfunc** to obtain information on the functions. You cannot issue **rs_helpfunc** directly on a system function but must qualify it with the replication definition name.

rs_helpfunc [rep_def_name [, function_name]]

With no parameters you get a full list of functions, including the user defined functions.

rs_helpfunc

System defined Replication Definition scope functions. (excluding system defined Replication Definitions.)

Function	Rep Def Name	PRS	Rep Def Type
rs_delete	def_jk	LNPRD_SRV1	R
rs_insert	def_jk	LNPRD_SRV1	R
rs_select	def_jk	LNPRD_SRV1	R
rs_select_with_lock	def_jk	LNPRD_SRV1	R
rs_update	def_jk	LNPRD_SRV1	R
rs_delete	def_jk1	LNPRD_SRV1	R
rs_insert	def_jk1	LNPRD_SRV1	R
rs_select	def_jk1	LNPRD_SRV1	R
rs_select_with_lock	def_jk1	LNPRD_SRV1	R
rs_update	def_jk1	LNPRD_SRV1	R

User defined functions.

Function	Rep Def Name	PRS	Rep Def Type
def_jk1prc	def_jk1prc	LNPRD_SRV1	F
def_jk2prc	def_jk2prc	LNPRD_SRV1	F

def_jk6prc	def_jk6prc	LNPRD_SRV1	F
def_jkprc	def_jkprc	LNPRD_SRV1	F
jk2prc	jk2prc	LNPRD_SRV1	F
jk4prc	jk4prc	LNPRD_SRV1	F
jk5prc	jk5prc	LNPRD_SRV1	F
jk7prc	jk7prc	LNPRD_SRV1	F

Function String Class Scope Functions.

Function

rs_begin

rs_check_repl

rs_commit

rs_dump

rs_dumpdb

rs_dumptran

rs_get_charset

rs_get_lastcommit

rs_get_sortorder

rs_get_thread_seq

rs_get_thread_seq_noholdlock

rs_initialize_threads

rs_load

rs_marker

rs_repl_off

rs_rollback

rs_set_isolation_level3

rs_setuser

rs_triggers_reset

rs_trunc_reset

rs_trunc_set

rs_update_threads

rs_usedb

With a replication definition name you get the functions for that replication definition:

rs_helpfunc def_jk

Functions and Parameters for Replication Definition: 'def_jk'

Replication definition Type: 'Table'

System Function Names

rs_insert
rs_delete
rs_update
rs_select
rs_select_with_lock

Parameter(s)	Datatype	Length
@a	int	4
@b	int	4

And with the function name you get the detail for the function as defined for the replication definition.

rs_helpfunc def_jk, rs_insert

Functions and Parameters for Replication Definition: 'def_jk'

Replication definition Type: 'Table'

System Function Name(s)

rs_insert

Parameter(s)	Datatype	Length
@a	int	4
@b	int	4

Function string class scope

This includes the functions which are independent of the data and execute the same for all replication definitions. These may be grouped as:

Transaction control

rs_begin	rs_check_repl	rs_commit
rs_dumpdb	rs_dumptran	rs_get_charset
rs_get_sortorder	rs_get_thread_seq	rs_get_thread_seq_noholdlock
rs_initialize_threads	rs_repl_off	rs_triggers_reset
rs_set_isolation_level3	rs_setproxy	rs_setuser
rs_truncate	rs_update_threads	rs_usedb

Replication coordination

rs_get_lastcommit   rs_marker

These functions need to be defined for all function string classes (except for the default) and they are available for all replication definitions which use that function string class. So replication definitions using the default function string class *rs_sqlserver_function_class* have all of the above available. An explanation of the implementation of these functions is given in table 8.1.

Function	Description
rs_begin	This begins a transaction in a data server. Replication Server executes an **rs_begin** function at the beginning of each transaction it distributes.
rs_check_repl	This is used internally by Replication Server to check if a table is marked for replication.
rs_commit	This ends a transaction with a commit.
rs_datarow_for_writetext	This provides an image of the data row associated with a text or image column update.
rs_delete	This deletes a row in a replicated table.
rs_dumpdb	This initiates a coordinated database dump by placing **rs_dumpdb** function calls in the same

	place in the transaction stream distributed to each Replicate Replication Server.
rs_dumptran	This initiates a coordinated transaction dump by placing **rs_dumptran** function calls in the same place in the transaction stream distributed to each Replicate Replication Server.
rs_get_charset	This returns the character set used by a data server to allow Replication Server to print a warning message if the character set is not what is expected.
rs_get_lastcommit	This returns a row from the *rs_lastcommit* system table.
rs_get_sortorder	This returns the sort order used by a data server to allow Replication Server to print a warning message if the sort order is not what is expected.
rs_get_textptr	This retrieves the text pointer for a text or image column.
rs_get_thread_seq	This returns the current sequence number for the specified entry in the *rs_threads* system table. The sequence number is used in parallel DSI threads to check for conflicting updates.
rs_get_thread_seq_noholdlock	The same as *rs_get_thread_seq* but issued with no holdlock.
rs_initialize_threads	This sets the sequence number of *rs_threads* to zero.
rs_insert	This inserts a row into a table in a replicate database.
rs_marker	This provides Replication Server with a method to insert data into the transaction log so that it can be retrieved by the LTM.
rs_repl_off	This specifies whether transactions executed by the maintenance user in the SQL Server database are replicated.

rs_rollback	This ends a transaction with a rollback. This should be issued only when parallel DSI threads are implemented. In this case large transactions are sent to the Replicate Database before the commit/rollback is received by Replication Server. If the transaction is subsequently rolled back, a rollback must be issued to the Replicate Database. This is the only occasion when non-committed transactions are sent to the Replicate Database.
rs_select	This issues a **select** when materializing a subscription.
rs_select_with_lock	As for **rs_select** but issued with *holdlock* to maintain data consistency.
rs_set_isolation_level3	This function is executed when the DSI connects to SQL Server and turns on transaction isolation level 3 locking in the SQL Server. This is used when the *isolation_level_3* method of serialization is defined for multiple DSI threads.
rs_setproxy	This changes the login name in a data server.
rs_textptr_init	This allocates a text pointer for a text or image column.
rs_triggers_reset	This turns off triggers in the SQL Server. By default this is set to 'off' in warm standby databases and to 'on' in Replicate Databases.
rs_truncate	This truncates a table in the Replicate Database.
rs_update	This updates a row of a table in the Replicate Database.
rs_update_threads	This updates the sequence number for the specified entry in the *rs_threads* system table. The *rs_threads* table is used to control transaction serialization when using parallel DSI threads.
rs_usedb	This is issued when Replication Server first connects to the Replicate Database to change the database context.

rs_writetext	This updates text or image data in the Replicate Database.

Table 8.1: System functions

Function strings and function string classes

A **function string** is a language template defined at the Replicate Replication Server to interpret the function instance received from the Primary Replication Server. The default T-SQL functions have corresponding default function strings with the same names as the default functions.

The **function string class** is a grouping of all function strings used by a specific data server or database. Each database connection must have a function string class defined. Replication Server provides two default function string classes for ASE 11.5 and one for DB2.

rs_sqlserver_function_class — This function string class supplies the default T-SQL function strings. This function string class is assigned to all databases that are initialized with **rs_init**. You may customize function strings in this class but you cannot use it as a parent class.

rs_default_function_class — This function string class was introduced in 11.5 and also supplies the default T-SQL function strings. You cannot customize this class but you may use it as a parent class.

rs_db2_function_class — This is a derived class of *rs_default_function_class* which supplies the default DB2 function strings. You cannot customize this class but you may use it as a parent class.

The processing of the function instance by the Replicate Replication Server is shown in figure 8.2.

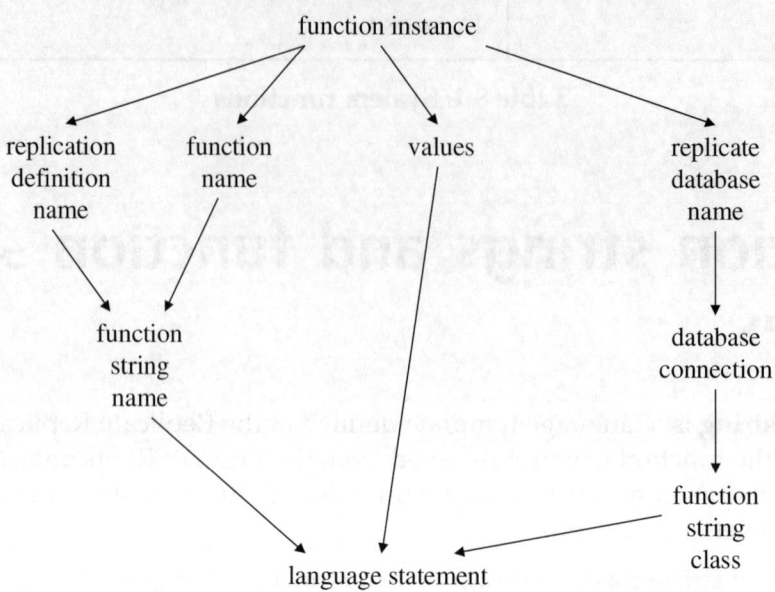

Figure 8.2: Function instance processing

When the function instance is received, the Replicate Replication Server uses the function instance to determine the replicate database, replication definition and functions. The replicate database then defines the function string class to use based on the database connection information. The replication definition and function information identifies the specific function string to be used and the values in the function instance are applied to the function string to create the language statement that is to be run against the Replicate Database tables.

Function string class

Creating function string classes

A function string class is created with the **create function string class** command.

create function string class function_string_class_name

[set parent to parent_class_name]

where

set parent to   Defines the name of an existing function string class to be used as the parent class for the class being created. If this clause is used the new function string class inherits the function strings of the parent class. This avoids the pre-11.5 need to define every function string for a new function string class. The *rs_sqlserver_function_class* cannot be used as a parent class.

create function string class jk_function_class

This command is entered at the Primary Replication Server. The name must be unique in the replication domain. The function string class is then associated with the database connection using the **alter connection** (or **create connection**) command. Before you relate the function string class to the database connection, you must define all of the function strings for the function string class. If you relate the function string class to the database connection before all of the function strings have been defined for the function string class, the connection will be suspended with an error. In 11.5 you can use the *rs_default_function_class* function string class to inherit the T-SQL function strings.

create function string class jk_function_class
set parent to rs_default_function_class

If you do not do this inheritance but create a base class, you will need to add all of the default function strings and any customized function strings to the new class before you can assign it to a database connection. You need to add all of the function string class scope function strings and whatever replication definition scope function strings that you need. If you are using 11.5, I would recommend this inheritance from *rs_default_function_class* as it saves a lot of time – although most of you will already have created scripts to add the function strings when you create a new function string class.

To relate the function string class to a database connection use the **alter connection** command, first suspending the connection.

suspend connection to PRSLN1.sales_db

alter connection to PRSLN1.sales_db
set function string class jk_function_class

resume connection to PRSLN1.sales_db

Displaying function class information

Information on the function string class is provided by the **rs_helpclass** system procedure. This displays both error class and function string class information

rs_helpclass [function_string_class_name]

The function string class name is wildcarded at the end by the procedure so **rs_helpclass** may return several classes beginning with the input string.

rs_helpclass

Function String Class(es)	PRS for CLASS	Parent Class
rs_default_function_class	Not Yet Defined.	Base Class
rs_sqlserver_function_class	Not Yet Defined.	Base Class

Error Class(es)	PRS for CLASS
rs_sqlserver_error_class	PNY1_RS

NOTE

If the PRS for your system supplied class has been labeled 'Not Yet Defined.', You may define it with — create {function string | error} class CLASS_NAME at

the Primary Replication Server (PRS).

rs_helpclass jk1_function_class

Function String Class(es)	PRS for CLASS
jk1_function_class	PNY1_RS

Error Class(es)	PRS for CLASS

The function string class information is held in the system table *rs_classes*.

select * from rs_classes

classname	classid	classtype	prsid
jk1_function_class	0x010f435001000065	F	17777488
rs_default_function_class	0x0000000001000003	F	0
rs_sqlserver_error_class	0x0000000001000002	E	17777488
rs_sqlserver_function_class	0x0000000001000001	F	0

Changing the primary site of a function string class

The primary site of a function string class is important because all function strings with function string class scope must be defined at the primary site of the function string class. This is normally the Replication Server where you create the function string class but occasionally you will need to change it. This is most common when a new routing configuration is created and you need to distribute the function strings throughout the new configuration.

To change the primary site use the **move primary** command at the new primary site Replication Server.

move primary of function string class function_string_class_name

to replication_server_name

The default function string class *rs_sqlserver_function_class* does not have a default primary site and you need to define this with the **move primary** command. Before you issue this you need to issue the **create function string class** command for the default function string class name.

create function string class rs_sqlserver_function_class

move primary of rs_sqlserver_function_class

to NYPRD_RS

Altering a function string class

You may alter the class status i.e. base or derived with the **alter function string class** command.

alter function string class f_s_class_name

set parent to {parent_class | null}

where

null   Specifies that the class is to be changed to a base class.

alter function string class jk_function_class

set parent to rs_default_function_class

This specifies that *jk_function_class* is changed to a derived class and that it inherits function strings from *rs_default_function_class*.

Dropping a function string class

You may drop a function string class with the **drop function string class** command.

drop function string class f_s_class_name

This removes the function string class and all associated function strings of the class.

drop function string class jk_function_class

You may not drop a function string class that is currently in use on a database connection and you may not drop a function string class that is parent class for a current derived class. And you cannot drop any of the three system provided function string classes: *rs_sqlserver_function_class,   rs_default_function_class, rs_db2_function_class.*

Function string

Creating a function string

A function string is created with the **create function string** command.

create function string

[rep_def_name.]function_name [; function_string_name]

for function_string_class_name [with overwrite]

[scan 'input_template']

[output {language 'output_template' |

rpc 'execute proc_name [@param=] {constant|?var!mod?}

[,[@param=] {constant|?var!mod?}] … ' |

writetext [use primary log | with log | no log] |

none}]

where

rep_def_name.function_name	The replication definition and function to which the function string is related e.g. *def_jk.rs_insert.*
function_string_name	The function string name if different from the function name. You must specify a function string name for the functions **rs_select**,

rs_select_with_lock, rs_get_textptr, rs_textptr_init and rs_writetext. For the three text functions a function string is required for each text/image column and it must have the same name as the column.

'input template' | 'output template'   A language template which defines the resulting command format. 'output template' is the command which will be applied to the Replicate Database. 'input template' is used for retrieving materialization data and may be used only with **rs_select** and **rs_select_with_lock**.

function string class name   The function string class name for the new function string.

with overwrite   Drops and recreates the function string if it already exists, identically to using **alter function string**.

writetext   Instructs Replication Server to use the **ct_send_data** function call when using the **rs_writetext** function.

use primary log   Used with *writetext* this logs the text in the replicate database if the logging option was specified in the primary database.

with log   Used with *writetext* this logs the text in the replicate database irrespective of the primary logging option.

no log   Used with *writetext* this does not log the text in the replicate database, irrespective of the primary logging option.

none   Does not replicate the text/image data when using the **rs_writetext** function.

create function string def_jk.rs_insert
    for rs_sqlserver_function_class
    output language
        ' insert into jk values (?a!new?, ?b!new?);
        update ctrl_tab set ctrl_col = ctrl_col + 1

```
                    where key_col="jk"'
create function string rs_commit
     for jk_function_class
     output language
          'execute rs_update_lastcommit
               @origin = ?rs_origin!sys?,
               @origin_qid = ?rs_origin_qid!sys?,
               @secondary_qid = ?rs_secondary_qid!sys?,
               @origin_time = ?rs_origin_commit_time!sys?;
          commit transaction'
```

As for any procedure execution, if the parameter names are not supplied, the parameter values must be supplied in the correct sequence to the procedure.

The most common processing against function strings is to alter the existing system functions for a specific replication definition. As the syntax for **alter function string** is the same as for **create function string** I shall concentrate on the alter command for the rest of the chapter. However remember that you need to create all of the function strings used by a function string class before you can define it against a database connection.

Altering a function string

A function string is altered with the **alter function string** command:

```
alter function string
     [rep_def_name.]function_name [; function_string_name]
     for function_string_class_name
     [scan 'input_template']
     [output {language 'output_template' |
     rpc 'execute proc_name [@param=] {constant|?var!mod?}
                         [,[@param=] {constant|?var!mod?}] ... '}]
     writetext [use primary log | with log | no log] |
     none} ]
```

where the definitions of the clauses are as before for the **create function string** command.

The language or rpc templates provide the means to alter the execution of the replication transaction at the Replicate Database. Note that the Replication Server does not interpret the contents of the language templates when they are defined; any errors are not picked up until run-time. So always check the function strings.

The language and rpc templates are enclosed in single quotes and run-time values may be accepted into function string variables of the format **?varable!modifier?**. The start and end question marks and the separating exclamation mark are mandatory. Multiple commands are separated by a semi-colon (;). If you need a real semi-colon use two (;;). If you need to quote a literal use two single quotes for each embedded quote. The resulting function string template has a maximum size of 64K.

Language templates

A language template is any valid T-SQL command. In the extreme you could issue a language template of:

alter function string def_jk.rs_delete

> **for rs_sqlserver_function_class**
>
> **output language 'drop table jk'**

Not recommended, but it is permissible, although do not blame me if you get into trouble with this type of rubbish. It's only an example for emphasis.

Run-time values are accepted to function string variable place holders of the format:

?varable!modifier?

?name!new?

?pkey!old?

The modifier may have the values shown in table 8.2:

Modifier	Action
new	The data substituted is the new value of the column for an inserted or updated row.
old	The data substituted is the old value of the column for an inserted or updated row.

sys	The variable name is a reference to a system variable. The system variables are defined in table 8.4 below.
param	The variable name is a reference to a function parameter.
text_status	The text status value for text/image data.
	0x0000 The text field contains NULL values and the text pointer has not been initialized. 0x0002 The text pointer is initialized. 0x0004 The text data follows. 0x0008 No text data follows because the text data is not replicated. 0x0010 The text data is not replicated but it contains NULL values.
user	The variable is defined in the input template of an **rs_select** or **rs_select_with_lock** function string.

Table 8.2: Language template modifier values

```
alter function string def_jk.rs_insert
    for rs_sqlserver_function_class
    output language
        'insert into jk values
            ("1", ?col_1!new?, ?col_2!new?)'
```

The suffix '_raw' may be appended to the modifier to change how the data is formatted. During function mapping the embedded variables are replaced with literal values formatted according to the T-SQL defaults for datatypes as shown in table 8.3. If the _raw suffix is added to the modifier the Replication Server does not format the variable when substituting the column value.

Datatype	Formatting of Literals
int, smallint, tinyint, rs_address	Integer number.
decimal, numeric, identity	Exact decimal number.

float, real	Decimal number.
char, varchar	Encloses value in single quotes if not already done.
	Adds a single quote to embedded quotes to generate double quotes.
	Adds an additional backslash and newline (\n) to an existing \n as ASE treats \n as a continuation character and deletes the additional \n, leaving the original.
money, smallmoney	Prefixed with a dollar sign.
datetime, smalldatetime	Encloses value in single quotes if not already done.
	Adds a single quote to embedded quotes to generate double quotes.
binary, varbinary	Prefixed with 0x.
bit	1 or 0.

Table 8.3: Formatting of function string variables

The system variables which may be used in function string templates with the *sys* or *sys_raw* modifier are shown in table 8.4.

System Variable	Datatype	Description
rs_default_fs	text	The default generated function string text for the function.
rs_deliver_as_name	varchar(200)	The name of the procedure to be invoked at the destination when executing a replicated function.
rs_destination_db	varchar(30)	Name of the database where a transaction was sent.
rs_destination_ds	varchar(30)	Name of the data server where a transaction was sent.

rs_destination_ldb	varchar(30)	Name of the logical database where a transaction was sent.
rs_destination_lds	varchar(30)	Name of the logical data server where a transaction was sent.
rs_destination_ptype	char(1)	Physical connection type for the database where a transaction was sent. ("A" for active or "S" for standby)
rs_destination_user	varchar(30)	User who will execute the transaction at the destination.
rs_dump_dbname	varchar(30)	Name of the database where a database or transaction dump originated.
rs_dump_label	varchar(30)	Label information for a database or transaction dump. For SQL Server, this variable holds a *datetime* value that is the time the dump originated.
rs_dump_timestamp	varbinary(16)	Timestamp of a database or transaction dump.
rs_lorigin	int	ID of the originating logical database for a transaction.
rs_origin	int	ID of the originating database for a transaction.
rs_origin_begin_time	datetime	The time that a command was applied at the origin.
rs_origin_commit_time	datetime	The time that a transaction was committed at the origin.
rs_origin_db	varchar(30)	Name of the origin database.
rs_origin_ds	varchar(30)	Name of the origin data server.
rs_origin_ldb	varchar(30)	Name of the logical database for a warm standby application.
rs_origin_lds	varchar(30)	Name of the logical data server for a warm standby application.

rs_origin_qid	varbinary(36)	Origin queue ID of the first command in a transaction.
rs_origin_user	varchar(30)	User who executed the transaction at the origin.
rs_origin_xact_id	binary(120)	The system assigned unique ID of a transaction.
rs_origin_xact_name	varchar(30)	User assigned name of the transaction at origin.
rs_secondary_qid	varbinary(36)	Queue ID of a transaction in a subscription materialization or dematerialization queue.
rs_last_text_chunk	int	If the value is 0, this is not the last chunk of text data. If the value is 1, this is the last chunk of text data.
rs_writetext_log	int	If the value is 0, **rs_writetext** has not finished logging text and image data at the primary database transaction log. If the value is 1, **rs_writetext** has finished logging text and image data at the primary database transaction log.

Table 8.4: Replication Server system-defined variables

Rpc templates

Rpc templates are used to convert a command into a procedure execution at the Replicate Database. This can also be done in the language template with a simple execute procedure command. I find this particularly useful to protect against **insert/ update/delete** errors at the Replicate Database caused by local user activity against the data.

For example you could alter the **insert** as:

alter function string def_jk.rs_insert

for rs_sqlserver_function_class

output rpc 'execute sales_ins_prc

```
                    @pkey=?pkey!new?, @name=?name!new?,
                    @salary=?salary!new?'
```

and define the procedure at the Replicate Database along the lines of:

```
create proc sales_ins_prc
(@pkey int, @name varchar(30), @salary numeric(8, 2))
as
begin
if not exists (select * from jk where pkey = @pkey)
begin
       insert into jk values (@pkey, @name, @salary)
end
else
begin
       update jk set name = @name, salary = @salary
             where pkey = @pkey
end
end
```

I know that it's not very sophisticated but it's just for illustration. Anyway once you have overwritten the local change a few times it will certainly initiate a discussion.

Restoring default function string

If you have made a change to the function string of a replication definition and need to reset it to the original default value, simply enter the **alter function string** command with no output template.

```
alter function string def_jk.rs_delete
       for rs_sqlserver_function_class
```

This restores the default **rs_delete** function string for the **rs_delete** function for the replication definition *def_jk*.

Dropping function strings

A function string may be dropped with the **drop function string** command.

> **drop function string [rep_def_name.]function_name[; f_s_name|all]**
>   **for function_string_class_name**

where   all   drops all function strings for a function

You need to suspend the database connection before you drop the function string.

> **suspend connection to RSLN1.sales_db**
> **drop function string def_jk.rs_delete**
>   **for jk_function_class**
> **resume connection to RSLN1.sales_db**

Dropping a function string is extremely rare as you will normally not be able to replicate all transactions if a function string is missing. It is more common to use **alter function string** to restore the default function string. Dropping a customized function string from a base class i.e. one which was created without the **set parent to** clause, does not automatically restore the default function string; you must use **alter function string** to achieve this. However if you drop a function string from a derived class, the class will inherit the default function string from its parent class.

The **alter function string** actually executes a drop plus a create as a single transaction, so there is no time when the Replication Server sees the function string as missing. In 11.5 you can use the **with overwrite** clause in the **create function string** command to drop and recreate the function string, in the same manner as **alter function string**.

Function string help

The **rs_helpfstring** system procedure provides help on function strings for a replication definition.

> **rs_helpfstring rep_def_name [, function_string_name]**

The function string name is wildcarded at the end by the procedure so **rs_helpfstring** may return several function strings beginning with the input string.

> **rs_helpfstring def_jk1prc**
> **Function String information for Replication Definition: 'def_jk1prc'**
> **Valid Parameters are:**

Parameter Name	Datatype
@pkey	int

Rep. Def. Name	Function Name	FString Name	FSClass Name
def_jk1prc	def_jk1prc	def_jk1prc	rs_sqlserver_function_class

Output Type	Option
default	not applicable

— Beginning of Function String Text —

FString Text

*** System-Supplied Transact-SQL Statement ***

— End of Function String Text —

rs_helpfstring def_jk, rs_insert

Function String information for Replication Definition: 'def_jk'

Valid Parameters are:

Parameter Name	Datatype
@a	int
@b	int

Rep. Def. Name	Function Name	FString Name	FSClass Name
def_jk	rs_insert	rs_insert	rs_sqlserver_function_class

Output Type	Option
language	not applicable

— Beginning of Function String Text —

FString Text

update jk set b=?b!new? where a=?a!new?

— End of Function String Text —

The **rs_helpclassfstring** system procedure displays function string information for function string class scope function strings

rs_helpclassfstring f_s_class_name [, function_name]

The function string name is wildcarded at the end by the procedure so **rs_helpclassfstring** may return several function strings beginning with the input string.

rs_helpclassfstring rs_default_function_class, rs_usedb

Function Name	FString name	FSClass name
rs_usedb	rs_usedb	rs_sqlserver_function_class

FString Text
Use ?rs_destination_db!sys_raw?

System tables

rs_classes

The function string classes are held in *rs_classes*.

select * from rs_classes

classname	classid	classtype	prsid
jk1_function_class	0x010f435001000065	F	17777488
rs_default_function_class	0x0000000001000003	F	0
rs_sqlserver_error_class	0x0000000001000002	E	17777488
rs_sqlserver_function_class	0x0000000001000001	F	0

where   classtype   F: function string class, E: error class

Nothing particularly interesting here and **rs_helpclass** is quite sufficient.

rs_functions

The functions are held in *rs_functions*.

select * from rs_functions

prsid	funcname	funcid	objid
conflicting	*userdefined*	*rowtype*	
0	rs_begin	0x0000000004000001	0x0000000000000000
0	*0*	*1*	
0	rs_commit	0x0000000040000020x0	0
0	*0*	*1*	
17777488	def_jkprc	0x010f435004000083	0x010f43500000006b
0	*1*	*1*	
17777488	def_jk1prc	0x010f435004000084	0x010f43500000006c
0	*1*	*1*	
17777488	def_jk2prc	0x010f435004000086	0x010f43500000006e
0	*1*	*1*	
17777488	jk2prc	0x010f435004000087	0x010f43500000006f
0	*1*	*1*	
17777488	jk4prc	0x010f435004000088	0x010f435000000070
0	*1*	*1*	
17777488	rs_insert	0x010f435004000089	0x010f435000000071
0	*0*	*1*	
17777488	rs_delete	0x010f43500400008a	0x010f435000000071
0	*0*	*1*	

where   userdefined   1: user defined function, 0: system function

This has a foreign key (*objid*) to *rs_objects* which allows a simpler output than the system procedure **rs_helpfunc** to see the functions for a replication definition.

select o.objname, f.funcname

from rs_objects o, rs_functions f
where o.objid = f.objid
and o.objname = '<rep_def_name>'

Refine this as you wish but I find it simpler than the **rs_helpfunc** output.

rs_funcstrings

The function strings are held in *rs_funcstrings* and *rs_systext*.

select * from rs_funcstrings

prsid	classid	funcid	name	fstringid
attributes	*parameters*	*param_hash*	*expiredate*	*rowtype*
0	0x0000000001000001	0x0000000004000001	rs_begin	0x0000000008000001
48	*0*	*0*	*Jan 1 1900 12:00AM*	*1*
0	0x0000000001000001	0x0000000004000002	rs_commit	0x0000000008000002
16	*0*	*0*	*Jan 1 1900 12:00AM*	*1*
17777488	0x0000000001000001	0x010f435004000093	jk5prc	0x010f435008000093
48	*0*	*0*	*Jan 1 1900 12:00AM*	*1*
17777488	0x0000000001000001	0x010f435004000094	def_jk6prc	0x010f435008000094
48	*0*	*0*	*Jan 1 1900 12:00AM*	*1*
17777488	0x0000000001000001	0x010f435004000095	jk7prc	0x010f435008000095
48	*0*	*0*	*Jan 1 1900 12:00AM*	*1*

select * from rs_systext

prsid	parentid	texttype	sequence
textval			
0	0x000000000fffff17	O	1
execute rs_update_threads @rs_seq = ?rs_seq!param?, @rs_id = ?rs_id!param?			
17777488	0x010f435008000079	O	1
update jk set b=?b!new? where a=?a!new?			
17777488	0x010f43500800007a	O	1
select 1			
17777488	0x010f43500800007e	O	1
execute jk_fs_prc @a=?a!new?			

This gives some scope to write your own SQL to simplify the **rs_helpfstring** output. The following are some examples which you might like to expand on.

Function string text for a replication definition function string

```
select o.objname, fs.name, t.textval
    from rs_objects o, rs_functions f, rs_funcstrings fs, rs_systext t
    where o.objid = f.objid
    and f.funcid = fs.funcid
    and fs.fstringid = t.parentid
    and o.objname = '<replication_definition_name>'
    and f.funcname = '<function_name>'
```

Function strings for a function string class

```
select c.classname, fs.name, t.textval
    from rs_classes c, rs_funcstrings fs, rs_systext t
    where c.classid = fs.classid
    and fs.fstringid = t.parentid
    and c.classname = '<function_string_class_name>'
```

Function strings for class wide scope

```
select c.classname, fs.name, t.textval
    from rs_classes c, rs_funcstrings fs, rs_functions f, rs_systext t
    where c.classid = fs.classid
    and fs.fstringid = t.parentid
    and f.funcid = fs.funcid
    and f.objid = 0x00
    and c.classname = '<function_string_class_name>'
```

## 9

Function Replication and User Defined Functions

Introduction

Replication Server has the ability to replicate stored procedures which Sybase has called "Replicated Functions". Pre-11 procedure replication was very restrictive as it was directly related to the underlying data replication. In system 11 it is the execution of the procedure that is replicated and this does not need to update a table. Even when the procedure updates a table, the table need not be defined as replicated. Pre-11 procedure replication is still supported but the recommendation is to define any new requirements as a replicated function as supported by system 11. Sybase use the definitions: a **replicated stored procedure** is a stored procedure marked for replication with the **sp_setrepproc** system procedure and a **function replication definition** is the replicated stored procedure, its parameters and its location. Executing the replicated stored procedure invokes the function replication definition which, in turn, invokes the Replication Server function. The Replication Server function passes the parameters to the relevant stored procedure in the Replicate Database. I'm not sure that I agree fully with this distinction and I like to view 11.5 procedure replication as function replication definitions – but who cares?

The function replication is defined with the **create function replication definition** command. This function replication definition automatically creates user defined functions, similar to the data replication definition system functions, to carry out the transformation requirements of the replicated functions. The user defined function has the same name and parameters as the function replication definition.

There are two types of function replication based on the direction of replication.

Applied functions   These are defined in the primary database and replicate the function from primary to replicate. This is analogous to data replication.

Request functions   These are defined in the replicate database and replicate the function from the replicate to the primary. This has some specific requirements, not least the need for an LTM between the replicate and the primary to support the replication. The request function delivers the procedure action from the Replicate Database to the Primary Database so that it may be executed in the Primary Database. This Primary Database execution is then replicated as normal to the Replicate Database. This is an approach that may be used to control local changes to replicate data.

Function replication

The replication of a procedure execution is defined in much the same way that table replication is defined. Not all parameters of the procedure need to be replicated, but make sure that you define defaults at the Replicate Database if you do not pass a primary procedure parameter (assuming that the procedures are the same at both databases).

As with table replication there are a few pre-requisites for function replication.

- The name, parameters and datatypes that you specify for the function replication definition must be the same as those of the primary procedure. If there are no parameters you must specify an empty argument list as ().

- A connection to the Primary Database must exist at the Replication Server. Connections between Replication Servers and databases are defined with the **create connection** or the **rs_init** command.

- The datatypes specified in the function replication definition follow the same rules as a table replication definition.

  - You cannot use User Defined Datatypes but must specify the base system datatype. Unfortunately Replication Server has no knowledge of the User Defined Datatypes which you may be using in the SQL Server database.

  - The *numeric* datatype is quoted without any precision or scale. Replication Server processes *numeric* columns without affecting the precision or scale of the value.

  - *Timestamp* datatypes are defined as *binary(8)*.

  - You cannot use the *text/image* datatypes as parameters.

- Nested transactions are not supported in function replication.

  Nothing new here as nested transactions are not generally supported by Sybase. However, be careful, as Replication Server wraps commands in a **begin/commit tran** block and this can generate inconsistent results if the procedure contains a transaction.

Consider the procedure:

```
create proc jk_prc (@name varchar(32)) as
update ctrl_tab set proc_execs = proc_execs + 1
where id_key = @name
      begin tran
            ……
            ……
            ……
      if @cnt = 0 rollback tran
            else commit tran
  go
```

Replication Server will execute this as:

begin tran

execute jk_prc @name = 'Fred'

commit tran

If the **rollback tran** occurs, the **update** of *ctrl_tab* will be rolled back, which may not have been the original intention.

Create the function replication definition

The full function replication definition syntax is:

create function replication definition rep_def_name

with primary at server_name.db_name

[deliver as 'proc_name']

([@par_name datatype [, par_name datatype] …])

[searchable parameters (@par_name [, @par_name] …)]

[send standby {all | replication definition} parameters]

where

with primary at	This specifies the location of the primary data. Note that this does not need to be the location of the invoked procedure, although it is more usual for the data and the procedure to be co-located.
deliver as	This allows you to specify a different procedure name to execute in the replicate database. If this clause is omitted the procedure name is the same in both primary and replicate databases.
searchable parameters	These are the only parameters that a subscription to the function replication definition may use to restrict the executions of the procedure. Searchable parameters cannot have NULL values.

send standby all parameters

This specifies that all parameters should be replicated to the standby database. This is the default for warm standby.

send standby replication definition parameters

> This specifies that only the parameters defined in the replication definition are replicated to the standby database.

Replication Server creates a user defined function for each function replication definition. For each of these user defined functions, Replication Server then creates a default function string in each of the three system function string classes (*rs_sqlserver_function_class*, *rs_default_function_class*, *rs_db2_function_class*) and in any derived classes which used these as parent classes. If you have your own base function string classes, then you will have to add the function strings for the new user defined function to this class and any derived classes.

The simplest function replication definition is:

create function replication definition orders_del_prc

with primary at PS001.sales_db

(@order_no int)

If the procedure name is different at the Replicate Database you can use the **deliver as** clause.

create function replication definition orders_del_prc

with primary at PS001.sales_db

deliver as 'sales_order_del_prc'

(@order_no int)

If you want the subscription to the function replication to be able to restrict the procedure execution you can define searchable parameters.

create function replication definition orders_del_prc

with primary at PS001.sales_db

deliver as 'sales_order_del_prc'

(@order_no int)

searchable parameters (@order_no)

The following steps, shown in figure 9.1, are involved in creating the function replication definition.

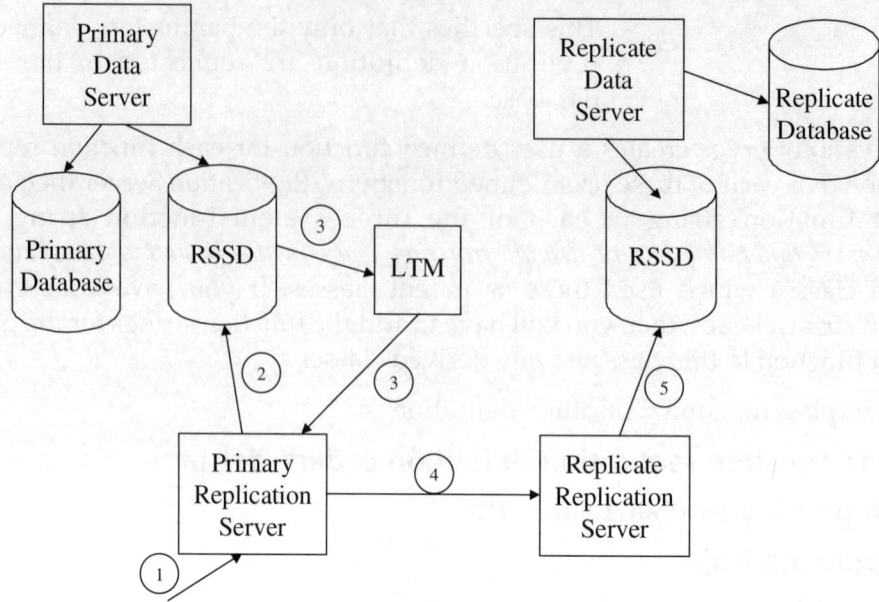

create function replication definition

Figure 9.1: Function replication creation

1. The **create function replication definition** is defined at the Primary Replication Server. Default user defined functions and function strings for the replication definition are created at the Primary Replication Server in the system defined function string classes.

2. The Primary Replication Server logs into the RSSD and updates the RSSD by inserting entries into the system tables.

3. The LTM reads the RSSD log and extracts the system table inserts to the Primary Replication Server.

4. The Primary Replication Server then distributes the replication definition inserts to all other Replication Servers in the replication domain.

5. Each Replicate Replication Server inserts the replication definition into its RSSD.

As for table replication we are not finished and we have to register the procedure for replication at the Primary Database with the system procedure **sp_setrepproc**.

sp_setrepproc [proc_name [, {'function'│'table'│'false'}]]

where

function	Enables System 11 function replication for a stored procedure.
table	Supports pre-system 11 stored procedure replication where the stored procedure replication is associated with a table replication definition. This type of stored procedure replication still requires the stored procedure to update a table. Removing this requirement from stored procedure replication is very useful as it allows you to define a function replication definition on a stored procedure which modifies a non-replicated table. Or even to specify a procedure for replication when it does not update any data.
false	Disables replication for the procedure.

If you drop and recreate the procedure, you must rerun **sp_setrepproc**.

Applied Function Replication

An applied function replicates execution of the procedure from the Primary to the Replicate Database. The steps involved are:

- Create a stored procedure at the Primary and the Replicate Database.

- Grant execute on the procedure in the Replicate Database to the Replication Server maintenance user.

- Create a function replication definition at the Primary Replication Server.

- Define a subscription to the function replication definition.

  If you use the **create subscription** command you must include the **without materialization** clause as the actual data is not replicated in a function replication and so atomic materialization cannot be done.

- Materialize the subscription using **activate subscription** and **validate subscription** commands.

- Mark the stored procedure as replicated using the **sp_setrepproc** system procedure.

An execution of the procedure in the Primary Database is then replicated as an execution of the corresponding procedure in the Replicate Database.

Create the procedure

Consider a procedure which updates a table based on name and status parameters.

```
create proc sales_upd (@name dt_name, @status dt_status)
as
update sales
     set discount = discount * 1.1
     where name like @name+'%'
     and status = @status
```

This stored procedure is defined at both the Primary and the Replicate Database with the same name.

Grant execute on the procedure to the maintenance user

In the replicate database you need to allow the maintenance user to execute the procedure.

```
grant execute on sales_upd to rsmnt_sales
```

Create the function replication definition

The function replication is defined in the Primary Replication Server using the **create function replication definition** command:

```
create function replication definition sales_upd
with primary at LNPRD1.sales_db
(@name varchar(32), @status tinyint)
```

Note the use of the system datatypes and the same names for the parameters and the function replication definition as the primary procedure.

Define and materialize the subscription to the replication definition

The subscription to the function replication definition is defined with the **define subscription** command:

```
define subscription sales_upd_sub
for sales_upd
```

with replicate at LNPRD1.sales_db

And then materialized with the **activate** and **validate** commands:

activate subscription sales_upd_sub

for sales_upd

with replicate at LNPRD1.sales_db

validate subscription sales_upd_sub

for sales_upd

with replicate at LNPRD1.sales_database

If you use **create subscription** you must include the **without materialization** clause.

create subscription sales_upd_sub

for sales_upd

with replicate at LNPRD.sales_db

without materialization

Mark the function replication definition for replication

Finally the procedure in the Primary Database is marked for replication so that the LTM will extract the executions from the transaction log.

sp_setrepproc sales_upd, 'function'

Request function replication

The request function can be used to prevent local updates to replicated data. The local process makes a call to a stub procedure at the Replicate Database which simply executes the principal procedure at the Primary Database. This Primary Database execution is then replicated normally to the Replicate Database, thus ensuring control over all local updates. Clearly this may not be the most performant activity as the procedure executions have to cross the network twice simply to make a change. You might find that an application design solution is better.

Consider that a user of the Replicate Database has to execute our *sales_upd* procedure locally. This could cause all sorts of problems with primary and replicate data getting out of synchronization. Using a request function solution we would define:

- A stub procedure at the Replicate Database.

- A function replication definition at the Replicate Database for the "stub" procedure.

- Mark the "stub" procedure for replication using **sp_setrepproc**.

The "stub" procedure at the Replicate Database could look like:

create proc sales_upd_stub (@name varchar(32), @status tinyint)

as

print "update passed to primary database for processing"

With a function replication definition defined at the Primary Replication Server:

create function replication definition sales_upd_stub

with primary at NYPRD_1.sales_db

deliver as 'sales_upd'

Note the *deliver as* clause which allows the request function to have a different name at the Replicate and the Primary Database. This is the most normal use of different procedure names as the content of the "stub" procedure is naturally different from the main procedure and so it is good practice to name them differently. Also there is no requirement to define a subscription for the 'request' function as the primary database is always the destination database.

Altering a function replication definition

Altering a function replication definition with the **alter function replication definition** command allows you to add a parameter; add a searchable parameter; alter the name of the procedure executed at the Replicate Database or alter the warm standby parameter replication.

alter function replication definition rep_def_name

{ deliver as 'proc_name' |

add @par_name datatype [, @par_name datatype] …] |

add searchable parameters @par_name [, @par_name] …] |

send standby {all | replication definition } parameters}

where

deliver as   This allows you to specify a different procedure name to
                    execute in the replicate database. If this clause is omitted the
                    procedure name is the same in both primary and replicate
                    databases.

searchable parameters

                    These are the only parameters that a subscription to the
                    function replication definition may use to restrict the
                    executions of the procedure. Searchable parameters cannot
                    have NULL values.

send standby all parameters

                    This specifies that all parameters should be replicated to the
                    standby database. This is the default for warm standby.

send standby replication definition parameters

                    This specifies that only the parameters defined in the
                    replication definition are replicated to the standby database.

Add a parameter

alter function replication definition orders_ins_prc
add @total_qty float

Add a searchable parameter

alter function replication definition orders_ins_prc
add searchable parameter @total_qty

Alter the Replicate Database procedure name

alter function replication definition orders_ins_prc
deliver as 'sales_order_ins_prc'

As with any changes to Replication Server it is strongly advised that all activity is
stopped while you make any changes to function replication definitions. This
involves:

- Stopping updates on the primary if possible.

- Quiescing the Replication Server.

- Setting replication to false on the primary procedure if changing the procedure or underlying table.

- Alter any subscriptions or function strings.

- Check that the new definitions have arrived at all RSSDs.

- Set replication to true for the new procedure.

The commands involved are:

- Quiesce the Replication Server.

admin quiesce_force_rsi

This flushes the DSI and RSI queues until all outbound messages have been sent and an acknowledgement has been received. The effect of this is checked with:

admin health

If this does not show quiesced as TRUE, wait a little and retry the **admin quiesce_force_rsi**. If this does not quiesce the Replication Server you have a problem and need to check the errorlog to see if there are any indications of the reason. The reverse of this is probably more relevant: do not try to quiesce the Replication Server if you know that there is a problem with message delivery as the quiesce will still try to send messages. Stop activity in another manner such as **drop connection**.

- Set replication to false.

sp_setrepproc proc_name, false

Dropping a function replication definition

To drop a parameter you must drop and recreate the function replication definition. The function replication definition is dropped with the **drop function replication definition** command.

drop function replication definition rep_def_name

All subscriptions must be dropped before you drop the function replication definition and you need to reset the procedure replication status in the Primary Database.

sp_setrepproc proc_name, 'false'

User Defined Functions

A User Defined Function is created automatically for every function replication definition. A User Defined Function may also be created to carry out transformations that cannot be accomplished in the system functions. If the User Defined Function is called in the Primary Database (applied function) the function call is replicated to all Replicate Databases which have a subscription to the User Defined Function. If the User Defined Function is executed in the Replicate Database (request function) the execution is replicated to the Primary Database.

Create a User Defined Function

The User Defined Function is created using the **create function** command. The User Defined Function is the definition of the function name and its related replication definition, plus the parameters of the function call.

> **create function rep_def_name.function_name**
>
> > **@param_name datatype [,@param_name datatype …]**

The normal rules of no user defined types apply to the parameters.

> **create function sales_rep_def.fn_update_sales**
>
> > **@order_id int, @product_id int**

The actions/transformations which take place as a result of the User Defined Function are defined at the Replicate Replication Server by the associated function strings i.e. no different from a system function. This is a general situation: the function is defined at the Primary Replication Server to specify what is to be replicated and the function string is defined at the Replicate Replication Server to specify the actions that will take place at the Replicate Database for this User Defined Function.

We have done the definition of the function replication definition before, but let's look at the actual process of the replication in more detail. An applied function executed in the Primary Database is processed as shown in figure 9.2.

1. The Primary Database executes the procedure and this is logged.

2. The LTM reads the transaction log and forwards the execution of the procedure to the Primary Replication Server.

3. The Primary Replication Server then forwards the procedure execution to the Replicate Replication Server.

4. The Replicate Replication Server executes the procedure against the Replicate Database.

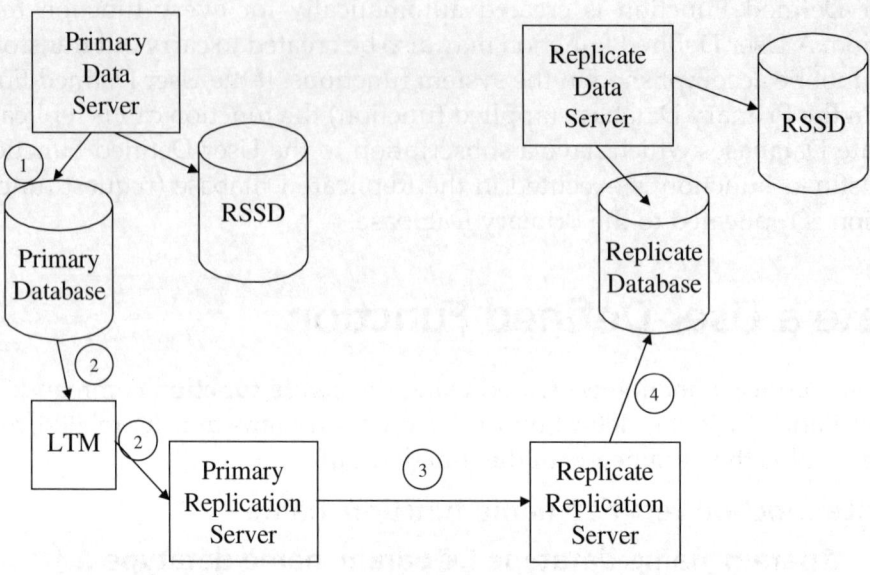

Figure 9.2: Applied function execution

A request function from the Replicate Database is the reverse of this as shown in figure 9.3.

1. The procedure is executed in the Replicate Database.

2. The LTM reads the transaction log and forwards the execution of the procedure to the Replicate Replication Server.

3. The Replicate Replication Server then forwards the procedure execution to the Primary Replication Server which executes the function against the Primary Database.

4. This Primary Database procedure execution is then extracted from the transaction log by the LTM and replicated to the Replicate Replication Server which executes the function against the Replicate Database.

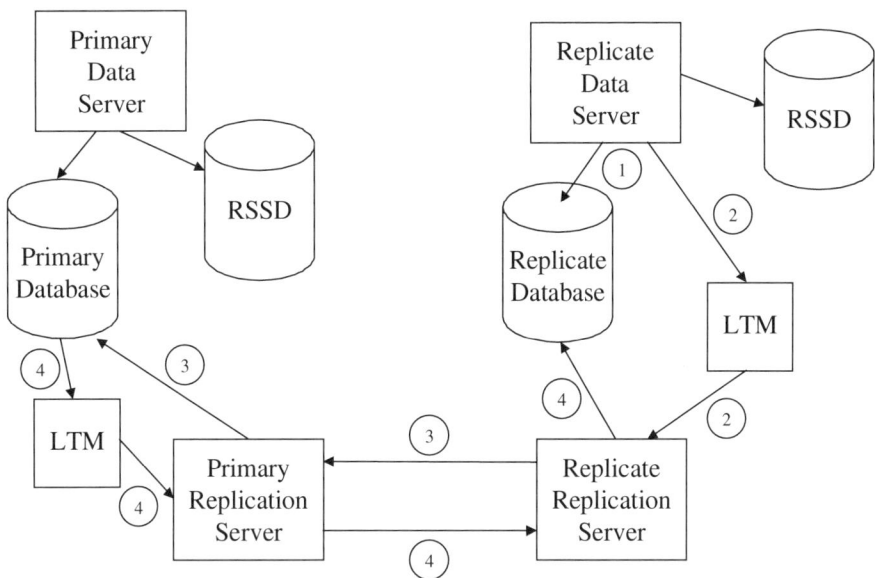

Figure 9.3: Request function execution

Dropping a User Defined Function

A User Defined Function is dropped with the **drop function** command.

drop function [rep_def_name.]function_name

drop function sales_rep_def.fn_update_sales

As with all changes to replication objects you should ensure that there is no activity against the replicated object before making the change.

Viewing function replication definition information

Existing replication definitions may be displayed with the **sp_helprep** system procedure which is run from the RSSD. This displays both table and function replication definitions.

rs_helprep [rep_def_name]

The rep_def_name is wildcarded at the end by the procedure so **rs_helprep** may return several replication definitions beginning with the input string. By itself the **rs_helprep** list the current replication definitions:

rs_helprep

Rep. Def. Name Type	PRS	Primary DS.DB	Primary Table	Creation Date
def_jk1prc *function repdef*	PRS1	LNPRD1.SALES_DB	def_jk1prc	Dec 14 1998
def_jk2prc *function repdef*	PRS1	LNPRD1.SALES_DB S	def_jk2prc	Dec 15 1998
def_jk4 *table repdef*	PRS1	LNPRD1.SALES_DB	jk4	Dec 15 1998
def_jk5 *table repdef*	PRS1	LNPRD1.SALES_DB	jk5	Dec 15 1998

The **rs_helprep** with a replication definition name displays the detailed information on the replication definition.

rs_helprep def_jk1prc

Rep. Def. Name	PRS	This Site	Creation Date	Type
def_jk1prc	PRS1	PRS1	Dec 14 1998 5:00PM	F

PDS.DB	Primary Table	Default Rep. Table
LNPRD1.SALES_DB	def_jk1prc	def_jk1prc

Parameter	Datatype	Length	Searchable
pkey	int	4	1

Function Name	FString Class	FString Source	FString Name
def_jk1prc	rs_sqlserver_function_class	Class Default	def_jk1prc

Subscriptions known at this Site 'LNPRS1'.

Subscription Name	Replicate DS.DB	Owner	Creation Date
sub_jk1prc	NYPRD1.SALES_DB	rssub_mkt	Dec 14 1998 5:03PM

System Tables

The system tables involved in function replication definition are *rs_objects*, *rs_columns*, *rs_functions*, *rs_funcstrings* and *rs_systext*.

rs_objects

One row per replication definition, the type identified by the *objtype* value (R: table, F: function).

select * from rs_objects

prsid	objname	objid	dbid	
	objtype	*attributes*	*ownertype*	*crdate*
	parentid		ownerid	rowtype
	phys_tablename			
	deliver_as_name			

17777439		def_jk1prc	0x010f431f00000082	100790
	RF	*0*	*U*	*Feb 19 1998 5:27PM*
	0x0000000000000000	0x0000000000000000		1
	def_jk1prc			
	jk1prc			

rs_columns

One row for each parameter of a function replication definition.

select * from rs_columns

prsid	objid		colname	colnum	coltype
	length	*searchable*	*primary_col*	*fragmentation*	*rowtype status*
17777439	0x0000000000000051		pkey	1	8
	4	*0*	*0*	*0*	*1 0*

rs_functions

Both system and user defined functions are held in *rs_functions*.

select * from rs_functions

prsid	funcname	funcid	objid
conflicting	userdefined	rowtype	
0	rs_begin	0x0000000004000001	0x0000000000000000
0	0	1	
0	rs_commit	0x0000000004000002	
0	0	1	
17777488	def_jkprc	0x010f435004000083	0x010f43500000006b
0	1	1	
17777488	def_jk1prc	0x010f435004000084	0x010f43500000006c
0	1	1	
17777488	def_jk2prc	0x010f435004000086	0x010f43500000006e
0	1	1	
17777488	jk2prc	0x010f435004000087	0x010f43500000006f
0	1	1	
17777488	jk4prc	0x010f435004000088	0x010f435000000070
0	1	1	
17777488	rs_insert	0x010f435004000089	0x010f435000000071
0	0	1	
17777488	rs_delete	0x010f43500400008a	0x010f435000000071
0	0	1	

where   userdefined   1: user defined function, 0: system function

As discussed in table replication definitions this has a foreign key (*objid*) to *rs_objects* which allows a simpler output than the system procedure **rs_helpfunc** to see the functions for a replication definition.

select o.objname, f.funcname
from rs_objects o, rs_functions f
where o.objid = f.objid
and o.objname = '<rep_def_name>'

Refine this as you wish but I find it simpler than the **rs_helpfunc** output.

rs_funcstrings

The system and user defined function strings are held in *rs_funcstrings* and *rs_systext*.

select * from rs_funcstrings

prsid	classid	funcid	name	fstringid
attributes	parameters	param_hash	expiredate	rowtype
0	0x0000000001000001	0x0000000004000001	rs_begin	0x0000000008000001
48	0	0	Jan 1 1900 12:00AM	1
0	0x0000000001000001	0x0000000004000002	rs_commit	0x0000000008000002
16	0	0	Jan 1 1900 12:00AM	1
17777488	0x0000000001000001	0x010f435004000093	jk5prc	0x010f435008000093
48	0	0	Jan 1 1900 12:00AM	1
17777488	0x0000000001000001	0x010f435004000094	def_jk6prc	0x010f435008000094
48	0	0	Jan 1 1900 12:00AM	1
17777488	0x0000000001000001	0x010f435004000095	jk7prc	0x010f435008000095
48	0	0	Jan 1 1900 12:00AM	1

select * from rs_systext

prsid	parentid	texttype	sequence
textval			
0	0x000000000fffff17	O	1
execute rs_update_threads @rs_seq = ?rs_seq!param?, @rs_id = ?rs_id!param?			
17777488	0x010f435008000079	O	1
update jk set b=?b!new? where a=?a!new?			
17777488	0x010f43500800007a	O	1
select 1			
17777488	0x010f43500800007e	O	1
execute jk_fs_prc @a=?a!new?			

This gives some scope to write your own SQL to simplify the **rs_helpfstring** output. The following are some examples which you might like to expand on. These are the same as the system function examples but are repeated here for completeness and to illustrate that there is no difference between them as far as Replication Server is concerned.

Function string text for a replication definition function string

```
select o.objname, fs.name, t.textval
    from rs_objects o, rs_functions f, rs_funcstrings fs, rs_systext t
    where o.objid = f.objid
    and f.funcid = fs.funcid
    and fs.fstringid = t.parentid
    and o.objname = '<replication_definition_name>'
    and f.funcname = '<function_name>'
```

Function strings for a function string class

```
select c.classname, fs.name, t.textval
    from rs_classes c, rs_funcstrings fs, rs_systext t
    where c.classid = fs.classid
    and fs.fstringid = t.parentid
    and c.classname = '<function_string_class_name>'
```

10

Warm Standby

Introduction

Warm Standby is a replication feature that allows the Replication Server to maintain a database as a copy of a primary database. The obvious use is in a Warm Standby architecture where the tasks running on the primary (active) database may be switched to the replicate (standby) database if the active fails. This is by no means a seamless switch and you will have to put considerable application and administration effort into making the switch. However the Replication Server will maintain the designated standby database with all active database updates to facilitate the switch to the standby.

There is no reason, of course, why this feature should be used simply to support standby databases. The principal facility of Warm Standby is the maintenance of a copy of the active database with a minimum of effort in specifying the replication. For example, to replicate all active database updates you do not have to specify any table replication definitions or subscriptions. Replication Server knows that a replicate database designated as a Warm Standby has to be kept up-to-date with all changes to tables in the active database which are marked for replication. Recognizing this, a common use of the Warm Standby feature is to maintain a Decision Support System for reporting purposes. The specification of this as a normal replication would be ponderous with replication definitions and subscriptions for all replicated objects. Using Warm Standby you simply inform Replication Server that the databases are in a Warm Standby relationship, mark all objects in the active for replication and Replication Server takes care of the replication.

This simplicity of replication definition does mean that there are some restrictions:

- The databases and replicated objects must be an exact schema copy of each other.

  This applies not just to the object definitions but also to the database sizes and disk allocations. It's not difficult initially but make sure that you action any changes to both databases.

- You cannot create a Warm Standby configuration for the RSSD or the master databases.

  The extension of this is that no system table changes are replicated. However version 11.5 does support the replication of DDL for Warm Standby so this is not a problem.

- Non-logged commands are not replicated.

  No difference here from normal replication: if the data changes do not get to the primary log they do not get replicated. Version 11.5 does provide support for **truncate table** replication.

- One Replication Server manages both active and standby databases.

  The active and standby databases are defined as a single logical connection and both physical databases must be managed by the same Replication Server. The logical database is seen by the Replication Server as a single unit and therefore may be defined as a single database for replication outside of the Warm Standby pair. However I believe that it is better to keep Warm Standby simple and not have the logical database involved in any other replication. There is no problem in having the active database involved in replication to other replicate databases: this is simply a case of making the appropriate connections and subscriptions.

- The Replication Server has no ability to switch applications between active and standby.

  When a failure occurs which requires a switch to the standby, there are commands to instruct the Replication Server to switch to the standby database. However the Replication Server has no knowledge of the application connections and therefore it has no ability to handle any switching of the applications.

If you are not using the standby database purely in a Warm Standby situation you do not need to be restricted by these conditions but you can define replication definitions and subscriptions as for a normal replication. There are additional clauses to the commands that we shall look at later. First I shall cover a simple Warm Standby definition without any replication definition or subscription commands.

Architecture

A typical Warm Standby architecture is shown in figure 10.1.

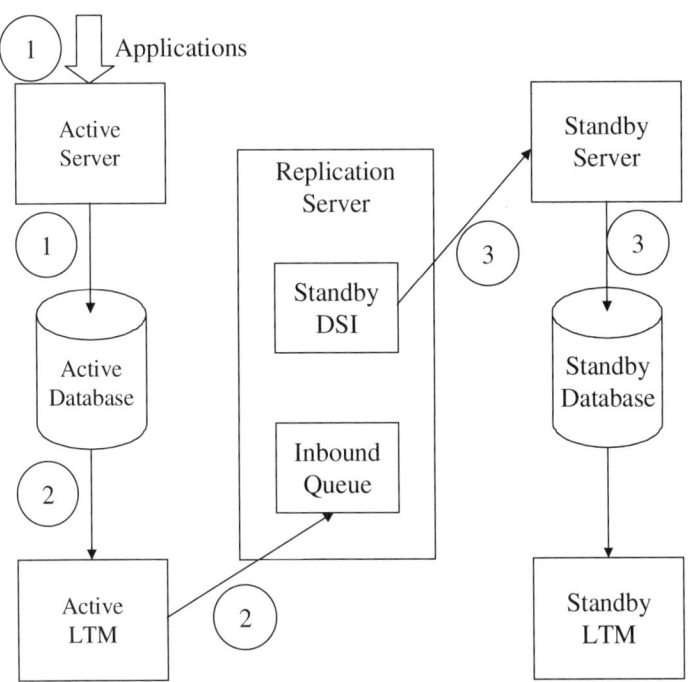

Figure 10.1: Warm Standby Architecture

1. The application processes the data in the active database and the changes are written to the transaction log.

2. The active database LTM reads the changes and adds them to the inbound queue of the Replication Server.

3. The Warm Standby DSI thread reads the transactions from the Replication Server queue and actions them against the standby database.

To set this up we need to define the following:

- Three database connections for the Replication Server.
  - A logical connection for the active:standby pair.
  - A physical connection for each of the active and standby databases.
- Two LTMs, one for each physical database with the standby LTM suspended. The standby LTM is required only when the active has failed and processing is switched to the standby database.

Warm Standby Setup

To setup Warm Standby we need to follow the steps:

- Create a logical connection for the active:standby pair.
- Add the active database to the Replication Server if necessary.
- Enable replication for the objects in the active database, if necessary.
- Create the maintenance user in the standby database with the correct permissions.
- Create the connection (suspended) between the standby database and the Replication Server.
- Initialize the standby database.
- Resume the standby connection.

This should work. However in practice do not worry if the **resume connection** command fails with duplicate insert messages. Simply **resume connection ... skip transaction** until these errors go away. We'll discuss this in more detail later in the chapter.

Create the logical connection

Creating the logical connection associates the standby database with the active database and defines a single logical database to the Replication Server. This is done with the **create logical connection** command.

create logical connection to server_name.db_name

When the active database is already defined to the Replication Server for another replication, you must use the real server and database name of the active database. However when the active database is not yet known to the Replication Server it is recommended that you use a different name for the logical connection. This makes it easier to switch databases when a failure occurs.

create logical connection to LNPRD_L.sales_db

Creating the Database Connection

rs_init

If the database has not yet been defined to a Replication Server use **rs_init** to create the connection between the database and the Replication Server. This is described in chapter 4 but there is the additional requirement to define the database as a physical database for a logical connection. When the database information screen is displayed answer *yes* to the logical connection item 10.

DATABASE INFORMATION

1. SQL Server name: PLON_MKT
2. SA user: sa
3. SA password: sa_pwd
4. Database name: sales_db
5. Will the database require an LTM: yes
6. Maintenance user: rsmnt_mkt
7. Maintenance password: rsmnt_mkt_ps1
8. DBO user: ltm
9. DBO password: ltm_pw
10. Is this a Physical Connection for Existing Logical Connection: yes
11. Logical DB Setup   Incomplete

This will then request further logical connection information.

LOGICAL CONNECTION INFORMATION

1. Is this an Active Connection or Standby Connection: Standby
2. Logical DS Name: MKT_L
3. Logical DB Name: sales_db
4. Active DS name :   PLON_MKT
5. Active DB name : sales_db
6. Active DB sa user : sa
7. Active DB sa password :   sa_pw
8. Initialize standby using dump and load : yes
9. Use Dump Marker to Start Replicating to Standby: yes

create connection

When the database has already been defined to a Replication Server, you create the database connection with the **create connection** command.

```
create connection to server_name.db_name
set error class [to] error_class_name
set function string class [to] function_string_class_name
set username [to] user_name
[set password [to] pass_word]
[set database_param [to] 'value']
[set security_param [to] 'value']
[with {log transfer on, dsi_suspended}]
[as active for logical_ds_name.logical_db_name I
as standby for logical_ds_name.logical_db_name
[ use dump marker ]]
```

where

error class   The name of an error class to handle errors on the database connection. The default error class is *rs_sqlserver_error_class*.

function string class	The name of a function string class to use for operations on the database. The default function string class is *rs_sqlserver_function_class*.
set username/password	This defines the maintenance user username and password used by the Replication Server to log into the database and execute the required operations. Make sure that you have defined the login at the database and granted the user the required permissions on tables and procedures for the Replication Server commands to be performed.
database_param	A database connection parameter as defined in the **configure connection** section of chapter 4.
security_param	A security parameter for the route as defined in table 10.1. Only the *use_security_services* parameter is implemented in the initial release of 11.5.
log transfer on	This indicates that the connection is to a Primary Database which has an LTM reading log transactions and passing them to the Replication Server. If you omit this clause for the database connection, the LTM will not be able to pass log transactions to the Replication Server. You should define this for both the active and standby databases to make the switch to the standby as simple as possible.
dsi_suspended	This creates the connection with the DSI thread suspended. This is a useful option to allow you to bulk materialize the standby database but still have the LTM extracting transactions from the active database log. You can resume the connection when the standby database is ready with the **resume connection** command and transactions in the DSI queue will be applied to the standby database.
as active/standby for	These define the location of the active and standby databases.
use dump marker	This specifies the use of the dump marker when materializing the standby database.

When defining the standby database we will use the clauses:

log transfer on	The standby database is defined as a primary but with the LTM suspended so that switching to it is simple. If you do not specify this clause the database may not have an LTM defined. Even if you are not using the standby database as a warm standby, I would still recommend that you get into the habit of creating the database connection to allow log transfer.

as standby for   The name of the logical server and database that this database is providing warm standby for.

use dump marker   This is used when materializing the standby database. This is not mandatory if you can suspend all activity against the active database but, as this is unlikely, it is recommended that you use this clause.

create connection to PSRV_LON2.sales_ws_db

set error class rs_sqlserver_error_class

set function string class rs_sqlserver_function_class

set username rsmnt_user

set password rsmnt_pw

with log transfer on, dsi_suspended

as standby for PSRV_LON1_L.sales_db

use dump marker

parameter	description
msg_confidentiality	Indicates whether Replication Server sends and receives encrypted data. If set to "required," outgoing data is encrypted. If set to "not required," Replication Server accepts incoming data that is encrypted or not encrypted.
msg_integrity	Indicates whether data is checked for tampering.
msg_origin_check	Indicates whether the source of data should be verified.
msg_replay_detection	Indicates whether data should be checked to make sure it has not been read or intercepted.
msg_sequence_check	Indicates whether data should be checked for interception.

mutual_auth	Requires remote server to provide proof of identify before a connection is established.
security_mechanism	The name of the third-party security mechanism enabled for the pathway.
unified_login	Indicates how Replication Server seeks to log in to remote data servers and accepts incoming logins.
	required: always seeks to log in to remote server with a credential.
	not_required: always seeks to log in to remote server with a password.
use_security_services	Tells Replication Server whether to use security services. If *use_security_services* is "off," no security features take effect. This Parameter can only be set by the **sp_configure** system procedure.

Table 10.1: Parameters affecting network based security

In this situation where Replication Server is not creating the LTM for you, you will have to manually alter the LTM *runserver* file to include the Warm Standby –W flag to identify this as a Warm Standby LTM. Do not forget this one.

Enabling objects in the active database

You do not need to define replication definitions or subscriptions for the objects in the active database but you must enable replication on every object that you wish to be replicated to the standby database.

> **sp_setreptable tab_name, 'true'**
>
> **sp_setrepproc proc_name, 'function'**

You may use the *function* or *table* option to **sp_setrepproc**: it makes no difference. My personal preference for Warm Standby is not to use procedure replication but simply define all tables for replication – it's much easier to control schema changes to tables than it is to control procedures changes.

Initializing the standby database

This is a bulk materialization problem and, as the complete database is being replicated, the suggestion is to use **dump** and **load**.

If you suspend processing against the active database during materialization then a simple **dump** and **load** is sufficient. Once the standby database is loaded you can create the connection to the standby database. In this case both databases will now be the same so you do not need to do anything before you restart processing against the active database.

However, as it is an active database, it is unlikely that you will be able to suspend processing during materialization. Now there will be some activity against the active database which is recorded in the active database transaction log and this activity has to be coordinated between the active and standby to allow processing to restart without any problem. To facilitate this, the Warm Standby standby activation writes two markers to the active transaction log. When the active database connection is created an *enable replication* marker is written to the log. When the load of the standby database is complete and the connection is created to the standby database, a *dump marker* is written to the active database log. This dump marker is now used as the start point for replication from the active database log to the standby database. I would recommend the use of the dump marker clause every time you use **dump** and **load** to initialize/refresh a standby database.

Let's look at this a bit more closely in figure 10.2.

When the active connection is created an *enable replication marker* is written to the active database log. When the load to the standby is completed a *dump marker* is written to the log. As the dump point is at the end of the dump, any transactions between the *enable replication* and the *dump marker* will be included in the dump and will be written to the standby database. In both cases replication, can start from the dump marker and no transactions will be lost.

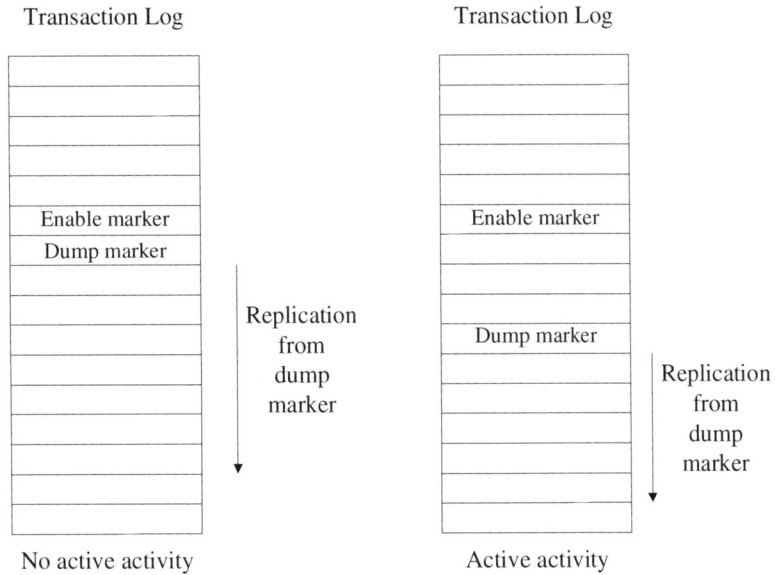

Figure 10.2: Initializing the standby database

Reinitializing a Standby Database

When you need to reinitialize the standby database you have the additional problem that replication has been occurring and there will be transactions in the Replication Server queues. If you have the chance you can quiesce the Replication Server and flush the queues before you dump and load the transaction logs from the active database. The steps involved in re-initializing a standby database are:

- Drop the connection to the standby database.
- Create the connection to the standby database using the *dsi_suspended* and *use dump marker* clauses.
- **Dump** and **load** the database.
- Reset the maintenance user permissions on the standby database.
- Resume the connection to the standby database.

In really extreme situations when the queues are very large and/or the transactions are large, it may be faster to clear the queues before refreshing the standby with a dump and load database. Identify the queue that you need to purge with an **admin who, sqm** and then purge the queue with **sysadmin sqm_purge_queue**.

sysadmin sqm_purge_queue, queue_number, queue_type

where

queue_number	The number of the queue.
queue_type	The queue type.

admin who, sqm

Spid	State		Info		Duplicates
	Writes	*Reads*	*Bytes*	*B Writes*	*B Filled*
	B Reads	B Cache	Save_Int:Seg		
	First Seg.Block		*Last Seg.Block*		
	Next Read	Readers	Truncs		
9	Awaiting Message		100512:0 LNRSSD_MKT.lnrssd_mkt		0
	0	*0*	*0*	*0*	*0*
	0	0	240:0		
	0.1		*0.0*		
	0.1.0	1	1		
10	Awaiting Message		100512:1 LNRSSD_MKT.lnrssd_mkt		80
	104442	*104748*	*34712951*	*16321*	*28*
	16366	16262	0:2773		
	2773.46		*2773.46*		
	2773.47.0	1	1		

sysadmin sqm_purge_queue, 100512, 1

This will delete the data from the queue – very quickly – and then you can refresh the standby database.

To setup the initialize and dump markers on the active database log you need to drop and recreate the standby database connection. Before you do this take a note of the standby database maintenance user. If you do not, the **drop connection** will remove all information on the maintenance user for that database from the Replication Server tables.

drop connection to server_name.db_name

Then recreate the connection as before:

create connection to PSRV_LON2.sales_ws_db

set error class rs_sqlserver_error_class

set function string class rs_sqlserver_function_class

set username rsmnt_user

set password rsmnt_pw

with log transfer on, dsi_suspended

as standby for PSRV_LON1_L.sales_db

use dump marker

Maintenance User Permissions

The maintenance user defined for the standby database requires all permissions against the objects in the standby database. Don't forget this. It's awkward enough resynchronizing Warm Standby, especially if the active is still processing. Do not be caught out by the simple requirement for the maintenance user to **insert**/**update**/**delete** the standby tables.

Resuming the Standby Database Connection

Once you have materialized the standby database you can resume the connection to the standby to allow replication to take place.

resume connection to PRSRV_LON2.sales_ws_db

You may find that the resume fails with duplicate inserts to the standby database. Check the status of the DSI with **admin who_is_down**. If it is still suspended check the errorlog for the reason. If it is a duplicate insert causing the failure resume the connection skipping the first transaction.

resume connection to PRSRV_LON2.sales_ws_db

skip transaction

and keep doing this until the connection resumes with no errors.

This can occur when there is activity against the active database while you are dumping it. The **dump database** dumps the data pages irrespective of whether they are being altered. At the end of this phase the transaction log is dumped and this can then be used by the **load database** to recover the changes against the loaded data pages. This approach ensures that the loaded database reflects the state of the database as at the end of the dump. Unfortunately replication is still running against the active database and a transaction which completes during the dump will be included in the loaded standby database as well as written to the Replication Server queues. Therefore when the connection to the standby is resumed there may be transactions in the Replication Server queues which have already been loaded against the standby database. You do not have any choice here – keep resuming until duplicate insert errors stop.

Defining replication definitions and subscriptions

Although it is not necessary for Warm Standby you may define the replication definitions and subscriptions.

Replication definition

The **create replication definition** and **create function replication definition** have additional clauses for Warm Standby.

> create replication definition rep_def_name
> with primary at server_name.db_name
> [with all tables named 'table_name' |
> [with primary table named 'table_name']
> [with replicate table named 'table_name']]
> (col_name [as replicate_column_name] datatype [null|not null]
> [, col_name [as replicate_column_name] datatype [null|not null]] …)
> primary key (col_name [, col_name] …)
> [searchable columns (col_name [, col_name] …)]
> [send standby [{all | replication definition} columns]]
> [replicate {minimal | all} columns]
> [replicate_if_changed (col_name [, col_name] …)]
> [always_replicate (col_name [, col_name] …)]

where

send standby … columns   all: replicates all columns

replication definition: replicates only the columns defined in the replication definition

You can change the standby definition with **alter replication definition**:

alter replication definition rep_def_name

{ with replicate table named 'table_name' |

alter columns with col_name as replicate_col_name

[, col_name as replicate_col_name]… |

add col_name [as replicate_col_name] [datatype [null | not null]]

[, col_name [as replicate_col_name] [datatype [null | not null]]] …|

add searchable columns col_name [, col_name] …|

send standby [off | {all | replication definition} columns] |

replicate {minimal | all} columns |

replicate_if_changed col_name [, col_name] … |

always_replicate col_name [, col_name] … }

Similarly, procedures may be defined specifically for Warm Standby replication:

create function replication definition rep_def_name

with primary at server_name.db_name

[deliver as 'proc_name']

([@par_name datatype [, par_name datatype] …])

[searchable parameters (@par_name [, @par_name] …)]

[send standby {all | replication definition} parameters]

With an identical ability to change the Warm Standby definition using the **alter function replication definition** command.

Subscriptions

The syntax for the **create** and **define subscription** commands is no different for Warm Standby.

Using bulk materialization you need to specify the **define subscription** followed by an **activate** and **validate subscription**.

define subscription subscription_name

for {rep_def_name I

publication pub_name with primary at server_name.db_name}

with replicate at server_name.db_name

[where predicate_expression]

[subscribe to truncate table]

[for new articles]

This will be the normal approach with Warm Standby as bulk materialization is the more feasible approach as you are initializing the whole database. In 11.5 you could of course use **create subscription without materialization**.

create subscription subscription_name

for {rep_def_name I

publication pub_name with primary at server_name.db_name}

with replicate at server_name.dbname

[where predicate_expression]

[incrementally I without holdlock I without materialization]

[subscribe to truncate table]

[for new articles]

11

Error Handling

Introduction

This chapter discusses the handling of Data Server errors by Replication Server. The handling of Replication Server and LTM errors from the related errorlog messages is discussed in chapter 15.

Data Server errors are processed by Replication Server using an error class for each database and assigning specific actions for each error in the error class. The default error class is *rs_sqlserver_error_class*. Although the assignment of a new error action to multiple error classes can sometimes be tedious, it can clearly be useful when you need to define different actions for a Data Server error depending on the server/ database.

Error Classes

Creating an error class

An error class is created with the **create error class** command.

   create error class error_class _name

   create error class jk_error_class

Defining the primary site

If the Replication Domain contains routes you will need to define a primary site for the error class so that the assigned error actions can be distributed to the other Replication Servers in the domain. Note that the default error class does not get assigned a default primary site and you need to define a primary site for the *rs_sqlserver_error_class*.

   An error class primary site is defined with the **move primary** command.

   move primary of error_class_name to RS_name

   move primary of rs_sqlserver_error_class to LONP_RS1

Initializing an Error Class

Once you have created an error class you can initialize it with error actions from an existing error class using the **rs_init_erroractions** system procedure.

   rs_init_erroractions new_error_class, existing_error_class

This is obviously most useful to initialize the new error class with the default error actions.

   rs_init_erroractions jk_error_class, rs_sqlserver_error_class

Dropping an error class

You can drop an error class using the **drop error class** command. This automatically unbinds all error action assignments.

drop error class error_class_name

You cannot drop an error class which is currently in use by a database and you cannot drop the default error class *rs_sqlserver_error_class*.

Associating an error class with a database

The error class and its assigned actions are associated with a database using the **create connection** and **alter connection** commands.

alter connection to PNY_MKT.sales_db

set error class to rs_sqlserver_error_class

Displaying error class information

Information on error classes is displayed with the **rs_helpclass** system procedure. This system procedure also displays function string class information.

rs_helpclass [error_class_name]

The error class name is wildcarded at the end by the procedure so **rs_helpclass** may return several classes beginning with the input string.

rs_helpclass

Function String Class(es)	PRS for CLASS	Parent Class
rs_default_function_class	Not Yet Defined.	Base Class
rs_sqlserver_function_class	Not Yet Defined.	Base Class

Error Class(es)	PRS for CLASS
rs_sqlserver_error_class	PNY1_RS
jk_error_class	PLN1_RS

NOTE
___

If the PRS for your system supplied class has been labeled 'Not Yet Defined.'. You may define it with — create {function string | error} class CLASS_NAME atthe Primary Replication Server (PRS).

rs_helpclass jk_error_class

Function String Class(es)	PRS for CLASS

Error Class(es)	PRS for CLASS

jk_error_class	PLN1_RS

The error class information is held in the system table *rs_classes*.

select * from rs_classes

classname	classid	classtype	prsid
jk1_function_class	0x010f435001000065	F	17777488
rs_default_function_class	0x0000000001000003	F	0
rs_sqlserver_error_class	0x0000000001000002	E	17777488
jk_error_class	0x010f3210010000042	E	17777488
rs_sqlserver_function_class	0x0000000001000001	F	0

Assigning error actions

By default each Data Server error number in an error class has an error action of *stop_replication*. This is clearly the most drastic action as it suspends the connection to the database and all replication to the database is halted. Transactions for the database will now accumulate in the Replication Server queue until the error is resolved and the connection resumed.

You will want to stop replication when most Data Server errors occur as they will need to be resolved before you can continue. However there are some errors for which you will want to alter the default to something less drastic as the error is transient and a retry may be appropriate. The most common example of this is a deadlock error (1205) which occurs at the target database. In this case you will want to retry the transaction on the basis that the retry should now succeed as the deadlocking conditions will have altered.

To assign a non-default action to a Data Server error number use the **assign action** command.

assign action action_option for error_class_name
to data_server_error [, data_server_error] ...

where

action_option

ignore	Replication Server ignores the error and continues processing.
warn	Replication Server displays a warning message but does not roll back the transaction or stop execution.
retry_log	Replication Server rolls back the transaction and retries it. The number of retry attempts is set with the *command retry* parameter of the **configure connection** command. The default number of retries is 3. If the error persists after retrying, Replication Server writes the transaction to the exceptions log and continues execution with the next transaction.
log	Replication Server rolls back the transaction, logs it in the exceptions log and continues execution with the next transaction.
retry_stop	Replication Server rolls back the transaction and retries it. The number of retry attempts is set with the *command retry* parameter of the **configure connection** command. If the error persists after retrying, Replication Server suspends the connection to the database.
stop_replication	Replication Server rolls back the current transaction and suspends the connection to the database.

To alter the action for a deadlock:

assign action retry_stop

for rs_sqlserver_error_class

to 1205

Displaying error action information

The error action for a specific error number is displayed using the **rs_helperror** system procedure.

rs_helperror server_error_number [, v]

where   v   verbose mode which displays any error message text

rs_helperror 1205

DS Error Num	Error Action	Error Class
1205	retry_stop	rs_sqlserver_error_class

Exceptions tables

Data Server errors may be written to the Replication Server exception log tables using the *retry_log* and *log* error actions and the *skip transaction* clause on the **resume connection** command. There are three exception log tables.

rs_exceptshdr   Header information about the origin and destination sites and information on why the error was logged.

rs_exceptcmd   Command information to retrieve the text of the command from the **rs_systext** system table.

rs_exceptslast   Queue ids and times about the last transaction written into the exception tables.

select * from rs_exceptshdr

sys_trans_id

rs_trans_id		
app_trans_name	orig_siteid	
orig_site	orig_db	
orig_time	orig_user	error_siteid
error_site	error_db	
log_time	ds_error	
ds_errmsg		
error_src_line error_proc	error_output_line	
log_reason trans_status	retry_status	app_usr
app_pwd		

0x010f432f00000067

0x0000000136851d9300095046494f4459315354535f544d000000000000000000
00000000000000000000000000000000000000000000000000000000000000000000
00000000000000000000000000000000000000000000000000000000000000000000
000000000000000000000000000000000000

_user_transaction	100943	
PLON_MKT	sales_db	
Mar 26 1998 5:42PM	sales_read	100944
PLON_MKT	sales_db	

Mar 27 1998 9:09AM	1205

0		0	
S	*0*	*2*	*sales_usr1*
NULL			

select * from rs_exceptscmd

sys_trans_id	src_cmd_line	output_cmd_index
cmd_type	*cmd_id*	

0x010f432f00000067	1	0
S	*0x010f432f2000006f*	
0x010f432f00000067	1	1
L	*0x010f432f20000070*	
0x010f432f00000067	8	0
S	*0x010f432f20000071*	
0x010f432f00000067	8	1
L	*0x010f432f20000072*	
0x010f432f00000067	8	2
L	*0x010f432f20000073*	

select * from rs_systext

prsid	parentid	texttype	sequence
textval			

0	0x0000000008000002	O	1

execute rs_update_lastcommit @origin = ?rs_origin!sys?,
@origin_qid = ?rs_origin_qid!sys?,
@secondary_qid = ?rs_secondary_qid!sys?,
@origin_time = ?rs_origin_commit_time!sys?; commit transaction

0	0x0000000008000007	O	1

execute rs_get_lastcommit

0	0x0000000008000008	O	1

use ?rs_destination_db!sys_raw?

0	0x0000000008000009	O	1

execute rs_marker @rs_api = ?rs_api!param?

0	0x000000000800000c	O	1

sp_serverinfo server_soname

You might find something along these lines useful:

Header error information on data servers and users

```
select
rtrim(hdr.orig_site) + '.' + rtrim(hdr.orig_db) + '.' +
rtrim(hdr.orig_user),
rtrim(hdr.error_site) + '.' + rtrim(hdr.error_db),
hdr.log_time, hdr.ds_error
from rs_exceptshdr hdr
```

Command text of error transactions

```
select
rtrim(hdr.orig_site) + '.' + rtrim(hdr.orig_db) + '.' +
rtrim(hdr.orig_user),
rtrim(hdr.error_site) + '.' + rtrim(hdr.error_db),
hdr.log_time, hdr.ds_error, txt.textval
from rs_exceptshdr hdr, rs_exceptscmd cmd, rs_systext txt
where hdr.sys_trans_id = cmd.sys_trans_id
and cmd.cmd_id = txt.parentid
```

Origin database and timing information on the last logged transaction

```
select
error_database, origin, origin_time, log_time
from rs_exceptslast
```

Transactions for a database

```
select * from rs_exceptshdr
where error_site = '<server_name>'
and error_database = '<database_name.'
```

The system procedure **rs_helpexception** displays information on the exception logs.

rs_helpexception [trans_id [, v]]

where   v   includes the text of the transaction

rs_helpexception

Summary of Logged Transactions on 'LNPRD_RS1'

Total # of Logged Transactions = 1

Xact ID	Org Site	Org User	Org Date	Dest Site	#Recs/Xact
101	LNPRD_1.mkt_db	sa	Dec 29 1998	NYPRD_1.mkt_db	3

rs_helpexception 101

Detailed Summary of Logged Transaction # 101 on 'LNPRD_RS1'

Origin Site	Origin User	Org. Commit Date	#Cmds in Xact
LNPRD_1.mkt_db	sa	Dec 29 1998 2:31	3

Dest. Site	Dest. User	Date Logged
NYPRD_1.mktdb	rsmnt_user	Dec 29 1998 2:35

This transaction was skipped due to a 'resume connection' command with the 'skip transaction' option.

The system procedure **rs_delexception** lists the records in the exceptions tables and also allows you to delete them.

rs_delexception [xact_id]
rs_delexception

Summary of Transactions on 'PRS1_MKT

Xact ID	Org Site	Org User	Org Date	Dest Site	#Recs/Xact
101	PRDLN.mkt_db	sa	Dec 29 1998	PRDNY.mkt_db	3

To delete a specific logged xact., type 'rs_delexception {Xact ID}'

12

Configuration Parameters

Introduction

This chapter describes the configuration parameters for Replication Server, LTMs and DSI/RSI connections.

Replication server parameters

Replication Server configuration parameters are displayed and altered with **rs_configure**.

rs_configure

Config Name	Config Value	Run Value
cm_max_connections	64	64
current_rssd_version	1103	1103
fstr_cachesize	200000	200000
id_server	PRS1_IDSRV	PRS1_IDSRV
init_sqm_write_delay	1000	1000
init_sqm_write_max_delay	10000	10000
md_source_memory_pool	100000	100000
memory_max	3	3
minimum_rssd_version	1100	1100
num_client_connections	30	30
num_concurrent_subs	10	10
num_msgqueues	178	178
num_msgs	45568	45568
num_mutexes	128	128
num_stable_queues	32	32
num_threads	100	100
oserver	PRSLN_MKT	PRSLN_MKT
password_encryption	0	0
queue_dump_buffer_size	1000	1000
rec_daemon_sleep_time	120	120
rssd_error_class	rs_sqlserver_error_class	rs_sqlserver_error_class
sqm_warning_thr1	75	75
sqm_warning_thr2	90	90
sqm_warning_thr_ind	70	70
sqt_max_cache_siz	131072	131072
sqt_max_prs_siz	262144	262144
sre_num_bitmaps	1000	1000
sre_reserve	0	0
sts_cachesize	100	100
sub_daemon_sleep_time	120	120

With the exception of a few connection related parameters all of the Replication Server parameters are static and require a server restart to be activated.

cm_max_connections

The maximum number of outgoing connections available, default 64. A connection is required for:

- Each outgoing route.
- Each database DSI.
- While a **create subscription** is executing.
- The RSSD.

Most of the memory for *cm_max_connections* is taken from the operating system with a small amount reserved from the global memory pool.

current_rssd_version

The replication server version supported by this RSSD.

This is automatically changed by the **rs_init** program while upgrading or downgrading the system and you should not need to change this value.

To support a Replication Server feature all Replication Servers need to be at least at the level of the feature introduction release. *Current_rssd_version* must not be less than *minimum_rssd_version* or the *rs_system_version* found in the *rs_versions* table of the ID Server.

fstr_cachesize

The function string cache size with a default value of 200,000 bytes.

The function string cache is global for the Replication Server and not related to each connection. When function strings are first used they are moved into cache for use by the DSI threads. A function string is never removed from cache until it is dropped. Replication Server automatically takes more memory when the cache size turns out to be too small and will continue to do so as long as there is available memory.

id_server

The name of the ID server set up at installation with **rs_init**.

init_sqm_write_delay

The initial write delay for the SQM thread, with a default of 1000 ms.

This is the length of time that the stable queue manager waits for a storage block to fill before writing the block to the queue on the stable device. If you are experiencing latency problems, set this to 100-200 ms and *batch_ltl_cmds* to off. However reducing *init_sqm_write_delay* will increase I/O and use more space on the stable queue as blocks are being written more often to the queue. *Init_sqm_write_delay* should be less than *init_sqm_write_max_delay*.

init_sqm_write_max_delay

The maximum write delay for the SQM thread, with a default of 10000 ms. A write to the queue is guaranteed after waiting for *init_sqm_write_max_delay*.

materialization_save_interval

The minimum time in minutes that materialization messages are retained in the queue after they have been successfully applied to the target database. This parameter applies to logical connections only with a default of "strict" which means that the data is deleted after it has been applied to the standby database.

It is not recommended that you alter this parameter as the Replication Server does not detect this type of loss.

md_source_memory_pool

An internal limit on the memory that the LTM can take from *memory_max* to hold pending writes. The default is 100,000 with a range of 65536 to 983040. Do not change this parameter as the default should be sufficient to hold all the pending writes. If something unusual occurs and the limit is reached the distributor will simply suspend itself until things move again.

memory_max

This specifies the memory available to the Replication Server, with a default value of 3MB.

At startup 2/3 of the *memory_max* value is allocated to 5 pools of segment sizes 256 bytes, 1 K, 4 K, 16 K and 64 K. Each pool has the same total allocation of memory equal to:

memory_max * 2/3 * 1/5

If there are no available segments in the pool, the pools are expanded from the remaining reserved memory up to a maximum of 64 pools. Subsequent pools will have a size of half the initial pool size:

memory_max * 2/3 * 1/10

This results in a real maximum memory of:

memory_max * ((5 * 2/3 * 1/5) + ((64-5) * 2/3 * 1/10))

4.6 * *memory_max*

If the replication server is running out of pools you will see error:

Cannot expand memory since '%ld' memory maps already exist

Increasing *memory_max* will allocate larger pools which provides more memory segments for allocation. If you are short of memory on the machine you might look at how the Replication Server connections are started. When Replication Server is started all threads are started in parallel and the appropriate memory pools allocated. This will result in a specific pool size allocation which might not be suitable later when Replication Server needs other pool sizes and the 64 pool limit is reached. You might consider starting the Replication Server with all connections suspended and resume them individually to control the memory pool allocation. But really, you should get more memory if you have to go to this extent.

minimum_rssd_version

The minimum Replication Server version supported by this RSSD.

This is automatically changed by the **rs_init** program while upgrading or downgrading the system and you should not need to change this value.

To support a Replication Server feature all Replication Servers need to be at least at the level of the feature introduction release. *Current_rssd_version* must not be less than *minimum_rssd_version* or the *rs_system_version* found in the *rs_versions* table of the ID Server.

num_client_connections

The maximum number of client connections with a default value of 30.

A client connection is used for:

- Each route into the Replication Server.
- Any isql sessions.
- Any RSM connections.
- Each LTM into the Replication Server.
- Each connection during a materialization.

Memory for client connections is taken from the operating system and each connection uses about 7000 bytes.

num_concurrent_subs

The number of concurrent subscriptions that can be created (using **create subscription)** or dropped, with a default of 10. Do not change this one. It is implemented to prevent concurrent subscription creation using too many resources – each create uses a connection, a stable queue and 1 or 2 threads.

num_msgqueues

The maximum number of Open Server message queues, with a default of 178. Message queues are required for:

- two global message queues for Replication Server – one for asynchronous IO and one for fadeouts
- one for each SQM
- one for each SQT

Every primary database requires four message queues (SQM and SQT for the inbound queue and an SQM and SQT for the database connection). Every replicate database requires two message queues (SQM and SQT for the database connection).

Every direct route requires one message queue. So the total number of message queues required is:

2 + (2 * # replicate databases) + (4 * # primary databases) + (1 * # direct routes)

Each subscription materialization not yet applied requires one message queue and each materialization being applied requires two message queues.

Memory for message queues is taken from the operating system with every queue using approximately 205 bytes.

num_msgs

The maximum number of Open Server messages, with a default of 45568. This determines the maximum number of messages that the Replication Server queues can hold and is also related to the number of message queues as:

*num_msgs = num_msgqueues * 60*

Internal memory for messages is taken from the operating system with every message using approximately 57 bytes.

num_mutexes

The maximum number of Open Server internal mutexes allowed, with a default of 128.

A mutex - mutual exclusion semaphore - is a logical locking object that Replication Server uses to protect shared resources.

Replication Server needs 12 global mutexes and 1 per SQM. The number of mutexes required is:

12 + (2 * # primary databases) + (1 * # replicate databases)

The error message for running out of mutexes is not that obvious. The Replication Server crashes with a stack trace that includes the function *srv_createmutex()*.

```
Thread GLOBAL RS(GLOBAL RS) infected with signal 11
***************STACK TRACE***************
*****thread GLOBAL RS(GLOBAL RS)*******
pc: 0x74084, exc_terminate ()
pc: 0x35af0, sun_svr4_catch_signal ()
pc: 0xef7c404c, _fini ()
```

```
pc: 0xef70a2b4, _fini ()
pc: 0xef70b570, _fini ()
pc: 0x157b3c, intl__strblist ()
pc: 0x156fbc, intl_cstrbuild ()
pc: 0xcb218, srv__builderr ()
pc: 0xc32c4, srv__seterr ()
pc: 0xc689c, srv_createmutex ()
pc: 0x37e50, sqm_start_queue ()
pc: 0x373f4, sqm_init ()
pc: 0x316a4, _init_rs_modules ()
pc: 0xd6b10, srv__spawnfunc ()
*****End of stack trace.****
```

Memory for mutexes is taken from the operating system with every mutex using approximately 205 bytes.

num_stable_queues

This variable is only used on HP platforms and specifies the maximum number of stable queues to be used. The default is 32.

num_threads

The maximum number of Open Server threads allowed with a default of 50. A thread is required for:

- Each incoming and outgoing RSI.
- Each SQT.
- Each SQM.
- Each LTM.
- Each DIST.
- Each DSI.

So each primary database requires 7 threads (four for the SQM/SQT for inbound queue and database connection plus one for each of LTM, DIST and DSI) and each replicate database requires 3 threads (two for the SQM/SQT database connection and one for the DSI).

During a subscription creation four threads are required for the Replication Server processes dSUB, dCM, dAIO and dALARM and one for the client process.

Memory overhead for threads is taken from the operating system with every thread using approximately 2800 bytes.

oserver

The Replication Server name set up during installation. Do not change.

parallel_dsi

A shortcut for setting parallel DSI settings, with a default of 'off'. Set to 'on', this sets the parallel DSI parameter settings to:

- *dsi_num_threads* to 5
- *dsi_num_large_xact_threads* to 2
- *dsi_serialization_method* to "wait_for_commit"
- *dsi_sqt_max_cache_size* to 1 MB.

password_encryption

The default of 'off' specifies that passwords are stored in clear text. This is set during installation or with **rs_init**. Note that this is internal RSSD encryption and passwords are still transmitted on the network in clear text.

queue_dump_buffer_size

The maximum number of characters of a command output when dumping queues with **sysadmin sqt_dump_queue**. The default is 1000 with a range of 1000 to 32768. Commands larger than this value are truncated when dumped.

rec_daemon_sleep_time

The time in ms that the recovery daemon sleeps before deleting strict save interval messages on a warm standby logical connection. The default is 120 with a range of 1 to 10000.

rssd_error_class

The error class for the RSSD set up at installation and altered using the **alter connection** command.

sqm_warning_thr1

The first warning threshold for the stable device space usage, with a default of 75%. The warning message is written to the error log.

sqm_warning_thr2

The second – and last - warning threshold for the stable device space usage, with a default of 90%. The warning message is written to the error log.

sqm_warning_thr_ind

A warning threshold when a single queue uses this percentage of the stable device space. The default is 70 with a range of 51 to 100.

The warning message is written to the error log.

sqt_max_cache_size

The maximum memory allocated to the SQT cache for processing messages. The default is 131,072 but this is seldom high enough and the recommendation is to set it to 256K.

If the *removed* column of **admin who, sqt** is regularly greater than zero, this indicates that messages have been removed from cache because there was not enough room. This can have a detrimental effect on Replication Server performance and should be avoided.

Memory for *sqt_max_cache_size* is taken from the global memory pool.

sqt_max_prs_size

The maximum cache used by the parser. This is no longer used in 11.5 but, in earlier versions, you should ensure that it is no less than *sqt_max_cache_size*.

sre_reserve

This specifies the space in the hash table pre-allocated for new subscriptions. The default is 0 with a range of 0 to 500 percent of current space. This should not be changed unless you have a **very** dynamic system with lots of subscription definition.

The s*re_reserve* space is taken from the global memory pool.

sts_cachesize

This specifies the number of slots in the hash table of the SQT cache for an RSSD table such as *rs_users, rs_objects* with a default of 100. This parameter defines the cache size for cached RSSD system tables. When no slot is available the least recently used object is removed. A warning is written to the error log.

sub_daemon_sleep_time

The time in seconds that the subscription daemon sleeps between attempts to materialize a subscription. The default is 120 with a range of 1 to 31536. There is no reason to alter this one.

Connection parameters

The connection configuration parameters are set using the **create connection**, **configure connection** or **alter connection** commands.

batch

Default of 'on' allows multi-command batches.

batch_begin

Default of 'off' allows the **begin tran** command to be included in the batch. You should alter this only when writing a special for connection to a foreign database.

command_retry

Specifies the number of times to retry a failed transaction when the error action is *retry_log* or *retry_stop*. The default is 3. If you suffer a high number of deadlocks at the replicate database this is a good one to increase as it reduces the number of times the connection will be down because of a number of consecutive deadlocks on the same transaction.

db_packet_size

This determines the maximum connection network packet size. This defaults to 512 bytes which should always be altered to 2048 (unless you are still using SQL Server 10.0 in which case leave it at 512).

dsi_charset_convert

This specifies the character set conversion for data applied to the database.

on   Converts the character sets and shuts down if there is an error. This is the default and worth leaving this setting as non-conversion will affect the replicate data.

allow   This converts when possible but applies any unconverted data to the replicate database.

off   No conversion is attempted. During a materialization 'off' functions as 'allow'.

dsi_cmd_batch_size

The maximum size of a command batch that Replication Server sends to a replicate database, with a default of 8192 bytes. If the majority of rows you change are greater than 500 bytes you should see if an increase in this value speeds things up. Be careful as setting this higher than 16K may cause some command batches to exceed the 64 pages parse limit.

dsi_cmd_separator

The command line separator, with a default of newline (\n). Change this one only if defining a connection to a foreign database – such as semi-colon (;) for DB2.

dsi_fadeout_time

The idle time in seconds before a DSI connection is closed, with a default of 600 seconds. If set to –1 the connection never fades out. There is obviously a network overhead in reconnecting but if the DSI is always connected you will not be able to shutdown the Replication Server until you have suspended the connection (or use the *nowait* clause – not recommended). Not worth the bother, leave this one alone unless you have serious network delays on connection or each separate connection costs you money.

dsi_keep_triggers

This specifies whether triggers fire for replicated databases. The default is 'on' except for standby databases. Note that 'off' issues a non-documented command **set triggers off** in the replicate database.

dsi_large_xact_size

The number of commands in a transaction which will cause the parallel DSI feature to treat the transaction as a large transaction. The default is 100 with a minimum of 3 and a maximum of *dsi_num_large_xact_threads* – 1.

This can be useful as large transactions are applied before the **commit tran** command is received by the Replication Server. However watch performance as transaction serialization must be maintained and a mixture of large and small transactions may cause the small transactions to be rolled back and re-executed serially to maintain transaction sequence at the replicate database.

dsi_max_cmds_to_log

The number of commands to write to the exceptions log. The default is –1 which logs all commands of a transaction.

dsi_max_text_to_log

The number of bytes to write to the exceptions log for a failed **rs_writetext**. The default is –1 which logs all text.

dsi_num_large_xact_threads

The number of parallel DSI threads to be reserved for use with large transactions. The default value is 0 and the maximum value is one less than the value of *dsi_num_threads*.

dsi_num_threads

This specifies the number of parallel DSI threads to be used. The default value is 1 and the maximum value is 20.

dsi_replication

This specifies if transactions applied by the maintenance user (DSI) are marked for replication in the replicate database transaction log. The default is 'off' for normal databases and 'on' for standby databases.

dsi_serialization_method

This specifies the method to maintain transaction serialization when using parallel DSI threads.

Wait_for_commit   The default which waits for one transaction to commit before applying the next.

Single_transaction_per_origin

     Applies transactions based on their origin database with only one transaction at time per origin allowed to be active.

None   No transaction serialization is used.

dsi_sql_data_style

This specifies the type of data server for the connection. The default is 'sql' with other values of 'db2', 'lotus' and 'watcom'. Note that warm standby supports 'sql' only.

dsi_sqt_max_cache_size

The maximum stable queue cache size for the connection when using parallel DSI threads. The default of 0 sets this to the value of *sqt_max_cache_size* which is the best way of setting this.

dsi_xact_group_size

The size of a grouped transaction which is simply a number of transactions from the same source that the Replication Server applies as one transaction. The default is 65536 and a value of –1 indicates no grouping.

If something fails within a grouped transaction the DSI performs all transactions separately. Note that the entire transaction must be in the SQT cache before it can be considered for grouping.

dump_load

This specifies if a replicate database participates in coordinated dumps. The default is 'off'.

save_interval

This specifies the minimum time in minutes to save messages in an outbound queue after they have been successfully applied to the replicate database. The default is 0 for physical connections and 'strict' for logical connections.

Saved messages can be used to resynchronize a database after it has been loaded from database and transaction log dumps using the **sysadmin restore_dsi_saved_segments** command.

The logical connection default of 'strict' means that the messages are not saved after they have been applied successfully.

send_standby_repdef_cols

For a warm standby database this specifies which columns are replicated.

off   All columns are sent to the warm standby.

on   Only the columns specified in a replication definition are sent to the warm standby.

standby_func_class

This specifies the function class to be used for the warm standby database. This is a strange one as the *rs_default_function_class* is the default function class set up for warm standby. Unfortunately this function class cannot be modified which may present you with problems as the standby may not function exactly as the active did when a switch is required. To alter this one you need to update the system table *rs_config* directly.

> **insert into rs_config**
>
> **values ("standby_func_class", 0x0000000000000000, "alternate", 0,**
>
> **"new function string class used by warm")**

Route parameters

The connection configuration parameters are set using the **create route**, **configure route** or **alter route** commands.

rsi_batch_size

The number of bytes sent by the RSI before requesting a truncation point. The default is 262144 bytes with a range of 1024 to 262144.

The RSI truncation point controls the deletion of messages from the stable queue – similar to the transaction log replication truncation point used by the LTM. The high default will result in transactions being resent when the Replication Server is restarted. Not really a problem but you may want to move the RSI truncation point more often.

rsi_fadeout_time

The idle time in seconds before the RSI connection is closed. The default is 120 seconds and a value of –1 indicates that the connection never closes. As for the DSI fadeout this should be left alone unless you must keep the connection open.

rsi_packet_size

The network packet size used by the connection with a default of 2048 bytes.

rsi_sync_interval

The number of seconds between RSI synchronization messages. The default is 60 seconds and the value must be greater than 0.

At each *rsi_sync_interval* the primary Replication Server requests the remote Replication Server locater value which tells the Primary Replication Server how much data has been received and processed by the Replicate Replication Server. A delete is then sent to the SQM to delete all messages up to and including the locater value from the Primary Replication Server queues.

save_interval

The minimum time in minutes to retain messages in the RSI queue after they have been successfully passed to the target Replication Server.

Similar to the DSI *save_interval* this allows transactions to be resent to a Replication Server after a target database has been recovered.

LTM Parameters

The LTM configuration parameters are defined at installation and held in the LTM config file.

```
# Configuration file for Log Transfer Manager 'LTM_PLN_MKT.
Created by rs_init.
#
SQL_server=PLN_MKT
SQL_database=SALES_DB
RS_source_ds=PLN_MKT
RS_source_db=SALES_DB
SQL_user=ltm
```

```
SQL_pw=ltm_pw
RS=PRS1_MKT
RS_user=rsltm_username
RS_pw=rsltm_pw
LTM_admin_user=sa
LTM_admin_pw=sa_pw
LTM_charset=iso_1
LTM_language=us_english
LTM_sortorder=binary
pwd_encrypt=0
#
# The parameters below have the given default values.
#
# scan_retry=15
# batch_sz=1000
# batch_ltl_cmds=on
# retry=10
# skip_ltl_cmd_err=off
# maint_cmds_to_skip=1000
# print_sproc_warning=on
```

scan_retry

The sleep time in seconds before checking for new log records, with a default of 15.

If there are no records in the log the LTM log scan thread sleeps for a minimum of *scan_retry* seconds. When new records arrive in the log the log scan thread is wakened and any remaining *scan_retry* time is added to the next sleep interval. Leave this one alone as decreasing *scan_retry* can have a negative performance impact on the SQL Server.

The *scan_retry* value determines the amount of time that you have to wait before the LTM process dies after the LTM has been shutdown as the thread within the SQL server will stay alive for 2*scan_retry after bringing the LTM down. When you shut down the LTM check that the LTM process has died before you restart the LTM as the LTM will not start if the old process is still running.

batch_sz

The number of log records requested before updating the replication truncation point, with a default of 1000. The default is normally the optimum setting for this. Increasing the value will cause more of the log to be retained as the truncation point moves less frequently. Decreasing the value will increase the CPU usage.

batch_ltl_cmds

The default of 'on' groups LTL commands into 16K buffers which are sent to the Replication Server when:

- The buffer is full.
- Five seconds have elapsed since writing the first LTL command in the buffer.
- The LTM log scan thread returns from the log scan.

When set to 'off' the LTM sends commands as soon as it receives them from the log scan thread. Setting *batch_ltl_cmds* to 'off' will provide the best improvement to latency but it will increase space usage in the stable queue.

retry

The time in seconds before the LTM tries to reconnect to the SQL Server or the Replication Server. The default is 10 seconds.

skip_ltl_cmd_err

This specifies whether to skip errors from the SQL Server or the Replication Server or to shut down the LTM. The default is 'off' which shuts down the LTM on receiving an error.

maint_cmds_to_skip

The number of commands to skip before forwarding a maintenance transaction **commit tran** to the Replication Server. The default is 1000 commands.

print_sproc_warning

Determines the warning messages printed if multiple replicated rows are modified within a replicated stored procedure. The default of 'off' prints one warning per row updated. The 'on' setting prints one warning per procedure execution.

13

Installation

Introduction

This chapter describes the installation of Replication Server and a database connection (DSI) on a Unix system. The **rs_init** examples used in the material refer to Replication Server 11.0.

System Planning

As Replication Server is such a complicated system, it is worth taking some time to consider defining some naming standards for the various system components. When you have several systems to look after, this will make maintaining the system so much easier, as all your Replication Servers will have the same 'feel' to them. This should apply to all parts of the system, from runserver file names to user names. Although Sybase has default component names you will probably want to define your own to suit your applications. Irrespective of the actual names, the point is to decide on a standard and stick to it rigidly.

Replication Servers

Replication Server names should contain the following information.

- The server name.
- The fact that it is a Replication Server.
- Whether it is production, development or test.

Consider a production Replication Server for a system known overall as 'TRADES'. To describe a Replication Server, including all of the information above, we could use the following format:

RS_TRADES_ P

The trouble with this is that the Replication Server installation program **rs_init** will not allow Replication Server components with the prefix **rs_** in either upper or lower case. A better way to describe the server above would be to prefix it with **PRS** for **P**roduction **R**eplication **S**erver like this:

PRS_TRADES

This contains all of the necessary information, **RS** - it is a Replication Server, **TRADES** - it is called TRADES, and **P** - it is a production server. So a test Replication Server for a system called 'DEALS' would be:

TRS_DEALS

Of course you may wish to include a number to cope with multiple Replication Servers for a system.

PRS1_TRADES

Log Transfer Managers

Again the name of the LTM should describe what the LTM does. Consider the LTM which connects to the 'TRADER' database on the 'PDS_MARKETS' SQL server. If we give this LTM a name to describe what it does, we could name it:

LTM_PDS_MARKETS_TRADER

This adequately describes that this is an LTM and it connects to the TRADER database on the PDS_MARKETS SQL Server. Numbers are not important in LTM names as the combination of server and database name will be unique.

Replication Server Users

There are many different users within a replication system and they reside on different components of the system. Even if you decide to name your Replication Servers and LTMs after your grandchildren or your favorite whiskies, please use a standard naming convention for the Replication Server user names that you need. You need to define the users listed below.

ID Server user	Each Replication Server needs to connect to the ID Server using this login and password which must obviously be defined at the ID Server.
	Suggested naming format: rsid_rsname
	e.g. rsid_PRS_TRADES
Primary user	The primary user accesses the RSSD to modify the Replication Server system tables when objects are created.
	Suggested naming format: A global name of rssdprm.
Maintenance user	The maintenance user accesses the SQL Server databases, including the RSSD, to apply the replicated changes.
	Suggested naming format: rsmaint_dbname
	e.g. rsmaint_sales
RSSD LTM user	RSSD system table changes are read by the RSSD LTM and distributed to the other Replication Servers in the domain. This login allows the LTM to access the RSSD to extract the transaction log information.
	Suggested naming format: ltm_dbname

Do not allocate a global name for the LTM user. When you have multiple LTMs to a server this means that you will probably default the LTM user to the *master* database. In this case you can hit trouble on a server start. Once the default database of the LTM user has started, the LTM can log into the server and start issuing commands. As these are **dbcc** commands, they bypass the basic checks to see if the database is online and can write to the transaction log while the database is being recovered. This causes the recovery routine to fail and to mark the database as suspect.

Even if you only have one LTM on a server, use a different user for each LTM and default the database of the LTM user to the Primary Database. This means that the LTM connection issues a **use database** which fails until the database is online. Or you can shutdown all LTMs which attach to the server – not always possible if you do not have *sa* control of them.

Primary database LTM user

The primary database changes are read by the primary database LTM and written to the inbound queue of the Replication Server stable device. This login allows the LTM to access the primary database to extract the transaction log information. It is recommended that this user is aliased to the dbo of the primary database.

Suggested naming format: ltm_dbname as above.

RSSD LTM Replication Server user

The LTM process needs to access the RSSD system tables to determine the replication requirements of the transaction. A separate user of the RSSD is required for this.

Suggested naming format: rssdltm_system_name

e.g. rssdltm_TRADES

LTM administration user

An administration user is necessary to execute the few administration commands supported by the LTM. The most common of these is **shutdown**. The default for this is *sa* which is as good as anything.

Suggested naming format: A global use of sa.

Subscription creation user

> It is recommended by Sybase to define a separate user at the Replication Server to create subscriptions. Unlike the other users in this section this user is not created during the installation. This user is not mandatory but, if you create subscriptions as *sa* and the primary database is owned by another user, the *sa* may not automatically have the correct permissions on the primary database tables. Using a subscription creation user supports the situation where the tables are owned by the database owner and permissions are granted individually.
>
> Suggested naming format: rssub_system_name
>
> e.g. rssub_TRADES

Managing Replication Server users

Replication Server users are defined separately from the **rs_init** process using the **create user** command. This command is input at the Replication Server.

create user user_name
set password {p_word | null}

Users may be altered or dropped with the **alter user** and **drop user** commands. Again these are input at the Replication Server.

alter user user_name
set password {p_word | null}
[verify password old_p_word]

where   the **verify password** clause must be entered by non-sa users to change their password.

drop user user_name

Replication Server user information is held in the *rs_users* and *rs_maintusers* system tables in the RSSD.

select * from rs_users

username permissions	uid use_enc_password	password enc_password
rsltm_trades 2	0x010f431f02000066 0	rs_ltm_trades_pw NULL
rssdprm 10	0x010f431f02000065 0	rssdprm_pw NULL
rssub_trades 4	0x010f431f02000067 0	rssub_trades_pw NULL
sa 1	0x0000000002000001 0	sa_pw NULL

select * from rs_maintusers

destid	username use_enc_password enc_password	password
100787	rssdmnt 0 NULL	rssdmntpw
100790	rsmnt_sales 0 NULL	rsmnt_sales_pw
100791	rsmnt_mkt 0 NULL	rsmnt_mkt_pw

The help procedure **rs_helpuser** provides all of the information that you need from these tables.

rs_helpuser [user_name]

rs_helpuser

Users and Privileges Known at Site PRS_MKT

Primary Users

User Name	Permission(s) Name
rsltm_trades	connect source
rssdprm	connect source, primary subscr
rssub_trades	create object
sa	sa

Maintenance Users

User name	Destination DS.DB
rssdmnt	LNPRD.prssd1_sales
rsmnt_sales	LNPRD.SALES
rsmnt_sales	NYPRD.SALES

rs_helpuser rsltm_sales

Users and Privileges Known at Site PRS_MKT

Primary Users

User Name	Permission Name
©rsltm_sales	connect source

The permissions that the Replication Server users may have are described in table 13.1.

Permission	Description
sa	The Replication Server administrator with permission to execute any command.
create object	Allows users to create objects such as replication definitions and subscriptions. Users with *create object* permission are automatically granted *primary subscribe* permission.
primary subscribe	Allows users to create subscriptions to primary data.
connect source	Allows the LTM and RSI to log into the Replication Server.

Table 13.1: Replication Server permissions

These permissions are either created automatically by **rs_init** or separately with the **grant** and **revoke** commands.

grant permission to user_name

revoke permission from user_name

The minimum permission to execute a Replication Server command is shown below.

<u>sa</u>	<u>create object</u>
abort switch	activate subscription (at replicate)
add partition	alter function
allow connections	alter function replication definition
alter connections	alter function string
alter logical connection	create function
alter route	create function replication definition
alter user	create function string
assign action	create replication definition
configure connection	create subscription (at replicate)
configure logical connection	define subscription (at replicate)
configure route	drop function
create connection	drop function replication definition
create error class	drop function string
create function string class	drop subscription (at replicate)
create logical connection	set autocorrection
create route	validate subscription (at replicate)
create user	
drop connection	
drop error class	<u>primary subscribe</u>
drop function string class	activate subscription (at primary)
drop logical connection	create subscription (at primary)
drop partition	define subscription (at primary)
drop route	drop subscription (at primary)
drop user	validate subscription (at primary)
grant	
ignore loss	

move primary	<u>any user</u>
rebuild queues	admin
resume connection	alter user ... verify password
resume distributor	
resume log transfer	
resume route	
revoke	
set log recovery	
shutdown	
suspend connection	
suspend distributor	
suspend log transfer	
suspend route	
switch active	
sysadmin	
wait for create standby	
wait for switch	

Disk space requirements

Before we start the installation we need to consider the disk space that we are going to need for the Replication Server. This breaks down into four components:

- The installation directory.
- The Replication Server error log.
- The Replication Server message queues i.e. the Stable Device.
- The Replication Server system catalog tables i.e. the RSSD.

The Installation Directory

The replication software is best kept in its own directory, though it can be stored in the $SYBASE directory. Using the $SYBASE directory can make upgrading difficult, and some locale files may be different from those used by SQL Server, therefore it is recommended to have a completely separate environment for the Replication Server.

The directory structure for Replication Server is the same as for a SQL server, i.e. a top level directory with the following directories under it:

- bin
- install
- scripts
- upgrade
- charsets
- locales
- diag

The bin directory contains the executable binary files:

repserver	The Replication Server executable.
repserver.diag	A Replication Server executable used in fault finding and diagnostic testing.
ltm	The log transfer manager executable.
ltm.diag	A log transfer manager executable used in fault finding and diagnostic testing.
rs_subcmp	A subscription comparison program, used to compare and if necessary, correct data in a primary/replicate table pair. This is described in Appendix E.

The install directory contains the set-up configuration and binary files and is where the RUN_SERVER files for the Replication Server and LTMs are created by the installation program. The install directory also contains the initialization routine **rs_init**.

Errorlog file

Like any other error log the Replication Server errorlog can grow at an alarming rate and you need to make sure that sufficient space has been allocated for its growth. A full errorlog will cause Replication Server to fail when it tries to write a message to the log. I normally use the default location for the errorlog but you can place this anywhere in the file system. As this file will get large, make sure that you cycle it at every restart of the Replication Server. A simple addition to the RUNSERVER file will achieve this. This will keep the errorlog as small as possible and will help with space usage as you can remove old log files.

The Stable Device

The location and size of the stable device must be determined. The stable device is used to store the messages being replicated. The location should be a raw Unix partition and will default to 20Mb if no size is specified, although it can be made smaller in 1Mb stages. You should try to make it as large as possible, as this will allow a primary database to keep operating in event of a network or replicate database failure, by storing all transactions on the stable device until the fault is rectified. Most large production systems should have stable devices of upwards of 2000Mb, and this may be significantly larger, made up of several physical devices. It depends on the size of the system and the transaction throughput expected. The partition should be mirrored using Operating System mirroring software, as Sybase do not provide mirroring functionality in the Replication Server.

The Replication Server System Database (RSSD)

We need a SQL server to store the RSSD database. This can be on an existing SQL Server, though I usually recommend that the Rep Server has its own RSSD SQL server. This improves reliability, especially if the Replication Server is replicating data from and to many different servers.

The RSSD location and size needs to be determined. For most applications a 50Mb database will be more than adequate, with at least the same size log device. It is better to overestimate the size of a RSSD log, as a full log on a RSSD is one of the worst recovery scenarios you can encounter on a replication system.

Installing the software

Software is loaded from CD or tape using the Sybase **sybload** utility, provided on the installation media. Most administrators will be familiar with this from Sybase SQL server installs.

Once the software is loaded on to the host machine, the Replication Server installation and initial configuration is set up using the **rs_init** program. This is very similar to **sybinit** for SQL server, and as with **sybinit**, it can be used interactively or with a resource file. Resource files will be explained later.

I know that we are computer experts which means that an installation holds no fears for us and we will dive in without any planning. This is not a good idea with Replication Server. Sybase provide a data sheet to fill in with the parameters required for installation of a Replication Server. It is worthwhile taking the time to fill it in, as it will be invaluable during the installation process. And remember to use a standard naming convention for all component and user names, and stick to it. So, with our completed data sheet to hand, we run **rs_init**.

When you run **rs_init** you are presented with a set of dialogue screens which begin with:

RS_INIT

1. **Release directory: /usr/sybase/repserver**
2. **Edit / View Interfaces File**
3. **Configure a Server product**

Set the release directory to the Replication Server software root directory by choosing the option number 1. Next, if you haven't already done so, enter the interfaces file entries by choosing 2. Finally choose 3 to configure the Replication Server. This option will present you with several other menu screens.

Product	Date Installed	Date Configured
1. Replication Server		Sep 28 98 16:45

Select 1. You will then see:

CONFIGURE REPLICATION SYSTEM

1. **Install a new Replication Server**
2. **Add a database to the replication system**
3. **Upgrade an existing Replication Server**
4. **Downgrade RSSD for an existing Replication Server**
5. **Upgrade an existing database in the replication system**
6. **Enable password encryption for a Replication Server**
7. **Enable password encryption for an LTM**
8. **Alter a Replication Server configuration file password**
9. **Alter a password in an LTM configuration file**

As we are installing a new Replication Server we select 1.

NEW REPLICATION SERVER

1. **Replication Server Information**   **Incomplete**
2. **ID Server Information**   **Incomplete**

3. Replication Server System Database   Incomplete

4. Disk Partition   Incomplete

5. Remote Site Connections   Incomplete

Each item is marked incomplete. As we enter information at each menu prompt, the item will be marked complete. Begin with 1. It will ask for the Replication Server name. Enter the name and the following menu will be presented to you.

REPLICATION SERVER INFORMATION

1. RSSD Requires LTM: no

2. Is this Replication Server the ID Server?   no

3. Replication Server error log:
         /usr/sybase/repserver/install/PRS_MARKETS.log

4. Replication Server configuration file:
         /usr/sybase/repserver/install/PRS_MARKETS.cfg

5. Replication Server password encryption: no

6. Replication Server character set: iso_1

7. Replication Server language: us_english

8. Replication Server sort order: binary

9. Replication Server Interfaces Information   Complete

You can now enter the information by selecting each item in turn. There are two points worth discussion:

- The RSSD will require an LTM as the replication objects must be replicated to all Replication Servers in the domain. Even if you only have one Replication Server initially it is recommended that you define a Replication Server LTM to prepare for any future expansion of the architecture.

- The ID Server is a Replication Server which contains the ids of all Replication Servers and databases in the replication domain. This must be the first Replication Server you create in the domain.

You should have all the information to hand on the Replication Server installation sheet which you have prepared earlier. Some menu items will generate further menus, and when the menu page is complete even more menus will be displayed. Keep selecting the menu items until you have entered all of the necessary data for the installation. You will then be prompted to install the Replication Server with a y/n prompt. Press y for yes and the Replication Server will be installed. If the installation fails, the reason for the failure will be printed in the screen or in the installation log file. You can then go back into the menus to correct the error.

If you quit the installation you will have to enter all of the information from scratch when you begin again. For this reason I recommend the use of **rs_init** resource files. These allow you to input the information once, and run **rs_init** with the filename as a parameter to the -r flag. If you make a mistake in the resource file, then you can simply correct it and run **rs_init** again.

Other uses for resource files are when you are installing a number of Replication Servers or you have a large number of databases to add to an existing Replication Server. In these cases the files can be automatically generated with parameter substitution to allow very rapid installation and setup of large systems.

The rest of this section discusses resource files and how to use them. Make the effort to understand how they work as they do save you time.

Using rs_init with resource files

Replication Server can be installed using **rs_init** with the **-r** parameter and a full path name for the resource file:

rs_init -r /usr/sybase/setup/rs_install_PRS_MARKETS.rs

The installation does not require user interaction as the data is already stored in the resource file. I find this method preferable to the interactive method as it allows you to generate multiple resource files for multiple installations.

The parameters used in the resource are discussed in table 13.2.

Resource file parameter	Description
sybinit.product	This denotes the product which is to be installed (rs - Replication Server). This is internal to the **rs_init** program. All of the following parameters will now be prefixed by *rs* as this is a Replication Server install.
rs.rs_operation	The operation to be carried out.
rs.rs_idserver_name	The name of the ID server. This can be any Replication Server that has been installed, including the Replication Server currently being installed.
rs.rs_id_server_is_rs_server	
	Set this parameter to yes if this Replication Server is to be an ID server. Remember you can only have one ID server per domain.

rs.rs_idserver_user   The ID server login name for this Replication Server. This in fact can be the same for every Replication Server you install using this ID server, however the recommendation is that you have a unique login for each one to ensure you comply with best security practices.

rs.rs_idserver_pass   The password for the previous login parameter.

rs.rs_start_db_id   The start database id parameter allows you to control the range of unique database ids held in the Replication Server domain. This parameter would only be used when installing an ID server and you wanted to start the database ids from 20000 for example.

rs.rs_name   The name of the Replication Server we are installing.

rs.rs_requires_ltm   Do we require a Log Transfer Manager on the RSSD? Yes if we intend to have routes to other Replication Servers, no if not. Recommendation is to define an LTM on every RSSD.

rs.rs_rs_errorlog   The full path and name of the Replication Server log file.

rs.rs_rs_cfg_file   The full path and name of the Replication Server configuration file.

rs.rs_charset   The Replication Server character set parameter. Only change if your Replication Server uses a charset other than 'iso_1'.

rs.rs_language   The Replication Server language parameter. Only change if your Replication Server uses a language other than 'us_english'.

rs.rs_sortorder   The Replication Server sort order parameter. Only change if your Replication Server uses a sort order other than 'binary'.

rs.rs_rssd_sqlsrvr   The SQL Server where the Replication Server RSSD is kept.

rs.rs_rssd_database   The name of the RSSD database.

rs.rs_create_rssd   This parameter flags the **rs_init** program to create the RSSD in the RSSD SQL Server. Only set this to yes if you have not already created the RSSD, as it will drop and recreate it if it already exists. In practice you will create the RSSD separately.

rs.rs_rssd_sa_login   The RSSD SQL server login required for installation. This has to be a user with 'sa' role.

rs.rs_rssd_sa_pass   Set the sa_role user password here.

rs.rs_rssd_prim_user   The RSSD primary user. Used by the Replication Server to communicate with the RSSD.

rs.rs_rssd_prim_pass   The RSSD primary user password

rs.rs_rssd_maint_user   The RSSD maintenance user. Used by Replication Server to apply transactions to the replicate databases.

rs.rs_rssd_maint_pass   The RSSD maintenance user password.

rs.rs_rssd_dbo_user   The RSSD dbo user (leaving this as DEFAULT uses sa).

rs.rs_rssd_dbo_pass   Leave as DEFAULT as above.

rs.rs_rssddb_size   The RSSD database size in MB for the data segment (include for informational purposes if you have already created the RSSD).

rs.rs_rssd_log_size   The RSSD database size in MB for the log segment (include for informational purposes if you have already created the RSSD).

rs.rs_rssd_db_device_name
                               The data segment data device name (informational only if we do not use **rs_init** to create it).

rs.rs_create_rssd_database_dev
                               Do not create the device if it already exists.

rs.rs_rssd_db_device_path

                               Path of DATA device for the RSSD. (Include for informational purposes if you have already created the RSSD.)

rs.rs_rssddb_device_size   The data device size. (Include for informational purposes if you have already created the RSSD.)

rs.rs_rssd_log_device_name

The log device name. (Include for informational purposes if you have already created the RSSD.)

rs.rs_create_rssd_log_dev Do not create the log device if it already exists.

rs.rs_rssd_log_device_path

Path of LOG device for the RSSD. (Include for informational purposes if you have already created the RSSD.)

rs.rs_rssd_log_device_size

The log device size. (Include for informational purposes if you have already created the RSSD.)

rs.rs_diskp_name   Physical path and name of Stable Device.

rs.rs_diskp_lname   The logical name of the Stable Device.

rs.rs_diskp_size   The size in MB of the Stable Device (maximum is 2040).

rs.rs_diskp_vstart   The offset in MB from the beginning of the physical device for the start of the Stable Device. Not normal to use anything else but 0.

rs.rs_rs_user   The RSI user (used to create routes).

rs.rs_rs_pass   The RSI user password.

rs.ltm_name   The RSSD ltm name. The suggestion is to create an LTM for the RSSD even if it is a stand alone Replication Server as it may need to connect to other Replication Servers in the future.

rs.rs_ltm_rs_user   The user that LTMs use to connect to the Replication Server.

rs.rs_ltm_rs_pass   The ltm user password.

rs.rs_ltm_admin_user   The LTM administrator.

rs.rs_ltm_admin_pass   The LTM admin user password.

rs.do_add_id_server   This is to add the ID server to the *interfaces* file. Recommended that you always edit the *interfaces* file separately so leave this as is.

rs.rs_id_server_connect_retry_count

Number of times to try and reconnect to the ID server.

rs.rs_id_server_connect_retry_delay_time

Number of seconds to wait before retrying to connect to the ID server.

rs.rs_id_server_notes   You could put a description of the ID server here, if you wished.

rs.rs_id_server_network_protocol_list

The transport protocol for the ID server *interfaces* file entry. This is redundant if you do not use this file to add the ID server entry to the *interfaces* file. Included for informational purposes if you add the server to the *interfaces* file separately.

rs.rs_idserver_hostname   The ID server hostname. Included for informational purposes if you add the server to the *interfaces* file separately.

rs.rs_idserver_port   The ID server port number. Included for informational purposes if you add the server to the *interfaces* file separately.

rs.do_add_replication_server

Do not add the ID server to the *interfaces* file. This should be done before installing the Replication Server.

rs.rs_rs_connect_retry_count

Number of times to try and reconnect to the Replication Server.

rs.rs_rs_connect_retry_delay_time

Number of seconds to wait before retrying to connect to the Replication Server.

rs.rs_rs_notes   You could put a description of the Replication Server here, if you wished. This information is written to the server startup file.

rs.rs_rs_network_protocol_list

The transport protocol for the Replication Server *interfaces* file entry. This is redundant if you do not use this file to add the Replication Server entry to the *interfaces* file. Included for informational purposes only.

rs.rs_rs_hostname   The Replication Server hostname. Included for informational purposes if you add the server to the *interfaces* file separately.

rs.rs_rs_port   The Replication Server port number. Included for informational purposes if you add the server to the *interfaces* file separately.

rs.do_add_ltm   Do not add the LTM server to the *interfaces* file. This should be done before installing the Replication Server.

rs.rs_ltm_connect_retry_count
                             Number of times to try and reconnect to the LTM.

rs.rs_ltm_connect_retry_delay_time
                             Number of seconds to wait before retrying to connect to the LTM.

rs.rs_ltm_notes   You could put a description of the LTM here, if you wished. This information is written to the server startup file.

rs.rs_ltm_network_protocol_list
                             The transport protocol for the LTM *interfaces* file entry. This is redundant if you do not use this file to add the LTM entry to the interfaces file. Included for informational purposes if you add the server to the *interfaces* file separately.

rs.rs_ltm_hostname   The LTM server hostname. Included for informational purposes if you add the server to the *interfaces* file separately.

rs.rs_ltm_port   The LTM server port number. Included for informational purposes if you add the server to the *interfaces* file separately.

Table 13.2: Replication Server resource file parameters

Creating DSI threads

Command Line Creation

You can create DSI threads using **rs_init**, or you can create them manually. The **rs_init** method is the usual way to create threads. However, **rs_init** is best used when the database is not already known to the Replication Server as it creates the necessary replication objects such as **rs_marker** and *rs_lastcommit*.

Consider a database which receives a data feed from a Replication Server in New York and we now want to add <u>another</u> feed from a Replication Server here in London. If we run **rs_init** to do this then we run the risk of it overwriting all of the replication objects which will mess up the existing DSI feed. Consider a development server which has a DSI feed into it, and the developers insist on refreshing the database with a dump from a non replicated production system? The problem with this is that none of the replication objects will exist in the database every time the database is loaded. The options here are to create the tables and stored procedures every time you load the database, or have the objects added to the database that supplies the dumps. (Most production system DBAs will reject the latter course). In both of these cases we need to create the DSI thread connection manually using the **create connection** command.

Database already has a DSI connection

For the first example we'll create a DSI into the database that already has a feed from another Replication Server. This database will have all of the replication objects already, so we create the DSI with the **create connection** command.

Log into the replicate Replication Server and issue the command:

create connection to server_name.db_name

set error class rs_sqlserver_error_class

set function string class rs_sqlserver_function_class

set username user01

set password passwd01

This will create the new DSI thread into the database, so this database will now have two feeds, but from different Replication Servers.

Load of dump from non-replicated database

Here things are a little different. In this case the database we will be replicating into does not have any replication objects, i.e. tables or stored procedures used by the replication system. This case usually occurs when a replicated database is refreshed from a non replicated source database dump. You can also use this approach to create a DSI into a database when you do not know the 'sa' password for the replicate target server.

The objects that are required by **rs_init** when defining a database for replication are shown in table 13.3.

Tables	Stored Procedures
rs_threads	rs_update_lastcommit
rs_dbversion	rs_get_lastcommit
rs_lastcommit	rs_update_threads
	rs_initialize_threads
	rs_marker
	rs_check_repl_stat

Table 13.3: Objects created by rs_init

You can get these from an existing replicate database using **defncopy** or from the **rs_init** script files in the Replication Server script directory. I would recommend writing and keeping a creation script to create the objects as and when needed. This script will need to do the following:

- Create the maintenance user login in the server.
- Create the maintenance user in the database and grant permissions for the tables that the maintenance user requires access to.
- Create the Replication Server objects in the database.
- Grant execute on all of the stored procedures to the maintenance user in the database.
- Run **sp_setreplicate rs_marker, true**.
- Create the connection by running the **create connection** command in the replicate Replication Server.

Creating DSI using rs_init

If the database does not already have a connection to a Replication Server in the domain, you should use **rs_init** to create the connection. This is described in detail in Chapter 4. The principal reason for using **rs_init** for a new database is that it creates the objects and users required by replication. These are defined in chapter 4.

If the connection is to a primary database which requires an LTM, the **rs_init** installation creates the RUNSERVER file, error log and configuration file for the LTM. The configuration file is important as it contains the user names and passwords for the users required by the LTM and the LTM configuration values.

> **# Configuration file for Log Transfer Manager 'LTM_PLN_MKT.**
> **Created by rs_init.**
>
> **#**
>
> **SQL_server=PLN_MKT**
>
> **SQL_database=SALES_DB**
>
> **RS_source_ds=PLN_MKT**
>
> **RS_source_db=SALES_DB**
>
> **SQL_user=ltm**
>
> **SQL_pw=ltm_pw**
>
> **RS=PRS1_MKT**
>
> **RS_user=rsltm_username**
>
> **RS_pw=rsltm_pw**
>
> **LTM_admin_user=sa**
>
> **LTM_admin_pw=sa_pw**
>
> **LTM_charset=iso_1**
>
> **LTM_language=us_english**
>
> **LTM_sortorder=binary**
>
> **pwd_encrypt=0**
>
> **#**
>
> **# The parameters below have the given default values.**
>
> **#**

```
# scan_retry=15
# batch_sz=1000
# batch_ltl_cmds=on
# retry=10
# skip_ltl_cmd_err=off
# maint_cmds_to_skip=1000
# print_sproc_warning=on
```

The rest of the connection information is held in the RSSD system tables *rs_databases* and may be displayed with the **rs_helpdb** system procedure.

rs_helpdb [server_name, db_name]

rs_helpdb

dsname	dbname	dbid
controlling_prs	*errorclass*	
funcclass		
status		
PRDLN_1	lnrs1_rssd	100787
LNRS1_PRD rs_sqlserver_error_class		
rs_sqlserver_function_class		
Log Transfer is ON, Distribution is ON		
PRDLN_1	SALES_DB	100790
LNRS1_PRD rs_sqlserver_error_class		
rs_sqlserver_function_class		
Log Transfer is ON, Distribution is ON		
PRDNY_1	SALES_DB	100791
LNRS1_PRD rs_sqlserver_error_class		
rs_sqlserver_function_class		
Log Transfer is ON, Distribution is ON		

The current status of the connections from the Replication Server may be seen with the **admin show_connections**.

admin show_connections

Server	Database	User State	Owner	Spid
LNPRS_PRD		rssdprm		
	lnprs_rssd	free		
LNPRD1	rsmnt_user			
	SALES_DB	already_faded_out	DSI EXEC	71
LNPRD2	rsmnt_user			
	SALES_DB	idle	DSI EXEC	67
NYPRD1	rsmnt_user			
	MKT_DB	already_faded_out	DSI EXEC	66

connection state	number	comments
connecting	0	in the process of connecting to a server
active threads	0	established connections owned and used by
idle	4	established connections owned but not being used
being_faded_out	0	idle connections that are being closed
already_faded_out	3	idle connections that have been closed
free	1	established connections not owned by any threads
closed	56	closed connections not owned by any threads
limbo	0	connection handles in state transition
total	64	total number of connection handlers available

Resource file for setting up DSI threads

If the database is a primary database, then it will have an LTM otherwise it will have a DSI only. The resource file in table 13.4 contains all of the information needed by **rs_init** to install a DSI thread including some redundant information regarding the Replication Server interfaces files, but the last time I checked **rs_init** wouldn't work without them. As with installing a Replication Server (described above), you should create all *interfaces* file entries for replicate servers and LTMs before beginning the DSI setup. The following file was used to create a DSI thread for a primary, therefore it has an LTM and the LTM information is present. I would recommend having the LTM information present even if you do not intend to install one as the database may be upgraded to a primary at a later date, and this will ensure that all relevant information is already here. Some of this resource file is applicable to warm standby setup only. Those parameters are described below in table 13.4, but as long as you answer no to *rs.rs_db_physical_for_logical* they will be ignored. The parameter that controls the installation of an LTM is *rs.rs_requires_ltm* which can be set to yes or no regardless of the other LTM parameter settings.

Resource file parameter	Description
sybinit.release_directory	The software release directory where the Replication Server files are located.
sybinit.product	This denotes the product which is to be installed (rs - Replication Server). This is internal to the **rs_init** program. All of the following parameters will now be prefixed by *rs* as this is a Replication Server install.
rs.rs_operation	The **rs_init** operation to be carried out. In this case a database setup.
rs.rs_name	The Replication Server name.
rs.rs_rs_sa_user	The Replication Server user.
rs.rs_rs_sa_pass	The Replication Server user password.
rs.rs_ds_name	The name of the SQL server where the database resides.
rs.rs_ds_sa_user	The sa login to the SQL server.
rs.rs_ds_sa_password	The SQL server sa login password.
rs.rs_db_name	The name of the database you are adding to the Replication Server.
rs.rs_requires_ltm	This database is a primary so we want an LTM. If it is a replicate only then answer no to this question.
rs.rs_db_maint_user	The name of the maintenance user on the SQL server. This user should already exist.
rs.rs_db_maint_password	The maintenance user password.
rs.rs_db_dbo_user	The database dbo user name.
rs.rs_db_dbo_password	The database dbo password.
rs.ltm_name	The name of the LTM.
rs.rs_ltm_rs_user	The user the LTM connects to the Replication Server as.
rs.rs_ltm_rs_pass	The LTM user password.

rs.rs_ltm_admin_user   The LTM administrator.

rs.rs_ltm_admin_pass   The LTM admin password.

rs.rs_ltm_errorlog   The full path and name of the LTM log file.

rs.rs_ltm_cfg_file   The full path and name of the LTM configuration file.

rs.rs_ltm_pwd_encryption

Do we want encryption of the LTM password. Say yes for encryption. Password encryption applies only to the values shown in the configuration files. The actual login does not encrypt the password.

rs.rs_charset   The Replication Server character set.

rs.rs_language   The Replication Server language.

rs.rs_sortorder   The Replication Server sort order.

rs.rs_db_physical_for_logical

Now the interesting bit. This is for warm standby setup. If you answer no to this then the next eight parameters do not have to be altered.   Answer yes if this is to be a warm standby database.   In such a case there will be a logical connection which will have already been created.

This parameter will let us create a physical connection for that logical connection and the following parameters will decide which connection it is (the primary or the contingency, also known as the active or standby).

Warm standby is discussed in chapter 10.

rs.rs_db_active_or_standby

There are two possible answers: active or standby.

rs.rs_db_logical_ds_name   The logical data server name.

rs.rs_db_logical_db_name   The logical database name.

rs.rs_db_active_ds_name   The active SQL server physical name.

rs.rs_db_active_db_name   The active database physical name.

rs.rs_db_active_sa   The active server sa login.

rs.rs_db_active_sa_pw   The active server sa password.

rs.rs_init_by_dump   Are we initializing the warm standby with a dump and load? I usually do – see the warm standby chapter.

rs.rs_db_use_dmp_marker

Use the dump marker to initialize the warm standby? I usually do – see the warm standby chapter.

rs.do_add_replication_server

Do not add the Replication Server to the *interfaces* file. Entries to the *interfaces* file are usually better done separately.

rs.rs_rs_connect_retry_count

Number of times to try and reconnect to the Replication Server.

rs.rs_rs_connect_retry_delay_time

Number of seconds to wait before retrying to connect to the Replication Server.

rs.rs_rs_notes

You could put a description of the Replication Server here, if you wished. This information is written to the server startup file.

rs.rs_rs_network_protocol_list

The transport protocol for the Replication Server *interfaces* file entry. This is redundant if you do not use this file to add the Replication Server entry to the *interfaces* file. Included for informational purposes if you have already added the server to the *interfaces* file.

rs.rs_rs_hostname

The Replication Server hostname. Included for informational purposes if you have already added the server to the *interfaces* file.

rs.rs_rs_port

The Replication Server port number. Included for informational purposes if you have already added the server to the *interfaces* file.

rs.do_add_ltm

Do not add the LTM server to the *interfaces* file. This should be done before installing the Replication Server.

rs.rs_ltm_connect_retry_count

Number of times to try and reconnect to the LTM.

rs.rs_ltm_connect_retry_delay_time

Number of seconds to wait before retrying to connect to the LTM.

rs.rs_ltm_notes   You could put a description of the LTM here, if you wished. This information is written to the server startup file

rs.rs_ltm_network_protocol_list

The transport protocol for the LTM *interfaces* file entry. This is redundant if you do not use this file to add the LTM entry to the *interfaces* file. Included for informational purposes if you have already added the server to the *interfaces* file.

rs.rs_ltm_hostname   The LTM server hostname. Included for informational purposes only if you have already added the server to the *interfaces* file.

rs.rs_ltm_port   The LTM server port number. Included for informational purposes only if you have already added the server to the *interfaces* file. If you do not have an LTM then this can be any number.

Table13.4: DSI resource file parameters

14

Monitoring

Introduction

Each component of replication system should be monitored as part of the Replication Domain that you are supporting. There are two ways to do this. Either write the system yourself, or use an existing GUI based monitoring system. Writing your own is time consuming and expensive, but it will be tailor made and easier to customize to your own needs.

Sybase have their own monitoring system called Replication Server Manager (RSM). This is a client server system with an Open Server monitoring the replication systems and interfacing to an Open Client GUI user tool which can run on different platforms. The client tool allows you to visually display the replication system as interconnecting icons within replication domains. It also allows you to set up server events that alert you to problems. You have to write the server events trigger scripts or programs yourself but this does allow you to interface to your current alert systems. Sybase are currently deploying a new tool called SQL Central which includes a combined SQL Server and Replication Server monitoring tool.

I shall concentrate on the Replication Server monitoring: what you should be monitoring and how you can collect the information. How you actually report on the monitoring statistics I leave to you as it will be specific to your requirements. However I will try to indicate what you should be looking for and the trigger levels and events that may cause concern and merit some action.

Although you may not collect all of these in a specific Replication Server implementation, you should consider monitoring for the following:

Processes	Each Replication Server process/thread to check that it is processing transactions.
Disk space	The free and used space for the Stable Device. The free and used space in each queue and the time spent in the queue by the replication transactions.
Latency	The transaction time from source to target, the time spent in the Replication Server queues and the time since the last commit at the target server.
Memory	The Replication Server cache hit ratio and the memory pool usage plus queue reads from disk and any external swap/paging activity.
CPU activity	The Replication Server CPU usage.
Disk Activity	The I/O activity for the disks used by Replication Server.
Network activity	The network usage such as bytes transferred, packet sizes and idle time.

Replication Server Thread Processes

These can be checked by examining the output from the **admin who** command, or reading the Replication Server log. Abnormal states can be detected with either method, though I prefer a combination of both to ensure greater reliability, as some thread errors may not be reported in the Replication Server log. A script to parse the output from **admin who** should be run on a regular basis. The value in the *state* column shows the current status of a thread and an alert can be raised if this state shows a problem exists.

admin who

Spid	Name	State	Info
24	DSI EXEC	Awaiting Command	10001(1) LONDON.MARKETS
15	DSI	Awaiting Command	10001 LONDON.MARKETS
18	DIST	Active	10001 LONDON.MARKETS
21	SQT	Awaiting Wakeup	10001:1 DIST LONDON.MARKETS
12	SQM	Awaiting Message	10001:1 LONDON.MARKETS
11	SQM	Awaiting Message	10001:0 LONDON.MARKETS
26	LTM USER	Awaiting Command	LONDON.MARKETS
23	DSI EXEC	Awaiting Command	10004(1) LONDON.LONDON_RSSD
16	DSI	Awaiting Command	10004 LONDON.LONDON_RSSD
19	DIST	Active	10004 LONDON.LONDON_RSSD
22	SQT	Awaiting Wakeup	10004:1 DIST LONDON.LONDON_RSSD
10	SQM	Awaiting Message	10004:1 LONDON.LONDON_RSSD
9	SQM	Awaiting Message	10004:0 LONDON.LONDON_RSSD
25	LTM USER	Awaiting Command	LONDON.LONDON_RSSD
14	RSI	Active	MDR_RS01
13	SQM	Awaiting Message	1777001:0 MDR_RS01
	RSI USER	Active	MDR_RS01
17	dSUB	Active	
6	dCM	Awaiting Message	
8	dAIO	Awaiting Message	
20	dREC	Active	dREC
50	USER	Awaiting Command	sa
53	USER	Awaiting Command	sa
59	USER	Active	sa
5	dALARM	Awaiting Wakeup	

The *state* values are shown in table 14.1.

State	Description
Active	The thread is processing a command
Awaiting Command	The thread is waiting for a client to send a command.
Awaiting I/O	The thread is waiting for an I/O operation to finish.
Awaiting Message	The thread is waiting for a message from an Open Server message queue.

Awaiting Wakeup	The thread has posted a sleep and is waiting to be awakened.
Connecting	The thread is in the process of connecting.
Down	The thread has not started or has terminated.
Getting Lock	The thread is waiting on a mutual exclusion lock.
Inactive	The status of an RSI User thread at the destination of a route when the source Replication Server is not connected to the destination Replication Server.
Initializing	The thread is being initialized.
Suspended	The thread has been suspended by the user.

Table 14.1: State column descriptions for admin who output

The ones that you should report on are *down* and *suspended* but it will always be useful to monitor *reading disk* and *getting lock*. *Reading disk* is often a pointer to a memory shortage and I have noticed that long periods in a state of *getting lock* can be an indication of a hung thread.

LTM processes

It is extremely important to monitor the LTMs. The log of a primary database cannot be truncated if the replication truncation pointer is not being incremented when rows are transferred to the Replication Server. This will cause the log to fill up until processes become suspended or abort. If this does happen, resolve the LTM problem before un-suspending the log. Once the LTM is running, log rows will be transferred and the log can be dumped to truncate it. When you are certain that the LTM is sending rows to the Replication Server, it will be safe to un-suspend the log and allow transactions to continue against the primary, providing you make provision to dump the log. Ideally you will have spotted the problem long before it fills the log.

The Unix level process can be checked to ensure that the LTM process is running. You can do this simply by logging in to it, then logging out. A successful login will indicate the process itself is healthy, but it will not tell you whether it is delivering transactions to the Replication Server. To do that, you will need to examine the output of the **admin who, sqm** command several times to ensure the inbound queue from the LTM is moving.

admin who, sqm

Spid	State		Info		Duplicates
	Writes	Reads	Bytes	B Writes	B Filled
	B Reads	B Cache	Save_Int:Seg		
	First Seg.Block		Last Seg.Block		
	Next Read	Readers	Truncs		
9	Awaiting Message		100512:0 LNRSSD_MKT.lnrssd_mkt		0
	0	0	0	0	0
	0	0	240:0		
	0.1		0.0		
	0.1.0	1	1		
10	Awaiting Message		100512:1 LNRSSD_MKT.lnrssd_mkt		80
	104442	104748	34712951	16321	28
	16366	16262	0:2773		
	2773.46		2773.46		
	2773.47.0	1	1		

If the queue is active, i.e. there are messages currently being processed in that queue, then the *Last seg* value will be greater than the *First seg* value and the *Next read* value will be between these two values. Run the **admin who, sqm** command again and note the values. If the queue is being processed, then the *Next read* value will have increased, or if the queue messages are small, the *First seg* and *Last seg* will have increased as the queue moves on.

If the difference between the *First seg* value and the *Last seg* value is large, then this indicates that the Replication Server is processing a large batch of commands. You can confirm this with an **admin who, sqt**. The troubleshooting chapter 15 discusses this in detail.

The important section of the output is:

admin who, sqt

SQM Blocked	First Trans
1	st:R,cmds:3,qid:50:57:24
1	st:O,cmds:1,qid:404:52:46

This shows the transaction in a number of states corresponding to where it is being processed in the Replication Server queue.

O   Open command being read in by the LTM

C   Closed command for which the **commit tran** command has been read and the command is now being processed by the DSI.

R   Read command which has been completely processed by the DSI and will be deleted after its *save interval*.

The *cmnds* figure indicates how large the transaction is and consequently how long it will take for the DSI to process the transaction and update the *rs_lastcommit* table.

I have seen situations where a LTM process checks out OK but there are no messages being delivered to the Replication Server. Restarting the LTM seems to fix this in most cases and the common factors in these cases are that the SQL Server has been bounced or there has been a network outage. Although the LTM log indicated a successful reconnection to the SQL Server, no messages were being delivered.

To confuse the issue further: an LTM failure to process transactions does not happen every time! Restarting a SQL Server without restarting the relevant LTM does not mean that replication will fail. In most cases it does not, so how do we know when there is a problem?

The answer is to set up some kind of 'heartbeat' monitoring that will tell you when the LTM is moving transactions. Create a table in the primary and replicate databases and regularly apply a number of inserts to the table. Check that these have moved the replication truncation point and been applied to the replicate database. This will force replication even when there is no business activity. You can check delivery at the replicate database from *rs_lastcommit*.

select origin, origin_time, dest_commit_time from rs_lastcommit

or simply monitor the *sqm* queue movement as above.

Hang on, I hear you say. Isn't that the same as latency monitoring?

Well yes it is, but here we are only trying to establish whether data is being transferred, we don't really care about the length of time taken. Of course we would have to set a time threshold on our test, but what will that be? Remember that during batch processing we will have significant increases in latency so the time threshold in a test like this will be dependent on the system it is running on and the position in the business cycle.

What I am trying to say here is that there is no easy way to monitor data flow in a Replication Server. It comes from knowing your system and fine tuning the monitoring to suit the system. Sometimes events out of the ordinary will cause a problem and people will get upset. All you can do is see whether you can avoid it happening again.

I would suggest a 30 minute heartbeat to check that the LTM is still processing transactions. If not, a simple restart of the LTM will normally start the queue moving. If this does not work you need to investigate further.

Replication server log files

A log checking program is a useful thing to have on your system. You can read all new lines added to the file then report on anything out of the ordinary. In other words you can write a program that ignores common messages or unimportant errors and warnings, but does report everything else. The same methodology can be used on LTM log files, although they tend not to produce as much useful information as the Replication Server log.

Primary SQL Server processes

The host level process should be checked along with a login (preferably using the LTM user) to ensure that the server is available and database log records can be processed. The Replication Server thread process checks should confirm a problem. As a Replication Server DBA you may not be responsible for the primary data servers, therefore you should ensure that the SQL Server DBA lets you know of any changes they intend to make or if they intend to shut down the server at any time. Your alarm bells will ring if they shutdown without telling you and this can cause unnecessary wake ups and phone calls.

A good tip here is to allow a delay between finding a SQL Server is not responding and reporting the fact to you. You should always check at least twice to avoid being alerted for minor network outages. There is nothing worse than a 2 am call and the server is up and running when you login. Most definitely you should implement a time delay on the LTMs – 5 minutes is good enough – before any paging starts.

Replicate SQL Server processes

The host level process should be checked along with a login (preferably using the maintenance user) to ensure that the server is available and records can be processed. The Replication Server thread process checks should confirm a problem. Again the checks should conform to the Primary SQL Server process model regarding reporting.

DSI

Efficient monitoring of DSI threads will ensure delivery of data to replicate databases with the minimum of interruption. Outbound queues should be large enough to tolerate long outages ensuring the primary can keep on working. Transactions will be queued until the DSI thread is able to resume when they will be applied to the replicate database.

Spotting this in time saves the embarrassment of having the replicate database users noticing the lack of 'up to date' data in their database, and calling you up to ask why. Monitor the DSI thread with an **admin who, sqm** and check the *state* column as discussed earlier.

RSI

Similarly when you are using routes RSI threads are important as they serve other Replication Servers which in turn will be distributing data to many replicate clients. A single RSI thread going down will affect everything down the line. This is usually caused by a network problem, or a problem with the Replication Server to which the route connects.

DIST

This is less of a problem as it will be unusual for the DIST thread to give you a problem independently of the LTM/DSI threads. Monitoring of the **admin who** output will catch when these are down.

Restarting a failed thread

If you find that a thread is suspended you can restart it with one of the following commands once you have corrected the problem. A thread which is *down* will need a bounce of the Replication Server.

DSI

> **resume connection to server_name.db_name**
> **[skip transaction]**

RSI

> **resume route to RS_name**

DIST

resume distributor server_name.db_name

Disk Space

Stable Device

Monitor how full the Stable Device is. This can give advance warning of problems not shown by other errors. Sometimes a Replication Server DSI may not be delivering messages due to it being suspended for maintenance purposes or due to some other problem. This will cause the Stable Device to fill up and is a good reason why you should over estimate the size of your Stable Device. A DSI thread may have to be out of action for some time and you will wish to keep the primary working as it may be distributing the data to several replicates. Set a sensible threshold for monitoring depending on the individual setup of your replication system and throughput of data. Each queue on a Stable Device will take up 1Mb of queue space when empty, so if you have 30 DSI connections your Stable Device will be permanently 30MB full. This is why I recommend having a very large Stable Device, something in the order of at least 2GB on a Unix machine. If you have high save intervals set on DSI queues remember that those queues will require even greater storage space as the transactions are kept after delivery. A save interval of 2 to 3 hours can dramatically increase the space needed for a Stable Device.

If your Stable Device does fill up, don't panic, you can add another partition to it which will allow the Replication Server to continue processing. I usually set aside a spare raw device for such emergencies. If you cannot afford the luxury of having an unused partition which will hardly ever, or maybe even never be used, you can add a temporary partition on a Unix filesystem. I must stress however, that this should be for emergencies only, and you should drop the partition when the crisis has passed. To add a new partition use the **add partition** command and to drop a partition use the **drop partition** command. When you drop a partition the Replication Server stops using it immediately and drops it once it is empty. You need to remove the operating system file independently.

Individual queue sizes

As well as the total disk space it is worth checking the individual queue sizes. The total space may be below your threshold but a single queue may be very large indicating a possible problem with the specific replication.

You check the queue sizes in the RSSD using **rs_helppartition**:

rs_helppartition MDR_RS01_SD

Information for stable device: 'MDR_RS01_SD' on 'MDR_RS01'.

This device is active.

Physical Name	Partition ID
/dev/MDR_RS01/QUEUE_0	101

Partition Size (MB)	Segments Allocated (MB)
2000	6

Inbound Database Queue(s) on this partition:

Connection Name	Number of Segments
MADRID.MARKETS	1

Outbound Database Queue(s) on this partition:

Connection Name	Number of Segments
MADRID.MARKETS	1

Outbound Replication Server Queue(s) on this partition:

Connection Name	Number of Segments
LND_RS01	1

Any decisions on thresholds or action for queue sizes are completely application dependent but a single queue which uses more than 50% of the Stable Device sounds like a good candidate for investigation.

Latency

Before we discuss latency monitoring, let me make it clear that this is not a 'catch all' for alerting the DBA to a Replication Server problem. Latency should be treated as a business requirement for data delivery within defined time bands. To someone who doesn't understand how Replication Server works latency checking seems like the ideal method of detecting a problem. After all, if latency increases dramatically then there must be a problem must there not? Well yes and no is the answer to that.

There are two types of latency that can be monitored: replication latency and queue latency.

Replication Latency

Replication latency is the difference between the *origin_time* date in the primary database and the *dest_commit_time* date in the replicate database allowing for time zone correction. Replication latency will tell you how long it took for a transaction in the primary database to be applied to the replicate database.

This is easily checked from the *rs_lastcommit* on the replicate database.

select origin, origin_time, dest_commit_time from rs_lastcommit

This is usually sufficient for the latency between primary and replicate. However treat this output with care. If you see a large time difference between the primary commit and the destination commit time but the transactions are still being processed (**admin who, sqm** or **admin who, sqt**) it usually indicates another problem such as too little memory or the transactions are too large.

Queue Latency

Queue latency is the age of the first block in a Stable Device. This block will remain the first block in the queue until the transaction it is a part of is either committed or rolled back and the block is processed. You can check this with an **admin who, sqm**.

Both types of latency monitoring have their uses, but both will increase in value during batch processing so a replication latency of ten to fifteen seconds during normal online transaction processing can suddenly increase to several minutes or even hours during a large batch job. Queue latency will also increase if large transactions are being processed by the replication system. A queue latency of four to ten seconds can suddenly become fifteen to thirty minutes.

Latency monitoring is useful to keep control of business service levels but it cannot be used by itself to determine the problem or where it is occurring. I find that the most common use of latency monitoring is as part of a heartbeat to check delivery or on an ad-hoc basis in response to a specific question on replication delays.

It is far better to monitor the individual components of a replication system (as explained earlier in the chapter) and be alerted when a component has a problem. This will alert you faster and will point you to the location of the problem straight away.

Memory

Replication Server Memory

Replication Server memory is difficult to judge.

The Replication Server memory is controlled by the *memory_max* configuration parameter which defaults to 3M. At start-up 66% of this is allocated to memory segment pools which have fixed block sizes of 256 bytes, 1K, 4K, 16K and 64K. The Replication Server memory is divided into 5 equal segment pools. For example if we leave *memory_max* at the default of 3M, then Replication Server will allocate 66% of this (2,076,162 bytes) to be split between the five segment pools i.e. 415,232 bytes each. The appropriate number of segments are then allocated to each of the pools. This is discussed in detail in chapter 2.

When Replication Server requests a segment of a specific size, it is allocated from the appropriate segment pool. If there are no available segments in the pool, the pool is expanded from the reserved memory (the remaining 34% left at start-up). If there is no free reserved memory an error is written to the log. If this becomes frequent, you need to seriously consider increasing the memory available to the Replication Server. The **admin statistics, mem** command shows the current allocation of memory to Replication Server:

admin statistics, mem

Segment_Size	Number_of_Segments	Number_Allocated
256	10813	3585
1024	2703	2703
4096	675	125

16384	168	82
65520	42	42
65520	21	21
65520	21	11
1024	1351	1351
16384	84	4
1024	1351	1351

A particular problem with the Replication Server memory is when the transaction in the queue does not fit into the available cache and has to be written to disk. The larger the transaction the bigger the problem. This can easily cause an increase in the transaction latency and both latency measures will indicate a delay. The transaction will not show as committed on *rs_lastcommit* until the complete transaction is committed in the replicate database. Also, if you see *reading from disk* on an **admin who** you should consider looking at memory usage.

An **admin who, sqt** is the best command to show how big the transaction is and what stage it is currently in.

admin who, sqt

Spid	State	Info		
21	Awaiting Wakeup	10001:1	DIST LONDON.MARKETS	
22	Awaiting Wakeup	10004:1	DIST LONDON.LONDON_RSSD	
15	Awaiting Command	10001	LONDON.MARKETS	
16	Awaiting Command	10004	LONDON.LONDON_RSSD	

Closed	Read	Open	Trunc	Removed	Full
0	17	1	18	0	0
0	0	1	1	0	0
0	0	0	0	0	0
0	0	0	0	0	0

SQM Blocked	First Trans
1	st:R,cmds:3,qid:50:57:24
1	st:O,cmds:38341,qid:404:52:46

Parsed	SQM Reader	Change Oqids	Detect Orphans
0	0	0	0
0	0	0	0
0	0	0	1
0	0	0	1

In this output we have two threads processing a small command (*cmds* = 3) and a large command (*cmds* = 38431). In the case of the small command it is in the Read status which means that it has been applied by the DSI to the target database. In the case of the large command it is Open which means that it has not yet been fully read in to the Replication Server queue by the LTM and therefore has not yet commenced DSI processing against the target database.

If you cannot reduce the transaction size, try parallel DSI threads as these process large transactions differently. Normal DSI processing of a transaction does not start until the **commit tran** command has been received. With parallel DSIs you can specify a large transaction size and commands above this limit will be processed by the DSI before the **commit tran** is received. It does not alter processing time but it can reduce the memory requirement as the complete transaction does not have to be read in before it can start being written to the replicate database.

LTM Memory

As discussed in chapter 2, allocation of memory by the LTM can be a little strange as it assumes that the largest transaction that it has processed is the amount of memory that it needs. So, if you have a very large transaction being replicated, the LTM will have allocated memory to process this and will retain this memory even although the subsequent transactions are smaller. If you see LTM memory usage as a problem simply restart the LTM and it should free memory – as long as the large transaction is not still being processed.

CPU Usage

Not a lot to be done here: a simple check of the CPU usage for the Replication Server process. How you do this depends on the Operating System you are running but a simple **top** command in Unix will show you all that you need. The threshold you set will depend on what else is running on the hardware.

Disk activity

As with CPU usage this is best monitored as the Operating System level and a simple **vmstat** command in Unix will show you the disk activity for the Replication Server Stable Device disks. Again it depends on what else is running on the hardware but any queues for the Replication Server disks should be investigated. And do not forget the RSSD disk devices as the RSSD can have a high access rate.

Network activity

Operating system commands are best for this and you need something that will show bytes transferred, packet usage and collisions. On Unix **netstat** should provide what you need. This information is best used as a back-up when other monitoring shows a problem and you are looking for a bottleneck. A long latency may be due to network outages or extremely high network activity.

15

Troubleshooting

Introduction

Replication Server is usually very reliable and robust. However, when something does go wrong, it can be difficult and time consuming to fix. Most day to day problems encountered will be easy to fix. They will be the simple things requiring a minimum amount of time and effort. Some problems though, such as replication recovery, can take hours to put right, and will involve down time to the system. The secret is to install efficient monitoring procedures to warn well in advance of any potential show stoppers. You should be prepared for the worst, and develop reliable recovery plans.

Do not hesitate to bounce a Replication Server component if messages are not being delivered. Restarting an LTM, DSI thread or even the Replication Server will often get things moving and you can then investigate the problem with less pressure on you.

The key to successful fault finding and repair is gaining a good understanding of what exactly happens to a transaction in all stages of its journey from the primary to the replicate, and learning how to interrogate the Replication Server in order to achieve this.

One of the most important tools is the errorlog. This will almost always contain a message indicating that there is a problem. Use this as a starting point to begin the fault finding process. If there isn't a message in the errorlog and you think there is a problem then you will have to analyze the replication system, pinpoint which part you suspect and run tests to prove your suspicions.

What commonly goes wrong?

The most common problem encountered in day to day support of a Replication Server system is the suspension of a DSI thread or an RSI route. DSI threads can go down for a number of reasons: the most common being network outages. This one is easy, the connection to the database will resume itself when the network comes back up. Other reasons and fixes are outlined below.

Duplicate row in replicate database

This occurs when the Replication Server delivers a row to a server with a unique primary key combination that already exists. In a well-designed system this should never happen, but unfortunately it does. The reason is usually because of user activity on the replicate database inserting a row which is subsequently replicated from the primary. Fixing this comes down to two choices. Do you keep the row that is already there, or remove it and replace it with the row that the Replication Server is trying to insert? You must bear in mind that although the primary keys are the same, other columns in the transaction row may contain different data. In the interests of consistency between primary and replicate, the replicate row should be removed, and the primary row inserted. Leaving the replicate row as it is will cause the primary and replicate rows to be out of step. The commands for resuming a connection in both cases are shown below.

To keep the primary row, delete the replicate row from the replicate database and resume the connection with the **resume connection** command in the Replication Server.

resume connection to replicate_rs.replicate_db

To keep the current replicate row you must tell the Replication Server to resume the connection and not insert the row in the DSI queue.

resume connection to replicate_rs.replicate_db skip transaction

When you issue this command, the **skip transaction** clause removes the transaction from the queue and stores it in the exceptions log, where it can be retrieved if necessary. The exceptions log is discussed in more detail in chapter 4.

Replicate database or log full

As a Replication Server administrator, you may not be responsible for monitoring the replicate database servers. Whether it is your problem or not, the replicate database will need to have the log enlarged or truncated or the database enlarged. When the replicate database problem is resolved, the connection can be resumed with the **resume connection** command.

Maintenance user cannot access replicate database

This can happen for a variety of reasons, the most common being the maintenance user does not have the correct permissions on the replicate table, or the maintenance user password is incorrect. This should never happen on a production system, but is a frequent problem on development servers. Replicate data server administrators should never alter the permissions or password of a maintenance user without coordinating any such change with the Replication Server administrator. Common sense you might say, but most data server administrators will not be aware they are causing a problem, and some are very big on regular password updates. If this problem arises, the Replication Server will have detailed error messages in the log, stating the SQL server error message. To fix this you can either have the maintenance user password reset to what it was originally, or you can change the password at the Replication Server with the following command.

alter user maint_user_name set password new_password

Sometimes the replicate database may be altered, e.g. a table definition may be changed to add or remove columns. If this is the case, the replication definition and subscriptions for that table will not match the new table definition, and if the table was dropped and recreated the permissions for the maintenance user will have to be granted on the new table. This is a common 'gotcha' on systems under development, and can happen on production systems when new releases of a database are rolled out. This can be avoided if procedures are in place to ensure that no changes are made to any system without coordinating those changes with the Replication Server administrator.

Troubleshooting Commands

Replication Server Queue and Thread States

To diagnose a problem we need information as to the state of a Replication Server. The **admin who** command shows the state of all of the threads, both inbound to and outbound from a Replication Server.

admin who

Spid	Name	State	Info
24	DSI EXEC	Awaiting Command	10001(1) LONDON.MARKETS
15	DSI	Awaiting Command	10001 LONDON.MARKETS
18	DIST	Active	10001 LONDON.MARKETS
21	SQT	Awaiting Wakeup	10001:1 DIST LONDON.MARKETS
12	SQM	Awaiting Message	10001:1 LONDON.MARKETS
11	SQM	Awaiting Message	10001:0 LONDON.MARKETS
26	LTM USER	Awaiting Command	LONDON.MARKETS
23	DSI EXEC	Awaiting Command	10004(1) LONDON.LONDON_RSSD
16	DSI	Awaiting Command	10004 LONDON.LONDON_RSSD
19	DIST	Active	10004 LONDON.LONDON_RSSD
22	SQT	Awaiting Wakeup	10004:1 DIST LONDON.LONDON_RSSD
10	SQM	Awaiting Message	10004:1 LONDON.LONDON_RSSD
9	SQM	Awaiting Message	10004:0 LONDON.LONDON_RSSD
25	LTM USER	Awaiting Command	LONDON.LONDON_RSSD
14	RSI	Active	MDR_RS01
13	SQM	Awaiting Message	1777001:0 MDR_RS01
	RSI USER	Active	MDR_RS01
17	dSUB	Active	
6	dCM	Awaiting Message	
8	dAIO	Awaiting Message	
20	dREC	Active	dREC
50	USER	Awaiting Command	sa
53	USER	Awaiting Command	sa
59	USER	Active	sa
5	dALARM	Awaiting Wakeup	

This shows you the state of all Replication Server threads. The example above shows a Replication Server in the normal (active) state.

The **admin who** command can take a supplementary parameter which gives more specific information regarding individual thread types. The syntax is:

admin who,

and the parameters are:

rsi	shows route thread information
dsi	shows database connection thread information
sqm	shows stable queue manager statistics
sqt	shows transaction manager statistics
dist	shows distributor thread information

admin who, rsi

This command shows information regarding the transfer of data across RSI routes to other Replication Servers. There will be an output row for each RSI route. This is not particularly useful in fault finding except to show that bytes are being moved from one Replication Server to another.

Spid	State	Info
14	Awaiting Wakeup	MDR_RS1

Packets Sent	Bytes Sent	Blocking Reads
13884.000000	18007016.000000	2570

Locator Sent
0x0000000000000000000000000000000000000000000000000000000000a600340002

Locator Deleted
0x0000000000000000000000000000000000000000000000000000000000a600340002

admin who, dsi

The **dsi** parameter shows information on the transfer of data across a connection to a replicate database. The output shows the connection configuration parameters and some information on the transactions processed.

Spid	State	Info
15	Awaiting Command	10001 LONDON.MARKETS
16	Awaiting Command	10004 LONDON.LONDON_RSSD

Maintenance User	Xact_retry_times	Batch
rsmnt_summit	3	on
rssdmnt	3	on

Cmd_batch_size	Xact_group_size	Dump_load	Max_cmds_to_log	Xacts_read
8192	65536	off	-1	0
8192	65536	off	-1	286

Xacts_ignored	Xacts_skipped	Xacts_succeeded
0	0	0
36	0	4

Xacts_failed	Xacts_retried	Current Origin DB
0	0	0
0	0	10002

Current Origin QID
0x00000000000000000000000000000000000000000000000000000000000000000000
0x00000001000cb4490000b8110004ffffffff000000008c480098402300000000000000001

Subscription Name
NULL
NULL

Sub Command
NULL
NULL

Current Secondary QID
NULL
NULL

Cmds_read	Cmds_parsed_by_sqt
0	0
0	0

IgnoringStatus	Xacts_Sec_ignored
Applying	0
Applying	0

GroupingStatus
on
on

TriggerStatus
on
on

ReplStatus	NumThreads	NumLargeThreads
on	1	0
on	1	0

LargeThreshold	CacheSize	Serialization
100	0	wait_for_commit
100	0	wait_for_commit

admin who, sqm

The **sqm** parameter is very useful for monitoring the movement of messages in the various queues. Using this command you can determine whether messages are being written to and read from the stable device queues. The useful columns in this output are the *First seg*, *Last seg* and *Next read*. They show the active part of the queue. This shows the location of the beginning, the end, and the current position in the queue that the sqm thread is reading from or writing to.

admin who, sqm

Spid	State		Info		Duplicates
	Writes	*Reads*	*Bytes*	*B Writes*	*B Filled*
	B Reads	*B Cache*	*Save_Int:Seg*		
	First Seg.Block		*Last Seg.Block*		
	Next Read	*Readers*		*Truncs*	
9	Awaiting Message		100512:0 LNRSSD_MKT.lnrssd_mkt		0
	0	*0*	*0*	*0*	*0*
	0	0	240:0		
	0.1		*0.0*		
	0.1.0	1		1	
10	Awaiting Message		100512:1 LNRSSD_MKT.lnrssd_mkt		80
	104442	*104748*	*34712951*	*16321*	*28*
	16366	16262	0:2773		
	2773.46		*2773.46*		
	2773.47.0	1		1	

Say we have a problem where we think messages are not being delivered, i.e. latency has increased but all our DSI threads and routes report as active. To prove that the Replication Server is moving messages we need to look at the queue we are concerned about. Run **admin who, sqm** and note the values for the *First seg, Last seg* and *Next read*. If the queue is active, i.e. there are messages currently being processed in that queue, then the *Last seg* value will be greater than the *First seg* value and the *Next read* value will be in between these two values. Run the **admin who, sqm** command again and note the values. If the queue is being processed, then the *Next read* value will have increased, or if the queue messages are small, the *First seg* and *Last seg* will have increased as the queue moves on.

If the difference between the *First seg* value and the *Last seg* value is large, then this indicates that the Replication Server is processing a large batch of commands. We shall see more of this later in the chapter when we look at some example problems.

admin who, sqt

The **sqt** parameter shows the state of the stable queue transaction managers.

admin who, sqt

Spid	State	Info
21	Awaiting Wakeup	10001:1 DIST LONDON.MARKETS
22	Awaiting Wakeup	10004:1 DIST LONDON.LONDON_RSSD
15	Awaiting Command	10001 LONDON.MARKETS
16	Awaiting Command	10004 LONDON.LONDON_RSSD

Closed	Read	Open	Trunc	Removed	Full
0	17	1	18	0	0
0	0	1	1	0	0
0	0	0	0	0	0
0	0	0	0	0	0

SQM Blocked	First Trans
1	st:R,cmds:3,qid:50:57:24
1	st:O,cmds:1,qid:404:52:46

Parsed	SQM Reader	Change Oqids	Detect Orphans
0	0	0	0
0	0	0	0
0	0	0	1
0	0	0	1

The interesting part of this output is the *First Trans* column. This shows the following information:

- The transaction state O open, C closed, R read or D deleted. (This is prefixed by st:)

  A read transaction is one that has been completely processed by the DSI and will be deleted after its *save interval*.

  An open transaction is one that is currently being written to i.e. has not received a **commit** or **rollback tran**.

  A closed transaction has been completely written to the replicate database and an acknowledgement has been received.

- The number of commands in the first transaction. (This is prefixed by cmds:)

- The queue id and segment, block and row information. (This is prefixed by qid:)

If an open transaction is currently being processed, repeated running of the **admin who, sqt** command will show the segment block and row information.

The open transaction is the one you need to look for when fault finding. If the same open transaction is shown over a period of time, it may be indicative of a problem with the transaction. For example, if a command was issued on a server, and the client process was disconnected before issuing a commit transaction, the transaction would never be closed, therefore the Replication Server could not process any more messages on that inbound queue. The queue would fill up with new incoming messages, but they could not be processed as the transaction manager would still be waiting to receive the **commit tran** for this transaction.

However care should be taken with this approach as the transaction could simply be a very large batch. Therefore the **admin who, sqt** should be used in conjunction with the **admin who, sqm** command to determine whether the queue is moving.

admin who, dist

The **dist** parameter shows statistics from the distributor threads. These threads examine transactions and pass them onto the relevant outbound queues, depending on the subscription information.

admin who, dist

Spid	State	Info
18	Active	10001 LONDON.MARKETS
19	Active	10004 LONDON.LONDON_RSSD

PrimarySite	Type	Status
10001	P	Normal
10004	P	Normal

PendingCmds	SqtBlocked	Duplicates	TransProcessed	CmdsProcessed
0	1	0	13234	54015
0	1	0	9805	28909

MaintUserCmds	NoRepdefCmds	CmdsIgnored	CmdMarkers
0	0	0	309
0	0	0	0

This does not really provide any significant assistance for troubleshooting and it's unlikely that you will use it much. A high number of duplicates can indicate a problem with the data in the queues but it is more likely to be a normal restart situation. The breakdown of the command types can be interesting as *CmdsIgnored* can indicate a problem with the replication definition to subscription matching but it is more likely that you will catch this from the Replication Server errorlog warning messages.

Stable Device Usage

You can also get overall disk space usage figures from the Replication Server with the **admin disk_space** command.

admin disk_space

Partition Logical	Part.Id	Total Segs	Used Segs
State			
/dev/PRS2_FIODY/QUEUE_02			
QUEUE_02 102		2040	602
ON-LINE//			
/dev/PRS2_FIODY/QUEUE_01			
QUEUE_01 103		2040	0
ON-LINE//			

This is more of a summary which gives a quick check on overall Stable Device usage. If you find that the *UsedSegs* is high use **rs_helppartition** to determine which queue is using up the space.

The system procedure **rs_helppartition** provides useful information on the Stable Device usage. This is run from the RSSD.

rs_helppartition <device_name>

Run this command to see which queues are causing the stable device to fill up. If you don't supply a parameter then it gives the totals for each stable device you have. Supplying a device name as a parameter will return statistics on each queue held on the device.

rs_helppartition

Displaying all partitions known to 'MDR_RS01'.

Logical Name	Size (MB)	Segments Allocated (MB)
MDR_RS01_SD	2000	6

rs_helppartition MDR_RS01_SD

Information for stable device: 'MDR_RS01_SD' on 'MDR_RS01'.

This device is active.

Physical Name	Partition ID
/dev/MDR_RS01/QUEUE_0	101

Partition Size (MB)	Segments Allocated (MB)
2000	6

Inbound Database Queue(s) on this partition:

Connection Name	Number of Segments
MADRID.MARKETS	1

Outbound Database Queue(s) on this partition:

Connection Name	Number of Segments
MADRID.MARKETS	1

Outbound Replication Server Queue(s) on this partition:

Connection Name	Number of Segments
LND_RS01	1

The specific queue output is particularly helpful as it shows which queues are using the Stable Device and may indicate a problem with a DSI/RSI thread which appears to be running correctly but is not draining the queue.

Analyzing Problems

DSI Suspended

Let's say we have a monitoring system keeping watch over our replication system, and it alerts us to a suspect DSI thread. We now have to identify the DSI thread (or threads) involved, and resolve the problem.

Let us start by examining the Replication Server threads and the error log. Log onto the Replication Server host and to the Replication Server itself. Now we run the **admin who** command to show us the state of the server thread processes.

The following shows that the *MADRID.MARKETS DSI* thread is suspended.

admin who

Spid	Name	State	Info
	DSI EXEC	Suspended	10003(1) MADRID.MARKETS
	DSI	Suspended	10003 MADRID.MARKETS
18	DIST	Active	10003 MADRID.MARKETS
21	SQT	Awaiting Wakeup	10003:1 DIST MADRID.MARKETS
12	SQM	Awaiting Message	10003:1 MADRID.MARKETS
11	SQM	Awaiting Message	10003:0 MADRID.MARKETS
26	LTM USER	Awaiting Command	MADRID.MARKETS
23	DSI EXEC	Awaiting Command	10004(1) LONDON.LONDON_RSSD
16	DSI	Awaiting Command	10004 LONDON.LONDON_RSSD
19	DIST	Active	10004 LONDON.LONDON_RSSD
22	SQT	Awaiting Wakeup	10004:1 DIST LONDON.LONDON_RSSD
10	SQM	Awaiting Message	10004:1 LONDON.LONDON_RSSD
9	SQM	Awaiting Message	10004:0 LONDON.LONDON_RSSD
25	LTM USER	Awaiting Command	LONDON.LONDON_RSSD
14	RSI	Active	MDR_RS01
13	SQM	Awaiting Message	1777001:0 MDR_RS01
	RSI USER	Active	MDR_RS01
17	dSUB	Active	
6	dCM	Awaiting Message	
8	dAIO	Awaiting Message	
20	dREC	Active	dREC

50	USER	Awaiting Command	sa
53	USER	Awaiting Command	sa
59	USER	Active	sa
5	dALARM	Awaiting Wakeup	

You could use the **admin who_is_down** command to display only the processes which are not running.

admin who_is_down

Spid	Name	State	Info
	DSI EXEC	Suspended	10003(1) MADRID.MARKETS
	DSI	Suspended	10003 MADRID.MARKETS

If we look at the state column, we can see that this shows the problem is the DSI thread for the MADRID.MARKETS thread which is suspended. The DSI has been suspended, either by the system, because of an error, or by the Replication Server administrator. By checking the log file for the Replication Server you should see an error relating to the suspended thread. Here are the Replication Server errorlog contents.

I. 97/02/20 11:08:46. A grouped transaction of 4 individual transactions has failed in database 'MADRID.MARKETS'. Each transaction in the group will be executed individually.

E. 97/02/20 11:08:47. ERROR #1028 DSI EXEC(10003(1) MADRID.MARKETS) - dsiqmint.c(2361)

   Message from server: Message: 2601, State 3, Severity 14 — 'Attempt to insert duplicate key row in object 'ref' with unique index 'AccountKey''.

I. 97/02/20 11:08:47. Message from server: Message: 3621, State 0, Severity 10 — 'Command has been aborted.'.

H. 97/02/20 11:08:47. THREAD FATAL ERROR #5049 DSI EXEC(10003(1) MADRID.MARKETS) - dsiqmint.c(2368)

   The DSI thread for database 'MADRID.MARKETS' is being shutdown. DSI received data server error #2601 which is mapped to STOP_REPLICATION. See logged data server errors for more information. The data server error was caused by output command #1 mapped from input command #2 of the failed transaction.

I. 97/02/20 11:08:47. The DSI thread for database 'MADRID.MARKETS' is shutdown.

The DSI has been suspended because it tried to insert a duplicate row into the replicate database. As can be seen, this is mapped to STOP REPLICATION within the errorclass, so has suspended the DSI thread. Now we know what the problem is. Fixing this is a matter of deciding which row to keep; the replicated row from the primary or the existing row in the replicate database. To keep the replicate row, skip the transaction when resuming the connection. To apply the primary row, delete the row from the replicate and resume the connection. Of course, you will need to ascertain why there is a duplicate in the first place. Before you skip a row, you can log it into the exceptions log and examine it. This will let you compare it to the row currently in the replicate. A point to note here is that the Replication Server cannot insert the row because of a duplicate primary key. The other data in the row may have changed, and deleting this row will lose the changes. So check with the user before making the decision to delete the existing row.

Logging the transaction into the exceptions log is done with the **sysadmin log_first_tran** command.

sysadmin log_first_tran

This enters the transaction into the *rs_exceptions* table where we can examine it with the RSSD stored procedure **rs_helpexception**. Run **rs_helpexception** without a parameter. This will give you a list of transactions currently held in the exceptions log.

rs_helpexception

Summary of Transactions on 'PRS_MKT'

Total # of Logged Transactions = 4

Xact ID	Org Site	Org User	Org Date	Dest Site	#Recs/Xact
159	PDS_MKT.report	report	Feb 26 1999	PDS_MKT_REP.report	4678
160	PDS_MKT.ref	ref	Feb 28 1999	PDS_MKT_REP.ref	3
161	PDS_MKT.ref	ref	Feb 28 1999	PDS_MKT_REP.ref	3
162	PDS_MKT.ref	ref	Feb 28 1999	PDS_MKT_REP.ref	3

For detailed information on a logged xact., type 'rs_helpexception {Xact ID}'

The transaction just logged will be the last on the list i.e. with the highest transaction id. Now run **rs_helpexception** with the *v* parameter. This will show the SQL for the transaction.

rs_helpexception 162, v

Detailed Summary of Transaction # 162 on 'PRS_MARKETS'

Origin Site	Origin User	Org. Commit Date	#Cmds in Xact
PDS_MKT.ref	ref_dbo	Feb 28 1999 2:18	3

Dest. Site	Dest. User	Date Logged
PDS_MKT_REP.ref	report_rs_maint	Feb 28 1999 11:56

This transaction was skipped due to a 'resume connection' command with the 'skip transaction' option.

Rejected Records

textval

A0110 05iso_1distribute 1 ~";Oct 28 1998 2:18:00:480PM,2 ~"!,3 1 begin transaction ~"%_ins for ~",ref_dbo/~",ref_dbo

begin transaction

A0110 05iso_1distribute 2 ~"!,3 1 applied ~!7FX_Group_Table_Map.~!*rs_insert yielding after ~$+group_name=~"(Country, ~$+table_name=~"7DS_REP_DB..CNTY

insert into FX_Group_Table_Map (group_name, table_name) values ('Country', 'DS_REP_DB..CNTY')

A0110 05iso_1distribute 1 ~";Oct 28 1998 2:18:00:480PM,2 ~"!,3 1 commit transaction

execute rs_update_lastcommit @origin = 101372,   @origin_qid = 0x0000000100319f340003fdfe0011ffffffff000000008cfe00eba8b00000000000000001, @secondary_qid = 0x0000000000000000000000000000000000000000000000000000000000000000000000000000, @origin_time = '199902

28 14:18:00:480'

   commit transaction

This is a bit messy but it is simple enough to isolate the **insert** command which shows that it is an **insert** into the *FX_Group_Table_Map* table.

You can now compare the row from the primary with the row from the replicate and you also have the changes replicated in the exceptions log. This will allow you to make a better informed decision regarding the validity of the replicate row.

Apparent Failure to Replicate

That was a simple and quite obvious problem. What about something more obscure. Say we are monitoring the replication latency between primary and replicate, and no transactions are appearing at the replicate but the LTM is running and all threads are up and active. There can be a lot of causes for this: the most likely being a very large transaction which is being written onto the Replication Server inbound queue. We need to establish that the queues are moving and transactions are being processed. To do this we will examine each stage in the replication process, from the primary to replicate.

LTM to Repserver inbound queue

Log onto the Replication Server and run **admin who, sqm**. Note the values for the inbound queue, for the *First seg*, *Last seg* and *Next read* columns. Run the command again and see if the values have changed, as explained earlier in the chapter. Run the command several times and take note of the values. If the values do not change, then the problem may be with the LTM. It may not be delivering messages to the Replication Server. To prove this, log onto the primary SQL server and use the primary database. Run **sp_spaceused syslogs** and note the value. Dump the transaction log then run **sp_spaceused syslogs** again. If the log is empty then the LTM is OK. If the value is only slightly less then this may be because the log has not been dumped since the problem began and you have only cleared previously transferred transactions. Therefore, dump the log again and run **sp_spaceused syslogs** again. The value should either be the same or, if there is still activity in the database, it will be increasing. If you can not clear the log, this shows that the LTM is not delivering messages to the Replication Server.

You can double check this by examining the replication truncation point.

select * from master..syslogshold

dbid	reserved *starttime* name	spid	page	xactid	masterxactid
21	0 *Jan 1 1900 12:00AM* $replication_truncation_point	0	66436	0x000000000000	0x000000000000

20	0	0	41109	0x000000000000	0x000000000000

Jan 1 1900 12:00AM
$replication_truncation_point

19	0	0	137533	0x000000000000	0x000000000000

Mar 25 1999 11:55AM
$replication_truncation_point

8	0	0	2228559	0x000000000000	0x000000000000

Mar 25 1999 9:31AM
$replication_truncation_point

1	0	0	1514	0x000000000000	0x000000000000

Mar 25 1999 9:27AM
$replication_truncation_point

This shows you the page number of the replication truncation point in the transaction log. If this is the first page of the log:

select first from sysindexes where id = 8

First
_____

2228559

then the log cannot be cleared with a **dump tran** and you have a problem with the LTM not moving the replication truncation point, presumably because it is not writing transactions to the Replication Server queue.

The first action to take here is to ensure that the LTM is running, and there are no errors in the LTM log. If it is not running, start it, or if there are errors in the log, restart the LTM and resolve any errors. After restarting the LTM run the inbound queue checks to see if the data is transferring to the Replication Server. If the LTM is running and there are no errors in its log, then the problem will be one of the following:

- The LTM truncation point in the log is not set.
- The tables in question are not marked for replication.
- There are no replication definitions for the tables in question.
- The database has been loaded from a dump and the gen_id is wrong.

However do not be shy in bouncing the LTM. Everything may check out OK but a simple bounce of the LTM will start the queue moving again. This is most common after a network outage and you may not see any errors.

The LTM truncation point in the log is not set.

Check this by logging onto the primary SQL server, use the database and run the **dbcc gettrunc** command. The LTM truncation state should be set to 1 for valid. If it is 0 run the **dbcc settrunc(ltm, valid)** command.

dbcc gettrunc

ltm_truncpage dbname	ltm_trunc_state ltiversion	db_rep_state	gen_id	dbid
1378276 SALES	0 300	6	1	8

dbcc settrunc(ltm, valid)

ltm_truncpage dbname	ltm_trunc_state ltiversion	db_rep_state	gen_id	dbid
1378276 SALES	1 30	7	1	8

The tables in question are not marked for replication

Log onto the primary SQL server, use the primary database and run the **sp_setreplicate** command against every table you are investigating.

sp_setreplicate SALES_TAB

The replication status for 'SALES_TAB' is currently true.

The state should be true if the table is to be replicated. I know that this sounds like an absolutely stupid reason for replication nor working but, especially if it is a new replication, you will be surprised how often this one can bite you.

There are no replication definitions for the tables in question

Log into the RSSD database. Run the **rs_helprep** command and look for replication definitions for the tables in question. In this case there will be lots of warning messages in the errorlog for the table which is marked for replication but has no replication definition defined.

The database has been loaded from a dump and the gen_id is wrong

This is a common problem in test or development systems. If you have not loaded the database yourself, or are unsure of the load status, you can run a test to prove that the *gen_id* is wrong. Set up a repeating update to one of the tables under investigation, ensure the LTM is running, then run **admin who, sqm** repeatedly as the update is running. If the *gen_id* is wrong, the *First seg*, *Last seg* and *Next read* columns will not change, but the *duplicates* column will increase indicating the Replication Server is ignoring transactions being passed from the LTM. The *gen_id* is the value used by the Replication Server to control the value of the *oqid*. The LTM will not process transactions which have an *oqid* less than the last *oqid* processed by the LTM. By increasing the *gen_id* this forces all new *oqids* to be greater than those previously processed by the LTM.

To resolve a *gen_id* problem, shutdown the LTM, log into the primary database and run **dbcc gettrunc**. The *gen_id* of the database is shown in the list returned. However this database may have been loaded from an external source so the *gen_id* could be wildly inaccurate. To get the *gen_id* that the Replication Server expects to find, run the **admin get_generation** command in the primary Replication Server and note the number returned.

admin get_generation, MADRID, MARKETS

Current generation for MADRID.MARKETS is 1.

Now increment the *gen_id* with **dbcc settrunc** so that it is at least one higher than the number just returned with the **admin get_generation** command. Using the above *gen_id* in the primary database that we have just loaded, we would run:

dbcc settrunc(ltm, gen_id, 2)

Restart the LTM and check the inbound queue with **admin who, sqm**. The queue should now be moving.

Everything is OK but still no Replication

In some cases the LTM may not show an error but will not be processing the log. Although this is not a common occurrence, I have known it to happen. In these cases first try recycling the LTM. If the log records are still not being forwarded by the LTM, you can reset the LTM log pointer to start at the beginning of the log by doing the following:

- Shutdown the LTM.

- Log onto the RSSD and run **rs_zeroltm** for the database in question.

   rs_zeroltm MADRID.MARKETS

   This sets the replication truncation point to the beginning of the log and the LTM will start to read the complete log. You can check this by watching the *duplicates* figure of an **admin who, sqm** steadily increase.

- Restart the LTM. The log records will now be transferred to the Replication Server.

The above process merely resets the LTM log pointer to start at the beginning of the log, so will do no harm. The LTM will process records already sent to the Replication Server, but these will be ignored as duplicates. I would only recommend this course of action in the case described above, i.e. where everything else has failed. Normally you would only use the **rs_zeroltm** command in conjunction with discarding log records.

I do not know why this happens, and Sybase technical support have been unable to help as it appears to be impossible to reproduce. However I have noticed that the most common occurrence of this is when there has been a network outage and the LTM has not crashed.

Inbound queue to outbound queue

If we have proved that the LTM is forwarding transactions to the Replication Server inbound queue, we can now check it is processing those transactions and passing them to the outbound queue. The results of **admin who, sqm** will show the inbound queue values increasing so we now look at the outbound queue we are interested in. First we must ensure that we are applying transactions to the primary that we know should be replicated to the outbound queue we are investigating. Once this is done we check **admin who, sqm** again. Do the outbound queue values for *First seg*, *Last seg* and *Next read* increment as expected, or are they static?

If the values do not change at all, then we have to go back to the inbound queue. Is it processing a very large transaction? Remember to check this we look at the *First seg*, *Last seg* and *Next read* values. If the *First seg* stays the same and the *Last seg* is constantly increasing, then there is a large transaction being written to the queue. Another test for this is to run **admin who, sqt**. This will show the transaction status as open, the *First seg* value returned in **admin who, sqm** and the number of commands in the transaction. A few iterations will show this number increasing as more commands are processed.

   admin who, sqt

Spid	State	Info
21	Awaiting Wakeup	100001:1 DIST LONDON.MARKETS
22	Awaiting Wakeup	100004:1 DIST LONDON.RSSD
16	Awaiting Command	100004 LONDON.RSSD

Closed	Read	Open	Trunc	Removed	Full
0	0	1	1	1	0
0	0	1	1	0	0
0	0	0	0	0	0

SQM Blocked	First Trans
2	st:O,cmds:528842,qid:147:51:3
0	st:O,cmds:1,qid:483:45:8

Parsed	SQM Reader	Change Oqids	Detect Orphans
0	0	0	0
1	0	0	0
0	0	0	0

We have an open transaction and the *cmds* figure is large and iterations will show it increasing.

If it is a very large transaction which is being written to the inbound queue then you should be able to let this continue until it has finished processing and the queue will begin to move again. In an emergency you may want to stop the Replication Server from processing these transactions or on a development system it may be because someone has accidentally fired off an enormous transaction and they want it stopped. You can remove the messages with the **sysadmin purge_first_open** command. This will tell the replication system to remove the messages from the queue. It will do this immediately but will put the primary and replicate databases out of sync if the primary transaction was not cancelled before the purge. Remember that Replication Server works asynchronously to the original transaction. So the command may have completed before you purge it from the Replication Server queue. This means that the transaction has been applied at the primary but not at the replicate database.

To remove the first open transaction, first get the inbound queue number with **admin who** then run:

sysadmin purge_first_open, q_id, q_type

On a production system it is best to leave the transaction to run and investigate what caused the problem, i.e. what did the transaction do, and what can you do to ensure it doesn't happen again. Check the Stable Device usage while this is running and watch the primary database transaction log as the replication truncation point will not be moving while the large transaction is processed by the Replication Server and you will not be able to clear space from the log. Most of these problems are caused by data deletions due to archiving. If you decide to delete all of the data for a specified period, run a **select** with a **where** clause and get the rowcount returned. If this is large, consider breaking the transaction into smaller units of work by using a cursor or some other method of batching the job into small transactions. Small transactions will run through the Replication Server faster. Although the Replication Server is multi threaded the SQM for the inbound queue is a single thread. While it is processing a large transaction from one user it cannot process the transactions of other users. Therefore they will have to wait in the SQL server log until the large transaction has been processed. Using smaller batched transactions for large jobs will allow transactions from other users to be processed concurrently by the Replication Server.

When the inbound queue thread has finished processing the transaction, it will be passed to the outbound queue and we will see the transactions being processed by using the **admin who, sqm** command. If the transaction does not appear on the outbound queue this may indicate that there is not a subscription for this information and the DIST thread has ignored it. If this is the case then check that there is a valid subscription for the data by logging into the RSSD and running **rs_helpsub** and looking for the replication definition name in the list returned.

The transactions in the outbound queue will now be read by the DSI thread and applied to the replicate database. The state of the DSI thread can be checked with the **admin who, dsi** command. This should only be necessary if you suspect transactions are not being applied and no errors are being reported. This can occur if a replicate database table has had changes made to it independently of the replication system. For example, if you **update** a date column in some rows in a table in the replicate database the values will obviously not match the corresponding rows in the primary database table. If you then **update** any of those rows in the primary table the Replication Server will put every column of the table in the **where** clause of the replicated updates. (Remember a simple **delete ... where column = value** which returns 20,000 rows will translate into 20,000 individual **delete** statements). Because the column values no longer match, the **update** will fail but without an error message as no rows are affected. The lesson to be learnt here is: do not under any circumstance change replicated data rows. This should be designed into the application before replication is enabled.

Any transactions that are making it is this far should be applied to the replicate database. Apart from differing data in the primary and replicate any errors due to the application of transactions will be shown in the Replication Server log file. These will be duplicate row inserts or maintenance user permission or perhaps data constraint problems which can be resolved as explained earlier.

Orphaned transaction

One exception to the above is when an orphaned transaction is blocking an inbound queue. This is very rare but does happen. This is where a transaction has been interrupted at the primary and the Replication Server has not received a rollback or cancel command. Usually in the case of a client connection being lost the SQL server will rollback the transaction and pass this onto the Replication Server. The offending messages in the queue will then be discarded. This can sometimes fail and the transaction is left orphaned while the Replication Server goes on to process new messages. These messages will back up behind the orphaned transaction and the queue will fill up. The Distributor thread can not pass the orphaned transaction to an outbound queue, as it is not committed, and the message cannot be purged from the queue because the first block is now on another transaction.

You can test for this condition as follows:

- Log into the Replication Server and ensure the queue is being processed with the **admin who, sqm** command (watch the *First seg*, *Last seg* and *Next read*).

- Check for an open transaction with the **admin who, sqt** command. If the *First Tran* column shows the same block, segment information as the **admin who, sqm** command, then this is an ordinary open transaction and can be purged with the **sysadmin purge_first_open** command. If is not, or there is no open transaction, you have an orphaned transaction.

To find the transaction in question you will have to dump the queue to a text file and search for it manually. Once you have identified the transaction, you can delete it with the **sysadmin zap_command** command. This is quite time consuming but it is straightforward and is the only way to get the queue moving apart from purging all transactions.

If we are going to dump the queue to a file we first want to set the filename we are dumping to, as by default the queue is dumped to the error log. Since the dumped file can be very large it is better to have it in its own file. Use the **sysadmin dump_file** command:

sysadmin dump_file, path_name

where   path_name is the full path for the file

sysadmin dump_file, "/usr/data/QDUMP"

Now dump the queue using the **sysadmin dump_queue** command.

sysadmin dump_queue, q_number, q_type, seg, blk, cnt [, RSSD | client]

where	q_number, q_type	identify the queue to dump
	seg, blk	identify the segment and block in the segment where the dump is to begin
		Setting seg to -1 starts with the first active segment in the queue.
		Setting seg to -2 starts with the first segment in the queue, including any inactive segments retained by setting a save interval.
		Setting seg to -1 and blk to -1 starts with the first undeleted block in the queue.
		Setting seg to -1 and blk to -2 starts with the first unread block in the queue.
	cnt	specifies the number of blocks to dump
		Setting cnt to -1, the end of the current segment is the last block dumped.
		Setting cnt to -2, the end of the queue is the last block dumped.
	RSSD	directs the output to RSSD tables – NOT a good idea as this output will usually be large.
		Client directs the output to the client – again not a good idea.

Note you now have a choice to dump either the whole queue or you can dump a specific section of the queue. As the queue is likely to be very large and the orphaned transaction will be at or near the front of the queue, we will only dump the first few segments.

sysadmin dump_queue, 10003, 1, -1, 1, 2

This dumps the first two segments of the queue to the file specified earlier with the **sysadmin dump_file** command. It will look like this:

```
I. 97/07/07 18:03:18.    Begin Transaction Origin User=markets_dbo Tran
Name=_upd

I. 97/07/07 18:03:18.     ENTRY ver=1100 len=324 orig=100001 lorig=0
oqid=000000890d6414300003a69c000d0003a69c000d00008b2000f
```

a3f840000000000000000 lqid=59126:52:6 st=4 tr= '000000890d' d '14' 0 '000d'
LONDON.MARKETS comlen=200 begin transaction

I. 97/07/07 18:03:18.   ENTRY ver=1100 len=736 orig=100001 lorig=0
oqid=000000890d6414300003a69c000f0003a69c000d00008b2000f

a3f840000000000000000 lqid=59126:52:7 st=2097152 tr= '000000890d' d '14' 0
'000d' LONDON.MARKETS comlen=612 update RLP_TYPE set id_grp_rpt=410,
id_db=1, dt_start='19970707 15:11:08:430', dt_end=NULL , ct_tries=1 where
id_grp_rpt=410

I. 97/07/07 18:03:19.   ENTRY ver=1100 len=324 orig=100001 lorig=0
oqid=000000890d6414300003a69c0012ffffffff000000008b2000f

a3f840000000000000000 lqid=59126:52:8 st=1 tr= '000000890d' d '14' 0 '000d'
LONDON.MARKETS comlen=200 commit transaction

I. 97/07/07 18:03:19.   Begin Transaction Origin User=markets_dbo Tran
Name=_del

I. 97/07/07 18:03:19.   ENTRY ver=1100 len=324 orig=100001 lorig=0
oqid=000000890d6414300003a69c00130003a69c001300008b2000f

a3f840000000000000000 lqid=59126:52:9 st=4 tr= '000000890d' d '14' 0 '0013'
LONDON.MARKETS comlen=200 begin transaction

I. 97/07/07 18:03:19.   ENTRY ver=1100 len=324 orig=100001 lorig=0
oqid=000000890d6414300003a69c0015ffffffff000000008b2000f

a3f840000000000000000 lqid=59126:52:10 st=1 tr= '000000890d' d '14' 0 '0013'
LONDON.MARKETS comlen=200 commit transaction

Pretty messy eh? Now comes the tricky bit. I find the best method for examining
the file, is to use a text editor and begin to break the transactions up into their **begin
transaction — commit transaction** blocks. After processing the file should be a little
easier to read, like this:

I. 97/07/07 18:03:18.   Begin Transaction Origin User=markets_dbo Tran
Name=_upd

I. 97/07/07 18:03:18.   ENTRY ver=1100 len=324 orig=100001 lorig=0
oqid=000000890d6414300003a69c000d0003a69c000d00008b2000f

a3f840000000000000000 lqid=59126:52:6 st=4 tr= '000000890d' d '14' 0 '000d'

LONDON.MARKETS comlen=200 begin transaction

I. 97/07/07 18:03:18.   ENTRY ver=1100 len=736 orig=100001 lorig=0
oqid=000000890d6414300003a69c000f0003a69c000d00008b2000f

a3f840000000000000000 lqid=59126:52:7 st=2097152 tr= '000000890d' d '14' 0 '000d'

LONDON.MARKETS comlen=612 update RLP_TYPE set id_grp_rpt=410, id_db=1, dt_start='19970707 15:11:08:430', dt_end=NULL , ct_tries=1 where id_grp_rpt=410

I. 97/07/07 18:03:19.   ENTRY ver=1100 len=324 orig=100001 lorig=0 oqid=000000890d6414300003a69c0012ffffffff000000008b2000f

a3f840000000000000000 lqid=59126:52:8 st=1 tr= '000000890d' d '14' 0 '000d'

LONDON.MARKETS comlen=200 commit transaction

I. 97/07/07 18:03:19.   Begin Transaction Origin User=markets_dbo Tran Name=_del

I. 97/07/07 18:03:19.   ENTRY ver=1100 len=324 orig=100001 lorig=0 oqid=000000890d6414300003a69c00130003a69c001300008b2000f

a3f840000000000000000 lqid=59126:52:9 st=4 tr= '000000890d' d '14' 0 '0013'

LONDON.MARKETS comlen=200 begin transaction

I. 97/07/07 18:03:19.   ENTRY ver=1100 len=324 orig=100001 lorig=0 oqid=000000890d6414300003a69c0015ffffffff000000008b2000f

a3f840000000000000000 lqid=59126:52:10 st=1 tr= '000000890d' d '14' 0 '0013'

LONDON.MARKETS comlen=200 commit transaction

The following line shows the Replication Server **begin tran** block:

I. 97/07/07 18:03:18.   Begin Transaction Origin User=markets_dbo Tran Name= Upd

This marks the beginning of a set of transactions. Each individual transaction follows, and each is ended with the following line:

LONDON.MARKETS comlen=200 commit transaction

If there is more than one transaction in the batch, then each individual transaction after the first will have the following line in front of it:

LONDON.MARKETS comlen=200 begin transaction

So the structure is:

I. 97/07/07 18:03:18.   Begin Transaction Origin User=markets_dbo Tran Name

transaction information

LONDON.MARKETS comlen=200 commit transaction

LONDON.MARKETS comlen=200 begin transaction

transaction information

LONDON.MARKETS comlen=200 commit transaction

The last command will be a **commit transaction**. An orphaned transaction will have one of these begin or end blocks missing. To find it you have to start at the beginning of the file and work your way down marking off begin/commit pairs, until you find the missing command. What you should see is this:

LONDON.MARKETS comlen=200 begin transaction

transaction information

LONDON.MARKETS comlen=200 commit transaction

I. 97/07/07 18:03:19.   ENTRY ver=1100 len=324 orig=100001 lorig=0 oqid=000000890d6414300003a69c0015ffffffff000000008b2000f

a3f840000000000000000 lqid=59126:52:10 st=1 tr= '000000890d' d '14' 0

LONDON.MARKETS comlen=200 commit transaction

In this example there is a commit with no corresponding begin. To get the queue moving you will have to remove the transaction. The physical location of where the transaction resides on the stable device is held in the *lqid*. Here the *lqid* is 59126:52:10 which is segment 59126, block 52 and row 10. To delete this transaction we must put the Replication Server into stand-alone mode[1] and issue the **sysadmin sqm_zap_command** command

sysadmin sqm_zap_command, q_id, q_type, seg, blk, row

For our above *lqid* we issue:

sysadmin sqm_zap_command, 100003,1, 59126, 52,10

This will mark the transaction as deleted. Restart the Replication Server in normal multi-user mode and the queue should begin to move. Check it is past the block that had the problem with **admin who, sqm**. If it is, then you will need to take action regarding the missing information in the replicate by running **rs_subcmp** on the primary and replicate tables.

---

[1] The Replication Server is put into single user mode using the –M option in the **repserver** command in the RUNSERVER file.

Dropping DSI when replication database has been dropped

Sometimes, a replicate database will be dropped from a replicate server without the knowledge of the Replication Server DBA. This causes a headache, as there are now queues building for the replicate, as well as subscriptions for the replicate in the RSSD tables. The DSI thread cannot be dropped as it has active subscriptions associated with it, and the subscriptions cannot be dropped as the DSI cannot connect to the replicate database.

On way to do it is to purge all of the queues and then delete the associated subscriptions from the RSSD along with any other records e.g. any records in the *rs_rules* table. This is possible but can be a little dangerous as unexpected things can occur in the system afterwards, such as repeated error messages saying subscriptions are missing.

A far better method is to create a dummy database on a test server, using a dump of the dropped database or a DDL script. Create the database and drop every index on all tables. Alter the *interfaces* file for the Replication Server so the entry for the missing dataserver now points to the dummy database server (keep the dataserver name the same as the old server). Now resume the DSI thread. The queues will empty and you can drop the subscriptions. When the subscriptions are all dropped, you can drop the connection to the database.

This method is the cleanest way to remove a DSI under these conditions and eliminates problems with orphaned rows in the RSSD.

Emergency RSI removal

You may at some time need to remove an RSI link to another Replication Server, and the other Replication Server is not available. Reasons for this are usually one of the following:

- The replication system is a development system and the replicate Replication Server has been decommissioned.

- The replication system is a production system and a catastrophic failure at the replicate side is causing your outbound RSI queues to fill. (You could add more partitions in this case).

To remove the outbound RSI, run the following command:

drop route to <replicate replication server> with nowait

The route will drop and all queues associated with the route will be purged. If the replicate Replication Server is still in service, then the following command will have to be run at the replicate Replication Server :

sysadmin purge_route_at_replicate <primary replication server>

This will remove all references to the primary Replication Server from the replicate Replication Server system tables. This command will have to be run at the primary replicate Replication Server if a two-way route was in operation.

Stable Device Full

If the stable device fills up you have two options: purge the queues or add a new Stable Device partition to allow replication to continue. The Replication Server errorlog will contain an error message when a Stable Device partition fills up.

Purging the queues is not a viable option on a production server and so you will have to add a new partition. You should plan for this in a replication installation and have a spare partition ready to hand. This partition can also be used if the main partition fails.

If you do not have a spare raw device you can use filesystem space as an emergency measure, and create partitions on filesystems. Here are methods for using both types of device.

Raw device

For this example we are going to add a new partition called TEMP_SD which will be on a raw device called /dev/rdsk/c3t0d2s7. Ensure the raw device belongs to the sybase user and has write permissions.

Log onto the Replication Server and issue the **add partition** command:

add partition TEMP_SD on '/dev/rdsk/c3t0d2s7' with size 1000

This will add a new Stable Device partition 1000Mb in size. When the Replication Server has added the partition, it will begin to use it immediately. You will see messages in the errorlog saying that the stable device usage percent is below its threshold. When the transactions in the queues are processed and the queues are empty, you can then remove the partition with the **drop partition** command:

drop partition TEMP_SD

A message will appear in the log saying that the device is in the process of being dropped. It may take a while to disappear, but it will eventually go. The dropped device is no longer used for new space and is dropped when the current space is freed. This may take some time especially if you have long save intervals on the queues.

You may wish to keep the Stable Device in which case you should choose a more permanent name for it when adding it.

Adding a temporary partition to a filesystem

This process should be used in an emergency only as filesystems are much more volatile and data could be lost in the event of a server crash.

First find spare disk space on a filesystem. You should make the partition as big as possible but if you do not have a contiguous length of empty space, you could make several smaller stable devices on any available space. Let us say we have 500Mb of filesystem space on one filesystem and we are going to use it to increase the Stable Device. You must first create an empty file on the file system. This will be the Stable Device partition.

For this example we will create a file called TEMP_SD in the filesystem directory /export/data.

Log onto the host server and create an empty file.

touch   /export/data/TEMP_SD

Now log into the Replication Server and add the new partition.

add partition TEMP_SD on '/export/data/TEMP_SD' with size 500

As with the raw device the partition will be added and used immediately. When the transactions have been processed and the queues are empty the partition should be removed. Do not be tempted to leave it in place 'just in case'. If you need more permanent Stable Device space add more disks and add a permanent raw partition.

16

Recovery

Introduction

Recovery procedures obviously depend on the type of failure and where the failure occurs. This chapter discusses those failures that make one or more of the databases unavailable to the Replication Server, either because of a database corruption or a hardware failure. The type of failure is not really relevant and I shall discuss only the recovery actions required to restore the replication system components to a usable state with as little loss of data as possible.

The recovery situations that we shall discuss are:

- Failure of a replicated database.
- Failure of a primary database.
- Failure of a Stable Device partition.
- Failure of the RSSD.

In all cases it is assumed that the databases are subject to normal dump practices so that – independent of any replication – a failed database may be restored from the database and transaction dumps.

General Principles

Consider the replication architecture of figure 16.1 below.

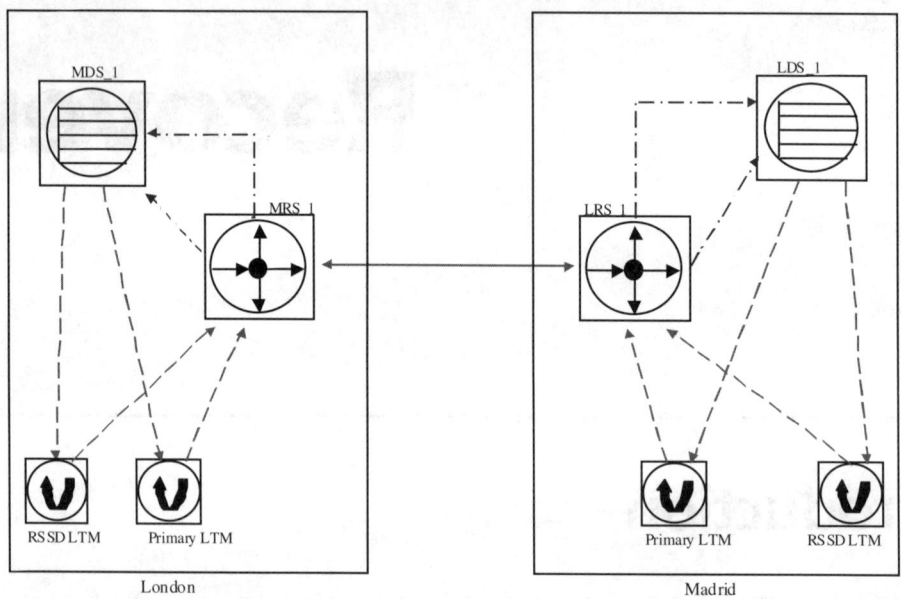

Figure 16.1: Typical two-way replication

In this architecture we have the same database schema at each site with a fragment of the data local to the site for update purposes. This is replicated to the other site on a read only basis. For example, the London site has write capability to its local London data which is replicated to Madrid which has read only access to this replicated data. At both sites the databases serve as both primary and replicate databases in the replication architecture. Global uniqueness of the data rows in the database could be implemented with a site id where users have read/write access to data identified as originating at their site, and read only access to the rest.

By its very definition replication is a copy of source data and one obvious point is that both sets of users can theoretically log into each other's servers and work. This is clearly an emergency possibility to allow production work to continue. However performance from the remote office across a network (and particularly a WAN) will be poor due to the amount of bandwidth required by each user.

So what do we do when things go wrong and we need to recover the system? Before we go into detail on this subject we need to discuss recovery issues, specifically the time taken to recover a replication system failure against allowable system downtime.

Before a replication system is deployed this issue should be fully resolved. This will allow you to design the best possible recovery procedure as few systems can afford many hours of downtime to allow the replication system to be resynchronized. In such a case a contingency setup, possibly using warm standby, should be deployed to support the production system. This will allow users to continue working while you fix the problem, then you can switch back to the primary system, probably at a quiet period to avoid further disruption to the production system.

Before we go into the actual failure scenarios and recovery options make sure that you can recover each data component in the system. The assumption at all times in this chapter is that:

- The primary and replicate databases and logs are being backed up regularly.
- The RSSD database and log are being backed up regularly.
- There are save intervals set on the DSI queues.

These are the most important conditions concerning any replication database recovery. If you can restore a database to a known point in time, then you have a chance of implementing a successful recovery plan.

In the system shown in figure 16.1 both databases will be backed up regularly to disk and the transaction logs dumped frequently, say every fifteen minutes. This gives us a maximum gap of 15 minutes where transactions will be lost in the case of a primary database failure. We would also have a recovery interval set on the outbound queues in the Replication Server, say 120 minutes. This means that all transactions will not be deleted until 120 minutes after they have been applied to the replicate. You can make this interval longer if you wish, it's a trade-off between disk space and peace of mind. Personally I would go for peace of mind and increase the disk space.

If we lose a database we can load database and transaction dumps up to the nearest point of failure. Apart from the transactions in progress at the time of failure there is the possibility that we can fully recover the data. Then we can concentrate on recovering the replication data.

In addition to the application databases the Replication Server has data storage components which may fail. The RSSD is a central component of replication and it is vital that you maintain dumps of the RSSD. The recommendation is that you treat the RSSD like the master database and dump it every time you make a change to it. The RSSD is not that big so a full database dump is not much of an overhead. But having to repeat replication definitions and subscriptions when replication is down because of a RSSD failure is not really a good idea. So keep up-to-date dumps of the RSSD – it will save you considerable grief.

Replicate Database Recovery

Let's say that we have lost a disk device on the replicate server. Assuming that we have the dump schedule described above, and the system failed 7 minutes after the last transaction log dump we will be in the state:

- All replicated transactions from the primary are now being queued up in the replication server stable device, so our incoming data is safe.

- Our replicate SQL Server is now down and the engineers are fitting and formatting a new disk.

- The DBA should be preparing the dump files to load into the server.

When the disk fault has been fixed we can load the last replicate database dump, then each log dump up until the most recent. This has brought the database up to the state it was in 7 minutes before the failure. We can now replay the transactions from the stable queue as we have a 120 minute save interval on the DSI queue.

To reapply the saved transactions ensure the DSI to the database is suspended, then issue the **sysadmin restore_dsi_saved_segments** command in the replication server.

> **sysadmin restore_dsi_saved_segments , server_name, db_name**

The replication server uses the **rs_get_lastcommit** stored procedure to get the last commit time from the replicate database and restore the transactions from that point on in the queue. Once this is complete you can resume the DSI connection to the replicate and the saved transactions will be applied.

```
suspend connection to PRS1_LN.SALES_DB
go
sysadmin restore_dsi_saved_segments , PRS1_LN, SALES_DB
go
resume connection to PRS1_LN.SALES_DB
go
```

This is relatively straightforward and you should have little trouble with it. However what do you do if this recovery fails? Well, it's only a replicate database and therefore it is a simple copy of the primary database which you can refresh from a primary database **dump** or by table **bcp**. (I know that real life may be more complicated but you should make some provision for this happening). **Bcp** of a complete database does not sound like an attractive proposition to me but it is the ultimate fallback. However I have frequently used **dump** and **load** with Warm Standby databases when the standby database has a problem and you may also find **dump** and **load** an effective solution for a normal replicate database.

If you take the **dump** and **load** approach you will need to discard any messages in the Replication Server queue so that they are not applied twice to the replicate database. This is done with the **sysadmin sqm_purge_queue** command.

sysadmin sqm_purge_queue queue_no, queue_type

You get the queue number and type from and **admin who** command.

Primary Database Recovery

A primary database failure is a bit more complicated as the primary database recovery may restore the database to a state prior to what it was before the failure. If you manage to recover up to the last committed transaction then your problems are minimized, but let's assume that you have recovered up to the end of the last transaction dump. In this case the user will repeat a number of transactions and these will be replicated to the replicate database. However these are repeated transactions which the Replication Server will already have applied – or will have in the queues – and the replicate database will reject them as duplicates when they get applied. You have no real option here but to manually intervene, check each error to ensure that it really is a duplicate – good case for a globally unique transaction id – and resume the connection, skipping the transaction until the duplicate errors stop.

Primary/replicate Database Recovery

In the case of the system shown in figure 16.1 at the beginning of the chapter, each database is both a primary and a replicate database. In this case I usually find that the simplest solution is to refresh the database. This is a little more complicated than a Warm Standby refresh as the refresh of the replicate database is made from a primary database which has an LTM and the a replication truncation point on the transaction log that have to be considered.

A reasonable approach is to:

- Shutdown the replication server and the LTM on the failed system.

- Get the generation number of the database to be recovered from the primary replication server with the **admin get_generation** command.

- Stop all processing in the primary replication server and quiesce it.

- Dump the primary database.

- Load this database into the replicate.

- In the replicate remove the truncation point on the failed database **dbcc settrunc(ltm, ignore)**.

- Truncate the log.

- Reset the truncation point with the **dbcc settrunc(ltm, valid)** command.

- Start the failed systems replication server in stand-alone mode.

- Purge the failed database queues with the **sysadmin sqm_purge_queue, q_number, q_type** command.

- Restart the replication server in normal mode.

- Increment the recovered databases generation id number, by running **dbcc settrunc(ltm, gen_id, n)** where **n** is the gen_id found above (from **admin get_generation**) incremented by 1. Do this in the recovered database.

- Restart the LTMs.

I have used this method to recover many times, however the people that make the big decisions usually want you to wait until users are not on the system before they will authorize the switch back to normal working. They prefer to leave all users on the contingency system at reduced capacity until a maintenance window allows downtime. Often this means doing it at the weekend.

Recovery from Offline Transaction Log Dumps

The above recovery scenarios assume that you have a 1:1 relationship between the primary and the replicate databases. This enables us to use database **dump** and **load** when necessary.

However in most cases you will have multiple replicate databases receiving feeds from one master primary. If you have to recover one of these replicates, you do not want to interrupt normal processing on the primary. To do this without interrupting normal processing you have to recover the replicate database from the primary database transaction log. If you have lost transactions that are no longer in the primary database log, you will have to recover the missing transactions from offline logs. This method entails creating a temporary recovery database from the last primary database dump, connecting the LTM to that database, then reloading all of the log files and replaying the transactions to the replicate.

For this method to work without interrupting primary processing, the primary log must be large enough to store all of the transactions processed while the replicate is being recovered, otherwise it will fill up and halt all processing.

The suggested steps to recover from offline logs are:

- Shutdown and restart the replication server in stand-alone mode.

- Create the recovery database.

- Load in the last full primary dump.

- Load the first subsequent transaction log dump.

- Edit the LTM configuration file and change the **SQL_server** and **SQL_database** parameters to point to the location of the recovery database.

- Restart the LTM in recovery mode.

- Look at the LTM log until you see the recovery complete message. This will say it is waiting for another log dump to be loaded. If you have more transaction log dumps to load then continue to load transaction logs as below otherwise skip direct to the Replication Server restart.

- Load the next transaction log dump.

- Log into the LTM and issue the **scan** command. This tells the LTM to replay this log.

- Wait for the recovery complete message as above.

- Continue restoring log dumps until you are back up to date.

- Shutdown and restart the replication server in normal mode.

- Shutdown the LTM.

- Edit the LTM configuration file and replace the original server values in the two variables **SQL_server** and **SQL_database**.

- Restart the LTM in normal mode.

The replicate will now be fully recovered. All of the backlogged transactions in the primary log will now be delivered to the replication server and all replicates will now start to receive the transactions. There is a risk here, as you could have a primary failure while you are recovering the replicate but you'd have to be severely unlucky for this to happen.

Recovering from Partition Loss

The above method (recovering from offline logs) is also used to recover from a stable device failure, but there are other steps required in this case. Before we go into this type of error, it is worth some discussion to see if we can prevent it from happening in the first place. A partition failure is very serious and will take some time to fix with subsequent downtime to the replicated system.

The best prevention method for this error is to have the stable device mirrored using proprietary hardware or software mirroring. The chances of losing both sides of the mirror are low and therefore the chances of you having to put this problem right are negligible also. There really isn't much of an argument, in my opinion, for not mirroring the stable device. If you want to recover from a failure, then you are going to have to have a partition to use in the stable device for recovery. If you have this space, why leave it redundant, why not use it as the mirror? If you do not leave a spare partition and have no mirror on the stable device, then you are going to have to add or replace a disk before any recovery takes place. Not an ideal scenario for a busy system.

If you insist on using non-mirrored stable devices, then you will have to create a new partition, rebuild the failed queues and get the replicate database up-to-date with the missing transactions. The suggested steps are:

- Drop the failed partition by entering the **drop partition <partition_name>** in the replication server.

- Add a new partition unless there are other stable devices already on the server when this is not strictly necessary.

- Issue the **rebuild queues** command in the replication server.

- If you get loss detection messages in the replication server error log then proceed with the next step otherwise you have been very lucky and you can skip to restarting the Replication Server.

- Shutdown and restart the replication server in stand-alone mode.

- Issue the **rebuild queues** command in the replication server.

- Check the replication server log and note which primaries the loss messages refer to. Make sure to note the date of the loss, this will help decide which log dumps to reload to replay the transactions.

- Create a temporary recovery database.

- Load in the last full primary dump from before the loss detection message date.

- Load the first subsequent transaction log dump.

- Edit the LTM configuration file and change the **SQL_server** and **SQL_database** parameters to point to the location of the recovery database.

- Restart the LTM in recovery mode.

- Look at the LTM log until you see the recovery complete message. This will say it is waiting for another log dump to be loaded. If you have more transaction log dumps to load then continue to load transaction logs as below otherwise skip direct to the Replication Server restart.

- Load the next transaction log dump.

- Log into the LTM and issue the **scan** command. This tells the LTM to replay this log.

- Wait for the recovery complete message as in step 13.

- Continue restoring log dumps until you are back up to date. You should not see loss detection messages. If you do, then you haven't gone back far enough with the database and log dumps and will have to start again.

- Shutdown and restart the replication server in normal mode.

- Shutdown the LTM.

- Edit the LTM configuration file and replace the original server values in the two variables **SQL_server** and **SQL_database**.

- Restart the LTM in normal mode.

The recovery will now be complete and you can continue normal processing. As you can see, this is a very time consuming and labor intensive procedure which is so easily avoided by using disk mirroring.

There is an alternative to following this procedure which involves ignoring the loss messages and resynchronizing the data by other means. Loss messages are recorded in the error log:

loss detected for <replicate_DS.replicate_DB> from <primary_DS.primary_DB>

After you have replaced the failed partition and rebuilt the queues you can issue the **ignore loss** command.

ignore loss from

<primary_DS.primary_DB> to <replicate_DS.replicate_DB>

This tells the replication server to ignore the loss messages and to continue processing the transactions for the database.

This is a bit dangerous as ignore loss messages prevent the replication server from processing the affected queues, so no messages will be delivered until either the problem has been fixed or the replication server is told to ignore the loss messages. If you instruct the replication server to ignore these messages, data processing can continue but data may be inconsistent between the primary and replicate. You will have to fix the inconsistencies with **rs_subcmp** if this is the case. This method may be faster than the previous method so make your decision depending on the time factors involved and the likelihood of problems occurring due to the data inconsistencies.

Be aware that the **rs_subcmp** program can take a very long time to execute. I ran this on about 600M of data and it took 30 hours. Interestingly this applied only to the first execution as subsequent, daily runs of **rs_subcmp** on the same data took 4 hours. I have not yet investigated why.

Recovering from a Failed RSSD

Of all problems you can encounter with a replication server, this is the worst you will come across, so before we go into the details of how to fix any problems with it, let's discuss what can be done to prevent it breaking in the first place.

Let us start with the RSSD database itself. Most DBAs will try and size a database depending on the expected volume of data it will store and base the log size on the expected transaction volume. Taking a typical replication server the RSSD would therefore be very small (10Mb) and the log smaller still (5Mb). I usually recommend a data segment of 50Mb to allow for future growth of the system. From experience, I found that a RSSD on a very large worldwide system had a data volume of 20 Mb (to store all of the server, definition, subscription and queue information) so the estimate of 50 Mb is a little high, but better this way. I also recommend a log segment of 50 Mb which seems way over the top but allows for backup system failures. If transaction log dumps fail for whatever reason the RSSD can still process transactions so your replication system will keep on working. If the log or database on a RSSD is full all replication will stop. Never look upon an oversized RSSD as a waste of data space, it may save you a lot of hassle one day.

The most important point of the RSSD recovery procedure is the backup schedule. It should be regular and reliable. As the database is small you should back it up regularly (say once every one or two hours) with very frequent transaction log dumps. The log will only take a few seconds to dump as it is very small (usually less than 1Mb). I would recommend you set up hourly database dumps and transaction log dumps every 5 minutes on every replication system RSSD.

In case of a failure, this schedule allows your recovered RSSD to be as up to the minute as possible. It also reduces the number of log dumps you will have to reload to recover the RSSD.

There are several procedures regarding RSSD recovery. The simplest recovery procedure is recovering a RSSD database where no DDL changes have occurred, and this should be the only one you ever need because if you create DSIs, routes, definitions or subscriptions you should immediately make a backup of the RSSD database. There really is no excuse for not doing so as it takes a few minutes to dump the RSSD and it will make recovery that much easier. The only time you should have to restore a RSSD database and re-enter object information is when the RSSD suffers a catastrophic failure between you making the changes and starting the dump. This will be very rare indeed.

Basic RSSD Recovery

Before we begin, check that you are not attempting to execute any DDL changes. Ensure the replication server is not running (its RSSD is down so it is unlikely to be). Now follow the steps outlined below.

- Shutdown all LTMs for this replication server if they are running.

- Restore the RSSD database from the latest database dump.

- Load all of the transaction dumps taken from the last full database dump to the point of failure.

- Start the replication server in stand-alone mode.

- Log into the replication server.

- Get the generation id of the RSSD with the **admin get_generation, <DS>, <RSSD_name>** command and make a note of it for later.

- Rebuild the stable device queues with the **rebuild queues** command.

- Start all LTMs except for the RSSD LTM in recovery mode using the -M flag.

- Check each LTM log until it states it has finished processing all log transactions.

- Now check the replication server log for loss detection messages. You should also do this in every replication server that has a route from the failed replication server. If loss is detected (this should only happen if a primary log has been truncated in the meantime) you will have to recover that database from offline logs as described earlier.

- Shutdown the LTMs.

- Log into the RSSD server and use the RSSD.

- Type **dbcc settrunc(ltm, ignore)** to disable the log truncation marker.

- Move the log truncation point to the next log page by issuing the following commands:

**begin tran
commit tran
go 40**

This will run an empty transaction 40 times to move the truncation point.

- Now restore the log truncation marker by typing **dbcc settrunc(ltm, valid)**.

- Take the value you obtained earlier for the generation id and increment it by one, then run the following command: **dbcc settrunc(ltm, gen_id, n)** where **n** is your incremented generation id value.

- Dump the RSSD database.

- Shutdown the replication server and restart it in normal mode.

- Restart all LTMs including the RSSD LTM.

The RSSD will now be recovered. This is by far the simplest RSSD recovery procedure. Make sure it is the only one you ever need by performing regular backups and always backing up the RSSD immediately after a DDL change, no matter how small.

If the loaded RSSD is still out-of-date you will have to recreate the missing objects. So make sure that you keep an up-to-date dump of the RSSD and that you have the appropriate Replication Server object scripts to rebuild from the ground up, if you really need to.

17

Replication Agent

Introduction

ASE 11.5 and Replication Server 11.5 have introduced a replacement for the LTM called RepAgent. RepAgent is an Adaptive Server thread which scans the transaction log and sends the replication transactions to the Replication Server. Therefore RepAgent replaces the LTM functionality in one Adaptive Server thread. RepAgent also provides recovery from transaction logs: both automatic on-line recovery and manual off-line recovery.

When the RepAgent detects an inconsistency it can reset the replication truncation point to the beginning of the log and rescan log records. When recovery is required from previous log dumps, RepAgent supports the transaction logs being loaded into a separate recovery database from which it can replay the transaction records.

Apart from the RepAgent specific commands and system procedures you can work with the RepAgent as you would with an LTM. For example you can suspend and resume log transfer with the **suspend/resume log transfer** commands.

I have never used RepAgent and so I cannot impart any practical experience. I have a deep distrust of the 'LTM' process being an integral part of ASE. I know that you can stop and start RepAgent independently of the server but I would hate to get any production system into the position where I have to bounce the server just to restart log transfer operations.

Enabling and disabling RepAgent

Enable RepAgent

You can enable RepAgent as for an LTM using **rs_init** or with the following command line options.

- Make sure that the SQL Server is defined using the **sp_addserver** system procedure.

    sp_addserver PLN_MKT, local

- Configure the SQL Server to use RepAgent using the **sp_configure** system procedure.

    sp_configure 'enable rep agent threads', 1

- Install the RepAgent using the **sp_config_rep_agent** system procedure. Make sure that you are in the primary database before you issue this procedure.

    sp_config_rep_agent db_name, 'enable',

    repserver_name, rs_username, rs_password

where

rs_username/rs_password

> The user and password used by RepAgent to log into the primary database. This user must have *connect source* permission in the primary database.

```
use SALES_DATABASE
go
sp_config_rep_agent SALES_DB, 'enable',
    PRS_MKT, ltm_sales, ltm_sales_pw
go
```

Disable RepAgent

If you no longer require the RepAgent, you can disable it with the **sp_config_rep_agent** system procedure.

```
sp_config_rep_agent db_name, 'disable' [, 'preserve secondary
truncpt]
```

You need to stop (see below) the RepAgent before you can disable it. Be careful of leaving the replication truncation point intact as you may have some problems in truncating the transaction log.

Configuring RepAgent

RepAgent configuration parameters are displayed and set with the **sp_config_rep_agent** system procedure.

```
sp_config_rep_agent  [ dbname
[, {'enable', 'repserver_name', 'rs_username', 'rs_password'} |
    'disable'[, 'preserve secondary truncpt'] |
    'rs_servername', 'repserver_name',
    'rs_username', 'rs_username',
    'rs_password', 'rs_password' |
    'scan_batch_size',  'no_of_qualifying_log_records' |
    'scan_timeout', 'scan_timeout_in_seconds' |
    'retry_timeout', 'retry_timeout_in_seconds' |
    'fade_timeout', 'fade_timeout_in_seconds' |
```

```
          'skip_ltl_errors', {'true' | 'false'} |
          'batch_ltl', {'true' | 'false'} |
          'send_warm_standby_xacts', {'true' | 'false'} |
          'connect_dataserver', 'connect_dataserver_name' |
          'connect_database', 'connect_database_name' |
          'send_maint_xacts_to_replicate',{'true' | 'false'} |
          'security_mechanism', 'mechanism_name' |
          'unified_login', {'true' | 'false' } |
          'mutual_authentication', {'true' | 'false' } |
          'msg_confidentiality', {'true' | 'false' } |
          'msg_integrity', {'true' | 'false' } |
          'msg_replay_detection', {'true' | 'false' } |
          'msg_origin_check', {'true' | 'false' } |
          'msg_out_of_sequence check {'true' | 'false' }]]
```

where

dbname	The database name.
enable	Enables RepAgent for the database and sets the secondary truncation point to valid.
rs_name	The name of the Replication Server to which RepAgent connects and transfers log transactions.
rs_username	The user name that RepAgent thread uses to connect to Replication Server.
rs_password	The password that RepAgent uses to connect to Replication Server.
disable	Disables RepAgent for the database and 'ignores' the truncation point. Use *preserve secondary truncpt* to retain the secondary truncation point.
scan_batch_size	The maximum number of log records to send to Replication Server in each batch. The replication truncation point is updated after this number of records. The default is 1000 records.

scan_timeout	The number of seconds that RepAgent sleeps once it has scanned and processed all records in the transaction log before requesting a new truncation point. The default is 15 seconds.
retry_timeout	The number of seconds RepAgent sleeps before attempting to reconnect to Replication Server. The default is 60 seconds.
fade_timeout	The number of seconds RepAgent remains inactive when there are no transactions on the log before disconnection. The default is 30 seconds.
skip_ltl_errors	Specifies whether RepAgent ignores errors in LTL commands or shuts down. The default 'false' shuts down the RepAgent when an error is received.
batch_ltl	Specifies whether RepAgent sends LTL commands to Replication Server in batches or one command at a time. The default of 'false' sends one command at a time.

send_warm_standby_xacts

Specifies whether RepAgent sends information about maintenance users, schema, and system transactions to the warm standby database. The default is "false."

connect_dataserver 'connect_dataserver_name'

The name of the data server RepAgent uses when connecting to Replication Server in recovery mode.

connect_database 'connect_database_name'

The name of the temporary database RepAgent uses when connecting to Replication Server in recovery mode.

send_maint_xacts_to_replicate

Specifies whether RepAgent should send records from the maintenance user to the Replication Server for distribution to subscribing sites. The default is "false."

security_mechanism

Specifies the network-based security mechanism RepAgent uses to connect to Replication Server. None of the security options are supported for Replication Server version 11.5.

unified_login	Specifies whether RepAgent seeks to connect to Replication Server with a security credential or password. The default is "false."

mutual_authentication

> Specifies whether RepAgent should require mutual authentication checks when connecting to Replication Server. The default is "false".

msg_confidentiality

> Specifies whether to encrpyt all messages sent to Replication Server. The default is "false."

msg_integrity   Specifies whether all messages exchanged with Replication Server should be checked for tampering. The default is "false".

msg_replay_detection

> Specifies whether messages received from Replication Server should be checked to make sure they have not been intercepted and replayed. The default is "false."

msg_origin_check   Specifies whether to check the source of each message received from Replication Server. The default is "false."

msg_out_of_sequence_check

> Specifies whether to check the sequence of messages received from Replication Server. The default is "false."

The configuration parameters are held in the *sysattributes* table on the primary database.

```
use SALES_DB
go
exec sp_config_rep_agent SALES_DB, 'fade_timeout', 60
go
```

Starting and stopping RepAgent

Starting RepAgent

RepAgent will start automatically when the SQL Server starts as long as it has been started once with the **sp_start_rep_agent** system procedure. If you have specifically stopped the RepAgent or it has crashed, you will need to restart it with **sp_start_rep_agent**.

> sp_start_rep_agent db_name
>
> > [, for_recovery [, connect_server, connect_db]
> >
> > [, 'repserver_name', rs_username', 'rs_password']]]

where

for_recovery	Starts the RepAgent in recovery mode.
connect_server	The name of the data server used to recover offline logs.
connect_db	The name of the database used to recover offline logs.
repserver_name	The name of the Replication Server to which RepAgent connects.
rs_username	The user name that RepAgent uses to connect to Replication Server.
rs_password	The password that RepAgent uses to connect to Replication Server.

> sp_start_rep_agent SALES_DB

Stopping RepAgent

The RepAgent is shut down using the **sp_stop_rep_agent** system procedure.

> sp_stop_rep_agent db_name [, nowait]
>
> sp_stop_rep_agent SALES_DB

The nowait option kills the RepAgent without waiting for currently executing operations to complete.

Help on RepAgent

Current RepAgent status information is available using the **sp_help_rep_agent** system procedure.

> **sp_help_rep_agent [database_name**
> **[, 'recovery' | 'config' | 'process' | 'scan' | 'security' | 'all']]**

where

recovery   Displays recovery status information.

config   Displays configuration information.

process   Displays information about the RepAgent process.

scan   Displays log-scanning information.

security   Displays current settings of the network-based security mechanism. This option is not supported for Replication Server version 11.5.

Appendix A

System Tables

rs_articles

One row for each article.

Column	Datatype	Description
articlename	varchar(30)	Article name.
articleid	rs_id	Unique article ID.
type	char(1)	T - table
		P - procedure
primaryname	varchar(30)	Primary table or procedure name.
primaryowner	varchar(30)	Primary table owner name.
objid	rs_id	Replication definition ID.
pubid	rs_id	Publication ID.
requestdate	datetime	Date and time the article was added to the publication.

Indexes

Unique clustered index on (articlename, pubid)

Unique index on (articleid)

rs_classes

One row for each function string class and error class.

Column	Datatype	Description
classname	varchar(30)	Class name.
classid	rs_id	Class ID.
classtype	char(1)	F - function string class.
		E - error class.

prsid	int	Primary site ID.
parent_classid	rs_id	parent class ID. 0 if base class.
attributes	int	0x01 rs_default_function_class
		rs_db2_function_class
		0x00 other class default

Indexes

Unique clustered index on (classname, classtype)

Unique index on (classid)

rs_columns

One row for each column used in each replication definition.

Column	Datatype	Description
prsid	int	Primary Replication ID.
objid	rs_id	Replication definition ID or function ID the column belongs to.
colname	varchar(30)	Column or parameter name.
colnum	smallint	Column number.
coltype	tinyint	Datatype of the column or parameter:
		0 - char
		1 - binary
		4 - text
		5 - image
		6 - tinyint
		7 - smallint
		8 - int
		9 - real

10 - float

11 - bit

12 - datetime

13 - smalldatetime

14 - money

15 - smallmoney

16 - numeric

17 - decimal

18 - varchar

19 - varbinary

length	tinyint	Length of the data.
searchable	tinyint	1 if searchable key, 0 if not.
primary_col	tinyint	1 if primary key, 0 if not.
fragmentation	tinyint	1 if fragmentation key, 0 if not.
rowtype	tinyint	1 if row is to be replicated, 0 if not.
status	int	0x01 - column is an IDENTITY column
		0x04 - column is an rs_address datatype
		0x08 - column has a status of replicate_if_changed
		0x10 - column allows null values in the replicate table (only for text or image columns)
basecolnum	smallint	Column position in base replication definition.
Repl_colname	char(30)	Column name in replicate table.

Indexes

Unique index on (objid, colname)

Unique index on (objid, colnum)

Unique index on (objid, basecolnum)

Clustered index on (objid)

rs_config

One row for each configuration parameter.

Column	Datatype	Description
optionname	varchar(30)	Name of the parameter.
objid	rs_id	ID of the object this option references. If set to 0, this applies to the whole system.
charvalue	varchar(255)	Character value for parameter.
status	tinyint	Not used.
comment	varchar(255)	Textual comment.

Indexes

Unique clustered index on (optionname, objid)

rs_databases

One row for each database known at a Replication Server site.

Column	Datatype	Description
dsname	varchar(30)	Data server name.
dbname	varchar(30)	Database name.
dbid	int	Unique database identifier for the database.
dist_status	tinyint	Status of the connection.
		0x1 - valid
		0x2 - suspended
		0x4 - suspended by a standby-related action

		0x8 - waiting for a marker
		0x10 - will issue dbcc ('ltm', 'ignore')
		0x20 - waiting for dump marker to initialize a standby database
		0x40 - switching related duplicate detection when ltype = 'P'
		0x40 - allow switching when ltype = 'L'
		0x80 - temporarily not doing any grouping
src_status	tinyint	Status of the source.
		0x1 - valid
		0x2 - suspended
		0x4 - suspended by a standby-related action
attributes	tinyint	1 - distribution
		2 - source
errorclassid	rs_id	Error class for the database.
funcclassid	rs_id	Function string class for the database.
prsid	int	ID of Replication Server managing the database.
rowtype	tinyint	1 if row is replicated, 0 if not.
sorto_status	tinyint	Indicates if the sort order check has been completed.
		0 - not checked
		1 - checked
ltype	char(1)	The type of database.
		P - physical database
		L - logical database connection
ptype	char(1)	The type of database in a warm standby application.

		A - the active database
		S - the standby database
		L - the logical database connection
ldbid	int	The dbid for the logical connection the database is associated with. If there is no logical connection, ldbid is the same as dbid.
enable_seq	int	The sequence number used during an active database switch or the creation of a standby database.

Indexes

Unique clustered index on (dsname, dbname, ltype)

Unique index on (ptype, ldbid)

Unique index on (dbid, ltype)

Unique index on (dsname, dbname, ptype)

rs_diskpartitions

One row for each disk partition.

Column	Datatype	Description
name	varchar(255)	Operating system name for the disk device.
logical_name	varchar(30)	Replication Server name for the partition.
id	int	Partition ID.
num_segs	int	Total size of the partition in segments.
allocated_segs	int	Number of segments currently used.
status	int	Status of the disk partition.
		1 - online
		2 - partition is being dropped

| allocation_map | binary(255) | Bitmap of allocated segments. |
| vstart | int | Offset at which Replication Server starts writing to the partition (in MB). |

Indexes

Unique clustered index on (logical_name)

Unique index on (name)

rs_erroractions

One row for each error action assigned to an error class.

Column	Datatype	Description
ds_errorid	int	Data server error number.
errorclassid	rs_id	Error class ID.
action	tinyint	Error action.
		1 - ignore the error
		2 - stop replication
		3 - output a warning message
		4 - write an entry in the exceptions log
		5 - retry the transaction and then log the transaction if it still fails
		6 - retry the transaction a certain number of times and then stop replication if it still fails
prsid	int	Primary site ID.

Indexes

Unique index on (ds_errorid, errorclassid)

Clustered index on (errorclassid)

rs_exceptscmd

One row for each command logged in the exceptions log.

Column	Datatype	Description
sys_trans_id	rs_id	System-assigned transaction ID.
src_cmd_line	int	Command-line number of the source within the logged transaction.
output_cmd_index	int	Line number of the output command within the logged transaction.
cmd_type	char(1)	S - source command
		L - language output command
		R - RPC output command
cmd_id	rs_id	Command ID – foreign key to rs_systext.

Indexes

Unique index on (cmd_id)

rs_exceptshdr

One row for each transaction written to the exceptions log.

Column	Datatype	Description
sys_trans_id	rs_id	System assigned transaction ID.
rs_trans_id	binary(120)	Replication Server unique transaction ID.
app_trans_name	varchar(30)	User transaction name.
orig_siteid	int	Origin database ID.
orig_site	varchar(30)	Origin database data server name.
orig_db	varchar(30)	Origin database name.
orig_time	datetime	Time the transaction was initiated.

orig_user	varchar(30)	User who submitted the transaction at the origin site.
error_siteid	int	ID of the site where the error occurred.
error_site	varchar(30)	Name of the data server where the error occurred.
error_db	varchar(30)	Name of the database where the error occurred.
log_time	datetime	Time the error occurred.
ds_error	int	Data server error number.
ds_errmsg	varchar(255)	Data server error message.
error_src_line	int	Line number of the command that caused the error.
error_proc	varchar(30)	Procedure for which the error occurred.
err_output_line	int	Line number of the output command that caused the error.
log_reason	char(1)	O - indicates an orphan transaction in the DSI queue
		E - a data server error mapped to *LOG* or *RETRY_LOG*.
		S - indicates the transaction was skipped because the resume connection command was executed with the skip transaction option
		D - the transaction was logged by a **sysadmin log_first_tran** command.
trans_status	smallint	Transaction status
		0x0001 - orphan transaction
		0x0002 - logged transaction was going to primary site
		0x0004 - conflicting transaction
retry_status	smallint	Retry status for the transaction

		1 - retry succeeded
		2 - transaction has not committed
app_usr	varchar(30)	Name of the user who applied the transaction at the error site.
app_pwd	varchar(30)	Password of the user who applied the transaction at the error site.

Indexes

Unique index on (sys_trans_id)

rs_exceptslast

One row for the last logged transaction written into the exceptions log.

Column	Datatype	Description
error_db	int	Database ID where the error occurred.
origin	int	Origin database ID of the transactions.
origin_qid	binary(36)	qid of the last transaction from this origin.
secondary_qid	binary(36)	Secondary qid of the last logged transaction from this origin.
status	tinyint	0 - Valid: no transactions were lost for this origin
		1 - Detecting losses: you should determine if any transactions have been lost in this origin
		2 - Rejecting messages after loss detected: transactions were probably lost for this origin
origin_time	datetime	Time at origin for the transaction.
log_time	datetime	Time the transaction was logged.
lorigin	int	Logical database ID where the message originated.

Indexes

Unique index on (error_db, origin)

Unique index on (error_db, origin, status)

rs_funcstrings

One row for each function string.

Column	Datatype	Description
prsid	int	Primary site ID.
classid	rs_id	Function string class ID.
funcid	rs_id	Function ID.
name	varchar(30)	Function string name.
fstringid	rs_id	Function string ID.
attributes	smallint	Attributes of the function string:
		0x01 - conflicting function
		0x02 - RPC
		0x04 - altered
		0x10 - default input
		0x20 - default output
		0x40 - writetext output is used for a **rs_writetext** function string
		0x80 - writetext output is used with the with log option for a **rs_writetext** function string
		0x100 - a function string for a **rs_writetext**, **rs_textptr_init**, or **rs_get_textptr** function
		0x200 - writetext output is used with the no log option for a **rs_writetext** function string
parameters	smallint	Number of parameters in the function string.

param_hash	int	Hash value of input template.
expiredate	datetime	Date the function string should expire.
rowtype	tinyint	1 if this row is replicated, 0 if not

Indexes

Unique clustered index on (classid, funcid, name)

Unique index on (fstringid)

rs_functions

One row for each function.

Column	Datatype	Description
prsid	int	Primary site ID.
funcname	varchar(30)	Function name.
funcid	rs_id	Function ID.
objid	rs_id	Object to which the function applies. NULL_OBJECT_ID (0x00000000) is stored in this column for class-wide functions.
conflicting	tinyint	1 if the function is conflicting, 0 if not.
userdefined	bit	1 if this is a user-defined function, 0 if not.
rowtype	tinyint	1 if this row is replicated, 0 if not.

Indexes

Clustered index on (objid)

Unique index on (objid, funcname)

Unique index on (funcid)

rs_idnames

One row for each Replication Server and database known to the ID server.

Column	Datatype	Description
name1	varchar(30)	Replication Server or data server name
name2	varchar(30)	Database name; "" for a Replication Server
type	int	8 - Replication Server
		9 - database
id	int	Replication Server or database ID.
ltype	char(1)	Database type
		'P' - Physical database
		'L' - Logical database

Indexes

Unique clustered index on (name1, name2, ltype)

rs_ids

Stores the last ID used for various types of objects.

Column	Datatype	Description
typename	varchar(30)	Name of this object type. Values are listed below under *objtype*.
objid	int	Last ID used for this object type
objtype	tinyint	1 - subscriptions
		2 - objects
		3 - classes
		4 - users
		5 - functions

6 - function strings

7 - error log

8 - Replication Server ID

9 - database ID

10 - disk partition IDs

11 – Not used

12 - reject transaction (an error log type)

13 - counter for subscriptions module

14 - recovery ID type

Indexes

Unique clustered index on (objtype)

rs_lastcommit

One row for each origin database.

Column	Datatype	Description
origin	int	Origin database ID.
origin_qid	binary	oqid for the last committed transaction in the stable queue for the origin database.
secondary_qid	binary	oqid for the last committed transaction in a subscription materialization queue.
origin_time	datetime	Commit time at origin for the transaction.
dest_commit_time	datetime	Destination commit time for the transaction.
pad1	binary(255)	Filler to pad the row to ensure record level locking.
pad2	binary(255)	Filler to pad the row to ensure record level locking.

pad3	binary(255)	Filler to pad the row to ensure record level locking.
pad4	binary(255)	Filler to pad the row to ensure record level locking.
pad5	binary(255)	Filler to pad the row to ensure record level locking.
pad6	binary(255)	Filler to pad the row to ensure record level locking.
pad7	binary(255)	Filler to pad the row to ensure record level locking.
pad8	binary(83)	Filler to pad the row to ensure record level locking.

Indexes

Unique clustered index on (origin)

rs_locater

One row per stable queue stable queues from each sender.

Column	Datatype	Description
sender	int	Sender site ID.
type	char(1)	Queue type.
		R - RSI (route)
		D - distributor locater used for subscriptions
		E - executor for LTM
		U - LTM locater at last system upgrade
		W - distributor locater used for a warm standby application
locater	binary(36)	Last queue ID received from this sender.

Indexes

Unique clustered index on (sender, type)

rs_maintusers

One row for each maintenance user.

Column	Datatype	Description
destid	int	Replication Server or database site ID.
username	varchar(30)	Maintenance user name.
password	varchar(30)	Maintenance user password.
use_enc_password	int	0 - use normal passwords
		1 - use encrypted passwords
enc_password	varchar(66)	Encrypted maintenance user password.

Indexes

Unique clustered index on (destid)

rs_msgs

One row for each localized error messages used during installation and by some Replication Server stored procedures.

Column	Datatype	Description
msgnum	int	Unique message ID.
langname	char(30)	Local language name of this version of the message text, corresponding to the @@language global variable in the RSSD SQL Server.
msgtxt	varchar(255)	Text of the message.

Indexes

Unique clustered index on (msgnum, langname)

rs_objects

One row for each replication definitions.

Column	Datatype	Description
prsid	int	Primary Replication Server ID.
objname	varchar(30)	Object name.
objid	rs_id	Object ID.
dbid	int	Unique database ID.
objtype	char(1)	R - table replication definition
		F - function replication definition
attributes	tinyint	0x01 - generate dynamic function strings
		0x02 - replication definition has fragments
		0x04 - minimum columns enabled for replication definition
		0x08 - replication definition has IDENTITY column
		0x10 - replicate_if_changed status
		0x20 - replication definition has a drop pending
		0x40 - replication definition has text or image column
		0x80 - replication definition is used by a standby
ownertype	char(1)	U - user
		S - System Administrator

crdate	datetime	Date and time created
parentid	rs_id	Parent object ID.
ownerid	rs_id	Owner ID.
rowtype	tinyint	1 if row is replicated, 0 if not
phys_tablename	varchar(200)	Physical table name.
deliver_as_name	varchar(200)	Procedure name by which a replicated function will be delivered.
phys_objowner	char(30)	Primary table owner.
has_baserepdef	rs_id	0x00 if base replication definition
		objid if not a base replication definition

Indexes

Unique clustered index on (objname)

Unique index on (dbid, phys_tablename, phys_objowner, objtype)

Unique index on (objid)

Unique index on (objid, dbid)

rs_oqid

One row for the last queue ID received from an origin site.

Column	Datatype	Description
origin_site_id	int	Origin site ID.
q_number	int	Queue number.
q_type	int	Queue type.
origin_q_id	binary(36)	Command ID at the origin database.
local_q_id	binary(36)	Local ID for the queue.
valid	int	0 - valid

		1 - detecting losses
		2 - rejecting messages after loss detected
origin_lsite_id	int	Site ID of the logical database of the origin site.

Indexes

Unique clustered index on (origin_site_id, q_number, q_type)

rs_publications

One row for each publication.

Column	Datatype	Description
prsid	int	Primary Replication Server ID.
pubname	varchar(30)	Publication name.
pubid	rs_id	Unique publication ID.
pdbid	int	Unique ID for the publication's primary data server and database
requestdate	datetime	Date and time the last article was added to the publication.
ownerid	rs_id	ID of the user who created the publication
status	int	0x00 - Invalid
		0x01 – Valid

Indexes

Unique clustered index on (pubname, pdbid)

Unique index on (pubid)

rs_queuemsg

Holds commands dumped from a Replication Server queue when the target is specified as the RSSD.

Column	Datatype	Description
q_number	int	Queue number.
q_type	int	Queue type.
q_seg	int	Queue segment.
q_blk	int	Queue block.
q_row	int	Queue row.
len	int	Length of the queue entry.
origin_site_id	int	Origin site ID.
origin_q_id	binary(36)	Queue ID assigned by the origin.
origin_time	datetime	Time transaction was initiated.
origin_user	varchar(30)	User who submitted transaction at origin site.
tran_name	varchar(30)	Transaction name.
local_q_id	binary(36)	Queue ID assigned by the local Replication Server.
status	int	Message status.
reserved	int	Reserved for future use.
tran_len	smallint	Length of tran_id.
txt_len	smallint	Length of command.
tran_id	binary(120)	Transaction ID.
lorigin_site_id	int	Site ID of the logical connection that is the source of the queue entries.
version	int	Release version of the message.

Indexes

Unique clustered index on (q_number, q_type, q_seg, q_blk, q_row)

rs_queuemsgtxt

One row for the command or text portion of messages in stable queues.

Column	Datatype	Description
q_number	int	Queue number.
q_type	int	Queue type.
q_seg	int	Segment that contains the message.
q_blk	int	Block within the segment that contains the message.
q_row	int	Row within the block that contains the message.
q_seq	int	Sequence number of the row for this entry.
txt	varchar(255)	Text of the entry.
txtbin	binary(255)	Text in binary.

Indexes

Unique default index on (q_number, q_type, q_seq, q_seg, q_blk, q_row)

rs_queues

One row for each Replication Server queue.

Column	Datatype	Description
number	int	Queue ID
type	int	1 - Replication Server
		2 - database

state	int	Current state of the queue.
		0 - failure
		1 - active
		2 - deleting
twosave	int	Save interval in seconds.
truncs	int	Number of truncation points

Indexes

Unique clustered index on (number, type)

rs_recovery

Actions that must be performed on Replication Server recovery.

Column	Datatype	Description
action	int	Represents the recoverable actions:
		1 - create_route
		2 - drop_route
		3 - stand-alone mode
		4 - rebuild queues
		5 - log recovery
		6 - restart LTM at the top of the log
		7 - create standby
		8 - switch active
		9 - strict save interval for DSI or materialization queue
		10 - quit DSI secondary duplicate detection after switch active

11 - drop standby

12 - alter distributor locater

13 - delete segments with replication definitions

14 - drop pending replication definitions

id	rs_id	Unique ID for the row.
seqnum	int	Row sequence number of actions with multiple rows.
state	int	Current state for recoverable actions.
text	binary(255)	Data required to complete the action.
textlen	int	Length of the text data.

Indexes

Unique index on (id)

rs_repdbs

One row for each database known by a primary Replication Server which has had a subscription entered for a database at a replicate site.

Column	Datatype	Description
dbid	int	Unique database ID.
dsname	varchar(30)	Data server name.
dbname	varchar(30)	Database name.
controllerid	int	Managing Replication Server for this database.

Indexes

Clustered index on (controllerid)

Unique index on (dbid)

Unique index on (dsname, dbname)

rs_repobjs

One row for each object showing auto correction status per database.

Column	Datatype	Description
objid	rs_id	Object ID
dbid	int	Database ID where the replicate data is stored
attributes	int	0x01 - autocorrection flag is on

Indexes

Unique clustered index on (objid, dbid)

rs_routes

One row per route.

Column	Datatype	Description
dest_rsid	int	ID of a data server or Replication Server
through_rsid	int	Destination is reached through this Replication Server
source_rsid	int	Replication Server where this route is defined
status	tinyint	1 - being initialized
		2 - route is valid at this site
		3 - dropping this route gracefully
		4 - dropping this route immediately
suspended	tinyint	0 - route is active
		1 - route is suspended

2 - route is being rebuilt. In the process of setting the truncation point.

3 - route is suspended. In the process of setting the truncation point.

8 (mask) - for an RSI outbound queue, instructs the replicate Replication Server to set the rs_locater to 0.

src_version	int	Version of source Replication Server for this route.

1000 - Pre-10.1 Replication Server

1010 - Version 10.1

1100 - Version 11.0

Indexes

Unique clustered index on (dest_rsid, source_rsid)

rs_routeversions

One row for each route.

Column	Datatype	Description
dest_rsid	int	Destination Replication Server ID.
source_rsid	int	Source Replication Server ID.
dest_rssd_id	int	ID of the RSSD of the destination Replication Server.
route_version	int	The minimum site version of the destination and source Replication Server.
min_path_version	int	Reserved for future use.
marker_serial_no	int	For internal use.
status	int	0x00 - Valid

		0x01 - Route upgrade/recovery in progress, or route upgrade/recovery needed.
		0x02 - Route upgrade/recovery complete. This is a temporary status used by RSMServer.
proposed_version	int	New route value in transition.

Indexes

Unique clustered index on (dest_rsid, source_rsid)

rs_rules

One row for each **where** clause in a subscription.

Column	Datatype	Description
prsid	int	Primary Replication Server ID.
subid	rs_id	Subscription ID.
objid	rs_id	Replication definition ID.
dbid	int	Subscription database ID.
subtype	int	0x01 - range subscription
		0x02 - equality subscription
primary_sre	int	If set, the subscription should be included in the subscription resolution engine at the primary Replication Server.
replicate_sre	int	If set, the subscription should be included in the subscription resolution engine at the replicate Replication Server.
colnum	smallint	Column number.
valuetype	tinyint	Datatype of operand, for example, SYBCHAR.
low_flag	tinyint	Bitmap for the type of the low value.

		0x01 - exclusive
		0x02 - inclusive
		0x04 - infinity
		0x08 - equality
		0x20 - rs_address
high_flag	tinyint	Bitmap for the type of the high value.
		0x01 - exclusive
		0x02 - inclusive
		0x04 - infinity
		0x08 - equality
		0x20 - rs_address
low_len	int	Length of low value.
high_len	int	Length of high value.
low_value	varchar(255)	Character representation of low value.
high_value	varchar(255)	Character representation of high value.

Indexes

Unique index on (subid, colnum, primary_sre, replicate_sre, subtype)

Unique index on (subid, colnum)

Clustered index on (objid, subtype, dbid)

rs_segments

One row for each segment allocation.

Column	Datatype	Description
partition_id	int	Partition ID.
q_number	int	Queue number for the partition.

q_type	int	Queue type.
partition_offset	int	Offset of segment within partition.
logical_seg	int	Offset of segment within queue.
used_flag	int	0 - inactive
		1 - active
		n - save interval in seconds
version	int	Current version of the segment. The version number increases after each use.
flags	int	Set to 1 on the last segment of the DSI queue after switch active.

Indexes

Unique clustered index on (partition_id, partition_offset)

rs_sites

One row for each Replication Server known at a site.

Column	Datatype	Description
name	varchar(30)	Replication Server name
id	int	Site ID assigned to this Replication Server
status	tinyint	Not used.

Indexes

Unique index on (name)

Unique clustered index on (id)

rs_subscriptions

One row for each subscription, trigger or fragment.

Column	Datatype	Description
subname	varchar(30)	Name of the subscription, trigger, or fragment.
subid	rs_id	ID for this subscription or fragment.
type	int	0x00 - subscription
		0x01 - range subscription
		0x02 - equality subscription
		0x04 - entire table
objid	rs_id	Replication definition ID.
dbid	int	Database ID.
pdbid	int	Primary database ID for the replication definition.
requestdate	datetime	Date and time the last DDL request (create, drop, alter) was entered
pownerid	rs_id	User ID at the primary Replication Server.
rownerid	rs_id	User ID at the replicate Replication Server.
status	int	Byte 1 holds the replicate materialization status.
		0x01 - subscription is new
		0x02 - bulk subscription is activating or atomic/non-atomic subscription has completed building materialization queue
		0x04 - bulk/non-atomic subscription is active
		0x08 - bulk subscription is validating or non-atomic has materialized
		0x10 - subscription is valid
		0x40 - subscription is valid at the standby

0x80 - subscription was removed at the standby

Byte 2 holds the primary materialization status.

0x0100 - new

0x0200 - activating

0x0400 - active

0x0800 - valid

Byte 3 holds the dematerialization status:

0x00010000 - dematerializing at replicate

0x00020000 - removing at replicate

0x00100000 - dematerializing at primary

Byte 4 holds the suspect status:

0x02000000 - suspect because of switch active

0x04000000 - suspect on drop at standby

recovering	int	Subscription recovery status:
		0x0 - subscription is OK
		0x1 - recovering
		0x2 - pending
error_flag	int	If set, subscription is unrecoverable.
materializing	int	If set, subscription is materializing.
dematerializing	int	If set, subscription is dematerializing.
primary_sre	int	If set, the subscription should be included in the subscription resolution engine at the primary Replication Server.
replicate_sre	int	If set, the subscription should be included in the subscription resolution engine at the replicate Replication Server.

materialization_try	int	Number of times this atomic materialization has been tried.
method	tinyint	Method for materializing the subscription:
		0x00 - default method
		0x01 - atomic
		0x02 - bulk
		0x04 - suspend
		0x08 - incremental
		0x10 - non-atomic
		0x80 - bulk materialization with suspended standby DSI
generation	binary	Generation number for the origin queue ID of the materialization queue.
parentid	rs_id	Subscription ID for publication if current subscription is for an article.
security	int	0x000　　default
		0x001　　unified_login
		0x002　　mutual_auth
		0x004　　msg_confidentiality
		0x008　　msg_integrity
		0x010　　msg_origin_check
		0x020　　msg_reply_detection
		0x040　　msg_sequence_check
mechanism	char(30)	Security mechanism name.

Indexes

Unique clustered index on (subid)

Unique index on (objid, dbid, subname)

Unique index on (subid, recovering, error_flag, materializing, dematerializing,

primary_sre, replicate_sre)

Unique index on (subid, status)

rs_systext

Stores the text of repeating groups for various other tables such as *rs_funcstrings*.

Column	Datatype	Description
prsid	int	Replication Server ID where the object is defined
parentid	rs_id	Object ID.
texttype	char(1)	Object type.
		S - input template for function string
		O - output template for function string
		C - command from a logged transaction in the exceptions log
sequence	int	Sequence of the text.
textval	varchar(255)	The text.

Indexes

Unique clustered index on (parentid, texttype, sequence)

rs_threads

One row for each parallel DSI thread to prevent deadlocks.

Column	Datatype	Description
id	int	Thread ID.

seq	int	The sequence number of the last update made to this entry.
pad1	char(255)	Filler to pad the row to ensure record level locking.
pad2	char(255)	Filler to pad the row to ensure record level locking.
pad3	char(255)	Filler to pad the row to ensure record level locking.
pad4	char(255)	Filler to pad the row to ensure record level locking.

Indexes

Unique clustered index on (id)

rs_users

One row for each Replication Server user.

Column	Datatype	Description
username	varchar(30)	User name.
uid	rs_id	User ID.
password	varchar(30)	User password.
permissions	smallint	0x0001 - sa
		0x0002 - connect source
		0x0004 - create object
		0x0008 - primary subscribe
use_enc_password	int	0 - use normal passwords
		1 - use encrypted passwords
enc_password	varchar(66)	Encrypted password.

Indexes

Unique index on (username)

Unique index on (uid)

rs_version

One row for each site.

Column	Datatype	Description
siteid	int	Replication Server ID.
		0 - site ID for the system-wide version number
		n - site ID of individual Replication Servers
version	int	Version number
		1000 - version 10.0 (assigned to any Replication Server whose version is unknown)
		1001 - version 10.0.1
		1002 - version 10.0.2
		1003 - version 10.0.3
		1010 - version 10.1
		1011 - version 10.1.1
		1100 - version 11.0

Indexes

Unique clustered index on (siteid)

rs_whereclauses

rs_whereclauses

One row for each **where** clause used in an article.

Column	Datatype	Description
articleid	rs_id	Article ID.
wclauseid	rs_id	Where clause ID.
type	int	0x01 - Range
		0x02 - Equality

Indexes

Unique clustered index on (wclauseid)

Appendix B

Replication Server Command Syntax

---

abort switch

abort switch for logical_ds.logical_database

Aborts the attempt to switch the active database in a warm standby environment.

activate subscription

activate subscription sub_name

for {table_rep_def | function_rep_def | publication pub_name

with primary at data_server.database}

with replicate at data_server.database

[with suspension [at active replicate only]]

Starts the distribution of updates from the primary to the replicate database for a subscription.

add partition

add partition logical_name on 'physical_name' with size size
[starting at vstart]

Adds a disk partition to Replication Server.

admin disk_space

admin disk_space

Displays the disk space usage.

admin echo

admin echo, character_string

Echoes the character string to the terminal.

admin get_generation

admin get_generation, data_server, database

Displays the generation number for the database.

admin health

admin health

Displays the Replication Server status.

admin log_name

admin log_name

Displays the path to the error log.

admin logical_status

admin logical_status [, logical_ds, logical_db]

Displays the logical connection status.

admin pid

admin pid

Displays the Replication Server process ID.

admin quiesce_check

admin quiesce_check

Checks to see if the Replication Server queues have been quiesced.

admin quiesce_force_rsi

admin quiesce_force_rsi

Checks to see if the Replication Server queues have been quiesced and forces delivery of RSI and DSI transactions.

admin rssd_name

admin rssd_name

Displays the RSSD server and database name.

admin security_property

admin security_property [, mechanism_name]

Displays the network security mechanisms and services.

admin security_setting

admin security_setting [, rs_idserver |, rs_server |, data_server.database]

Displays the Replication Server network based security parameters.

admin set_log_name

admin set_log_name, log_file

Closes the existing Replication Server log file and opens a new log file.

admin show_connections

admin show_connections

Displays information of RSI and DSI connections.

admin show_function_classes

admin show_function_classes

Displays function classes and their parents/inheritance.

admin show_route_versions

admin show_route_versions

Displays version numbers of routes to and from the Replication Server.

admin show_site_version

admin show_site_version

Displays the Replication Server site version.

admin sqm_readers

admin sqm_readers, q_number, q_type

Displays the read and delete points of the threads that are reading a stable queue.

admin statistics

admin statistics, {mem | md | reset}

Displays memory and message delivery statistics.

admin version

admin version

Displays the Replication Server version number.

admin who

admin who [, {dist | dsi | rsi | sqm | sqt}]

Displays information on the Replication Server queues.

admin who_is_down

admin who_is_down

Displays the threads that are down.

admin who_is_up

admin who_is_up

Displays the threads that are up.

allow connections

allow connections

Allows connection requests from LTMs started in recovery mode.

alter connection

alter connection to data_server.database {
set function string class [to] function_class |
set error class [to] error_class |
set password [to] passwd |
set log transfer [to] {on | off} |
set database_param [to] 'value' |
set security_param [to] 'value' |
set security_services [to] 'default']

Alters the properties of a database connection.

alter function

alter function table_rep_def.function_name
add parameters @param_name datatype [, @param_name datatype]...

Adds parameters to a user-defined function.

alter function replication definition

alter function replication definition function_rep_def
{deliver as 'proc_name' |
add @param_name datatype [, @param_name datatype]... |
add searchable parameters @param_name [, @param_name]... |
send standby {all | replication definition} parameters}

Alters the properties of a function replication definition.

alter function string

alter function string
[replication_definition.]function[;function_string]
for function_class
[scan 'input_template']
[output {language 'lang_output_template' |

rpc 'execute procedure

        [@param_name=]{constant I ?variable!mod?}

        [, [@param_name=]{constant I ?variable!mod?}]...' I

writetext [use primary log I with log Ino log] I none}]

Alters the properties of a function string.

alter function string class

alter function string class function_class

set parent to {parent_class I null}

Alters the status (base/derived) of a function string class.

alter logical connection

alter logical connection to logical_ds.logical_db {

set distribution {on I off} I

set logical_database_param to 'value' I

set send_truncate_table to {on I off} }

Alters the properties of a logical connection.

alter replication definition

alter replication definition replication_definition

{with replicate table named [table_owner.]'table_name' I

alter columns with column_name as replicate_column_name

    [, column_name as replicate_column_name]... I

add column_name [as replicate_column_name] [datatype [null I not null]]

    [, column_name [as replicate_column_name]

[datatype [null I not null]]]... I

add searchable columns column_name [, column_name]... I

send standby [off I {all I replication definition} columns] I

replicate {minimal I all} columns I

     replicate_if_changed column_name [, column_name]... |

     always_replicate column_name [, column_name]...}

Alters the properties of a replication definition.

alter route

     alter route to dest_replication_server {

     set next site [to] thru_replication_server |

     set username [to] 'user' set password [to] 'passwd' |

     set password [to] 'passwd' |

     set route_param [to] 'value' |

     set security_param [to] 'value' |

     set security_services [to] 'default' }

Alters the properties of a route.

alter user

     alter user user_name set password {new_passwd | null}

     [verify password old_passwd]

Alters the password of a user.

assign action

     assign action

     {ignore | warn | retry_log | log | retry_stop | stop_replication}

     for error_class

     to data_server_error [, data_server_error]...

Assign an error action in an error class to a data server error number.

check publication

     check publication pub_name

     with primary at data_server.database

Displays the publication status and the number of articles.

check subscription

check subscription sub_name

for {table_rep_def | function_rep_def | publication pub_name

with primary at data_server.database}

with replicate at data_server.database

Displays the subscription status.

configure connection

configure connection to data_server.database {

set function string class [to] function_class |

set error class [to] error_class |

set password [to] passwd |

set log transfer [to] {on | off} |

set database_param [to] 'value' |

set security_param [to] 'value' |

set security_services [to] 'default']

Configures a database connection.

configure logical connection

configure logical connection

to logical_ds.logical_db {

set distribution {on | off} |

set logical_database_param to 'value' |

set send_truncate_table to {on | off} }

Configures a logical database connection.

configure replication server

configure replication server {

set repserver_param to 'value' |
set route_param to 'value' |
set database_param to 'value' |
set logical_database_param to 'value'
set security_param to 'value' |
set id_security_param to 'value' |
set security_services [to] 'default' }

Configures the Replication Server.

configure route

configure route to dest_replication_server {
set next site [to] thru_replication_server |
set username [to] 'user' set password [to] 'passwd' |
set password [to] 'passwd' |
set route_param [to] 'value' |
set security_param [to] 'value' |
set security_services [to] 'default' }

Configures a route.

create article

create article article_name for pub_name
with primary at data_server.database
with replication definition {table_rep_def | function_rep_def}
[where {column_name | @param_name} {< | > | >= | <= | = | &} value
[and {column_name | @param_name} {< | > | >= | <= | = | &} value]...
[or where {column_name | @param_name} {< | > | >= | <= | = | &} value
[and {column_name | @param_name} {< | > | >= | <= | = | &} value]...]...]

Creates an article.

create connection

create connection to data_server.database

set error class [to] error_class

set function string class [to] function_class

set username [to] user

[set password [to] passwd]

[set database_param [to] 'value']

[set security_param [to] 'value']

[with {log transfer on, dsi_suspended}]

[as active for logical_ds.logical_db |

as standby for logical_ds.logical_db

[use dump marker]]

Creates a database connection.

create error class

create error class error_class

Creates and error class.

create function

create function replication_definition.function

([@param_name datatype [, @param_name datatype]...])

Creates a user defined function.

create function replication definition

create function replication definition function_rep_def

with primary at data_server.database

[deliver as 'proc_name']

([@param_name datatype [, @param_name datatype]...])

[searchable parameters (@param_name [, @param_name]...)]

[send standby {all | replication definition} parameters]

Creates a function replication definition.

create function string

create function string
[replication_definition.]function[;function_string]

for function_class [with overwrite]

[scan 'input_template']

[output {language 'lang_output_template' |

    rpc 'execute procedure

     [@param_name=]{constant | ?variable!mod?}

     [, [@param_name=] {constant | ?variable!mod?}]...' |

writetext [use primary log | with log | no log] | none}]

Creates a function string.

create function string class

create function string class function_class
[set parent to parent_class]

Creates a function string class.

create logical connection

create logical connection to data_server.database

Creates a logical database connection.

create publication

create publication pub_name with primary at data_server.database

Creates a publication.

create replication definition

create replication definition replication_definition
with primary at data_server.database
[with all tables named [table_owner.]'table_name' |
[with primary table named [table_owner.]'table_name']
[with replicate table named [table_owner.]'table_name']]
(column_name [as replicate_column_name] [datatype [null | not null]]
[, column_name [as replicate_column_name]
[datatype [null | not null]]]...)
primary key (column_name [, column_name]...)
[searchable columns (column_name [, column_name]...)]
[send standby [{all | replication definition} columns]]
[replicate {minimal | all} columns]
[replicate_if_changed (column_name [, column_name]...)]
[always_replicate (column_name [, column_name]...)]

Creates a table replication definition.

create route

create route to dest_replication_server {
set next site [to] thru_replication_server |
[set username [to] user]
[set password [to] passwd]
[set rsi_batch_size [to] 'value']
[set route_param to 'value']
[set security_param to 'value'] }

Creates a route.

create subscription

create subscription sub_name
   for {table_rep_def | function_rep_def | publication pub_name
   with primary at data_server.database}
   with replicate at data_server.database
   [where {column_name | @param_name} {< | > | >= | <= | = | &} value
   [and {column_name | @param_name} {< | > | >= | <= | = | &} value]...]
   [without holdlock | incrementally | without materialization]
   [subscribe to truncate table]
   [for new articles]

Creates a subscription.

create user

create user user_name set password {passwd | null}

Creates a user.

define subscription

define subscription sub_name
   for {table_rep_def | function_rep_def | publication pub_name
   with primary at data_server.database}
   with replicate at data_server.database
   [where {column_name | @param_name} {< | > | >= | <= | = | &} value
   [and {column_name | @param_name} {< | > | >= | <= | = | &} value]...]
   [subscribe to truncate table]
   [for new articles]

Creates a subscription when using bulk materialisation.

drop article

**drop article article_name for pub_name
with primary at data_server.database
[drop_repdef]**

Drops an article.

drop connection

drop connection to data_server.database

Drops a database connection.

drop error class

drop error class error_class

Drops an error class.

drop function

drop function [replication_definition.]function

Drops a user defined function.

drop function replication definition

drop function replication definition function_rep_def

Drops a function replication definition.

drop function string

**drop function string
[replication_definition.]function[;function_string | all]
for function_class**

Drops a function string.

drop function string class

drop function string class function_class

Drops a function string class.

drop logical connection

drop logical connection to data_server.database

Drops a logical database connection.

drop partition

drop partition logical_name

Drops a disk partition.

drop publication

drop publication pub_name
with primary at data_server.database
[drop_repdef]

Drops a publication.

drop replication definition

drop replication definition replication_definition

Drops a replication definition.

drop route

drop route to dest_replication_server [with nowait]

Drops a route.

drop subscription

drop subscription sub_name
for {table_rep_def | function_rep_def |

{article article_name in pub_name | publication pub_name}
with primary at data_server.database}
with replicate at data_server.database
[without purge [with suspension [at active replicate only]] |
[incrementally] with purge]

Drops a subscription.

drop user

drop user user

Drops a user.

grant

grant {sa | create object | primary subscribe | connect source}
to user

Grants permissions to users.

ignore loss

ignore loss from data_server.database
[to {data_server.database | replication_server}]

Instructs Replication Server to accept messages after a loss has been detected.

move primary

move primary of {error class | function string class} class_name
to replication_server

Specifies the primary site for a function string class or an error class.

rebuild queues

rebuild queues

Rebuilds stable queues from a failed partition.

resume connection

resume connection to data_server.database
[skip transaction | execute transaction]

Resumes a database connection.

resume distributor

resume distributor data_server.database

Resumes a distributor thread.

resume log transfer

resume log transfer from {data_server.database | all}

Instructs the Replication Server to accept connections for the LTM.

resume route

resume route to dest_replication_server

Resumes a route.

revoke

revoke {sa | connect source | create object | primary subscribe}
from user

Revokes permissions from users.

route_upgrade

route_upgrade source_rep_server.dest_rep_server

Upgrades a route to Replication Server 11.5.

route_upgrade_recovery

route_upgrade_recovery source_rep_server.dest_rep_server

Recovers a failed route upgrade.

route_upgrade_status

route_upgrade_status

Displays the routes that need to be upgraded or recovered.

set autocorrection

set autocorrection {on | off} for replication_definition with replicate at data_server.database

Sets autocorrection for a database.

set log recovery

set log recovery for data_server.database

Specifies databases whose logs are to be recovered from offline dumps.

set proxy

set proxy [to] [user_name [verify password passwd]]

Switches to another user.

shutdown

shutdown

Shuts down the Replication Server.

suspend connection

suspend connection to data_server.database [with nowait]

Suspends a database connection.

suspend distributor

suspend distributor data_server.database

Suspends a distributor thread.

suspend log transfer

suspend log transfer from {data_server.database | all}

Instructs the Replication Server to refuse connections from the LTM.

suspend route

suspend route to dest_replication_server

Suspends a route.

switch active

switch active for logical_ds.logical_database to data_server.database [with suspension]

Changes the active database in a warm standby application.

sysadmin apply_truncate_table

sysadmin apply_truncate_table data_server, database, {table_owner | ''}, table_name {'on'| 'off'}

Enables or disables replication of **truncate table**.

sysadmin dropdb

sysadmin dropdb, data_server, database

Drops a database from the ID Server.

sysadmin dropldb

sysadmin dropldb, data_server, database

Drops a logical database from the ID Server.

sysadmin drop_queue

sysadmin drop_queue, q_number, q_type

Drops a stable queue.

sysadmin droprs

sysadmin droprs, replication_server

Drops a Replication Server from the ID Server.

sysadmin dump_file

sysadmin dump_file [, file_name]

Specifies the log file when dumping a Replication Server stable queue.

sysadmin dump_queue

sysadmin dump_queue, q_number, q_type, seg, blk, cnt [, RSSD | client]

Dumps a stable queue.

sysadmin fast_route_upgrade

sysadmin fast_route_upgrade, dest_replication_server

Updates the route version to Replication Server 11.5.

sysadmin hibernate_off

sysadmin hibernate_off [, string_ID]

Switches Replication Server from hibernation mode to active mode.

sysadmin hibernate_on

sysadmin hibernate_on [, string_ID]

Switches Replication Server from active to hibernation mode.

sysadmin log_first_tran

sysadmin log_first_tran, data_server, database

Writes the first transaction in a DSI queue into the exceptions log.

sysadmin purge_all_open

sysadmin purge_all_open, q_number, q_type

Clears all open transactions from a queue.

sysadmin purge_first_open

sysadmin purge_first_open, q_number, q_type

Clears the first open transaction from a queue.

sysadmin purge_route_at_replicate

sysadmin purge_route_at_replicate, replication_server

Removes all references to a primary Replication Server from a replicate Replication Server.

sysadmin restore_dsi_saved_segments

sysadmin restore_dsi_saved_segments, data_server, database

Restores transactions held in a queue because of a save interval.

sysadmin set_dsi_generation

**sysadmin set_dsi_generation,
gen_number, primary_data_server, primary_database,
replicate_data_server, replicate_database**

Changes a database generation number in the Replication Server.

sysadmin site_version

sysadmin site_version [, version]

Sets the site version number for the Replication Server.

sysadmin sqm_purge_queue

sysadmin sqm_purge_queue, q_number, q_type

Clears all messages from a stable queue.

sysadmin sqm_unzap_command

sysadmin sqm_unzap_command, q_number, q_type, seg, blk, row

Undeletes a message in a stable queue.

sysadm sqm_zap_command

sysadm sqm_zap_command, q_number, q_type, seg, blk, row

Deletes a message in a stable queue.

sysadmin sqt_dump_queue

sysadmin sqt_dump_queue, q_number, q_type, reader [, open]

Dumps the transaction cache for an inbound or a DSI queue.

sysadmin system_version

sysadmin system_version [, version]

Displays or sets the version number for the replication system.

validate publication

validate publication pub_name with primary at data_server.database

Sets the status of a publication to VALID.

validate subscription

validate subscription sub_name
for {table_rep_def | function_rep_def | publication pub_name
with primary at data_server.database}
with replicate at data_server.database

Sets the status of a subscription to VALID.

wait for create standby

wait for create standby for logical_ds.logical_database

Blocks a client session in the Replication Server until the standby database creation process is complete.

wait for switch

wait for switch for logical_ds.logical_database

Blocks a client session in the Replication Server until the switch to the new active database is complete.

Appendix C

RSSD
System
Procedures

rs_capacity

rs_capacity TranDuration, FailDuration, SaveInterval, MatRows

Estimates stable queue size requirements.

rs_configure

rs_configure [config_param [, value]]

Displays or changes Replication Server configuration parameters.

rs_delexception

rs_delexception [transaction_id]

Displays or deletes transactions in the exceptions log.

rs_fillcaptable

rs_fillcaptable RepDefName, InChRateI, InChRateD, InChRateU, OutChRateI, OutChRateD, OutChRateU, InTranRate, OutTranRate, DelFlag

Records estimated transaction rates in the *rs_captable* table for an existing replication definition.

rs_helpclass

rs_helpclass [class_name]

Displays help on function string and error classes.

rs_helpclassfstring

rs_helpclassfstring class_name [, function_name]

Displays help on function strings with function string class scope.

rs_helpdb

rs_helpdb [data_server, database]

Displays help on databases.

rs_helperror

rs_helperror server_error_number [, v]

Displays help on error numbers.

rs_helpexception

rs_helpexception [transaction_id, [, v]]

Displays exception log information.

rs_helpfstring

rs_helpfstring replication_definition [, function_name]

Displays help on function strings.

rs_helpfunc

rs_helpfunc [replication_definition [, function_name]]

Displays help on functions.

rs_helppartition

rs_helppartition [partition_name]

Displays disk partition usage.

rs_helppub

rs_helppub
[publication_name, primary_dataserver, primary_db [, article_name]]

Displays help on publications.

rs_helppubsub

rs_helppubsub subscription_name, publication_name,
    primary_dataserver, primary_db,
    replicate_dataserver, replicate_database

Displays help on publication subscriptions.

rs_helprep

rs_helprep [replication_definition]

Displays help on replication definitions.

rs_helprepdb

rs_helprepdb [data_server, database]

Displays help on databases with subscriptions for replication definitions in the current Replication Server.

rs_helpreptable

rs_helpreptable <database>, [<owner>], <table>

Displays help on replication definitions created against a primary table.

rs_helproute

rs_helproute [replication_server]

Displays help on routes.

rs_helpsub

rs_helpsub [subscription_name [, replication_definition [, data_server, database]]]

Displays help on subscriptions.

rs_helpuser

rs_helpuser [user]

Displays help on users.

rs_init_erroractions

rs_init_erroractions new_error_class, template_class

Initializes a new error class.

rs_zeroltm

rs_zeroltm data_server, database

Resets the locator value for a database to zero.

Appendix D

ASE Commands and System Procedures

dbcc dbrepair

dbcc dbrepair(database_name, ltmignore)

Turns off replication for an offline database that has a valid secondary truncation point.

dbcc gettrunc

dbcc gettrunc

Displays LTM status.

dbcc settrunc

dbcc settrunc('ltm', {'valid' | 'ignore'})
dbcc settrunc('ltm', 'gen_id', db_generation)

Modifies LTM truncation point and generation id.

set replication

set replication ['on' | 'force_ddl' | 'default' | 'off']

Enables or disables replication of data definition language (DDL) and/or data manipulation language (DML) commands to the standby database.

sp_configure

sp_configure 'enable rep agent threads'[, 1 | 0]

Enables or disables RepAgent thread integration in the Adaptive Server.

sp_config_rep_agent

sp_config_rep_agent [dbname [,
{'enable', 'repserver_name', 'repserver_username',
'repserver_password'}|

'disable'[, 'preserve secondary truncpt'] |

'rs_servername', 'repserver_name',
        'rs_username', 'repserver_username',
            'rs_password', 'repserver_password' |

'scan_batch_size', 'no_of_qualifying_log_records' |

'scan_timeout', 'scan_timeout_in_seconds' |

'retry_timeout', 'retry_timeout_in_seconds' |

'fade_timeout', 'fade_timeout_in_seconds' |

'skip_ltl_errors', {'true' | 'false'} |

'batch_ltl', {'true' | 'false'} |

'send_warm_standby_xacts', {'true' | 'false'} |

'connect_dataserver', 'connect_dataserver_name' |

'connect_database', 'connect_database_name' |

'send_maint_xacts_to_replicate',{'true' | 'false'} |

'security_mechanism', 'mechanism_name' |

'unified_login', {'true' | 'false' }|

'mutual_authentication', {'true' | 'false' } |

'msg_confidentiality', {'true' | 'false' } |

'msg_integrity', {'true' | 'false' } |

'msg_replay_detection', {'true' | 'false' } |

'msg_origin_check', {'true' | 'false' } |

'msg_out_of_sequence check {'true' | 'false' }]]

Changes or displays the configuration parameters for the RepAgent thread.

sp_help_rep_agent

sp_help_rep_agent [dbname
[, 'recovery' | 'config' | 'process' | 'scan' | 'security' | 'all']]

Displays information about a RepAgent thread.

sp_reptostandby

sp_reptostandby dbname [, 'L1' | 'all' | 'none']

Sets or unsets replication to the standby database.

sp_start_rep_agent

sp_start_rep_agent dbname[, 'for_recovery'
[, 'connect_dataserver', 'connect_database'
[, 'repserver_name', repserver_username', 'repserver_password']]]

Starts a RepAgent thread for the specified database.

sp_stop_rep_agent

sp_stop_rep_agent dbname[, 'nowait']

Stops a RepAgent thread for the specified database.

sp_setrepcol

sp_setrepcol table_name [, {column_name | null}
[, { do_not_replicate | always_replicate | replicate_if_changed}]]

Sets or displays the replication status for *text* and *image* columns.

sp_setrepdefmode

sp_setrepdefmode table_name [,{'owner_on' | 'owner_off'}]

Changes or displays the owner status of tables marked for replication.

sp_setreplicate

sp_setreplicate [object_name [, {'true' | 'false'}]]

Changes or displays the replication status for an table or stored procedure.

sp_setrepproc

sp_setrepproc [proc_name [, {'function' | 'table' | 'false'}]]

Changes or displays the replication status for a stored procedure.

sp_setreptable

**sp_setreptable [table_name [, {'true' | 'false'}
[, {owner_on | owner_off}]]]**

Changes or displays the replication status for a table.

Appendix E

Replication Server Programs

ltm

The LTM executable.

ltm [-C config_file] [-S ltm_name] [-I interfaces_file] [-E errorlog_file] [-M] [-A] [-W] [-v]

where

-C	Configuration file location.
-S	LTM name.
-I	Interfaces file location.
-E	Error log location.
-M	Recovery mode.
-A	Include updates made by the maintenance user.
-W	Active LTM for warm standby.
-v	Displays version number.

repserver

The Replication Server executable.

repserver [-C config_file] [-i id_server] [-S rs_name] [-I interfaces_file] [-E errorlog_file] [-M] [-v] [-K keytab_file]

where

-C	Configuration file location.
-i	ID Server name.
-S	Replication Server name.
-I	Interfaces file location.
-E	Error log location.
-M	Recovery mode.

-v   Displays version number.

-K   Specifies the name and location of the DCE keytab file that contains the security credential for the user logging into the server.

rs_subcmp

The **rs_subcmp** executable compares the primary and replicate versions of a table, locating and optionally reconciling any missing, orphaned or inconsistent rows. Reconciliation of the data consists of insert/update/delete against the replicate data to make it the same as the primary. The differences are classified as:

Missing   Exists at the primary but not at the replicate. The row is inserted at the replicate.

Orphaned   Exists at the replicate but not at the primary. The row is deleted from the replicate.

Inconsistent   The primary keys match at primary and replicate but other columns are different. The replicate row is updated to the primary values.

rs_subcmp [-R | -r] [-v] [-V] [-z[1 | 2]]

[-f config_file] [-F]

[-S primary_ds] [-D primary_db] -s replicate_ds [-d replicate_db]

[-t table_name] [-T primary_table_name]

[-c select_command] [-C primary_select_command]

[-u user] [-U primary_user] [-p passwd] [-P primary_passwd]

[-B primary_init_batch] [-b replicate_init_batch]

[-n num_iterations] [-w wait_interval]

[-e float_precision] [-E real_precision]

[-k primary_key_column [-k primary_key_column]...]

[-i identity_column]

[-l text_image_column_name [-l text_image_column_name]...]

[-N text_image_column_name [-N text_image_column_name]...]

[-Z language] [-o sort_order] [-J rs_subcmp_charset] [-j rep_charset]

[-a replicate_column_name primary_column_name

[-a replicate_column_name primary_column_name]...]

where

-R	Reconciles the replicate data with the primary data making a final verification of any data inconsistencies at the primary database.
-r	Reconciles the replicate data with the primary data without making a final verification of any data inconsistencies at the primary database.
-v	Displays version information.
-V	Displays the results of the comparison. Text and image data are reported without the associated data values.
-z	Enables trace information.

       -z1   The default which provides basic trace information.

       -z2   Information on comparisons of all rows and commands.

-f config_file	Specifies the name of the configuration file for **rs_subcmp**. The syntax of **rs_subcmp** is not simple and recommendation is to use a configuration file.
-F	Displays the format (syntax) to use for the configuration file.

-S primary_ds

       The name of the data server containing the primary data for the subscription.

-D primary_database

       The name of the database containing the primary data for the subscription.

-s replicate_ds

       The name of the data server containing the replicate copy of the data.

-d replicate_database

       The name of the database containing the replicate copy of the data.

-t table_name The name of the table in the primary and replicate databases containing the data to be compared.

-T primary_table_name

> The name of the table in the primary database. Use this option when the table name is different in the primary and replicate databases.

-c select_command

> A **select** command that retrieves the data from both the primary and replicate copies of the data. Text and image datatypes may be included with the restrictions:
>
> - They cannot be primary key columns.
> - They must be placed at the end of the select list.
> - By default, the replicate table must not allow null values for the columns. To allow nulls you must use the –N parameter.
>
> The **select** command must order the data based on the primary key.

-C primary_select_command

> The **select** command that retrieves the data from the primary copy of the data. Use this option and -c when you need a different **select** command for the primary and replicate databases. The **select** command must order the data based on the primary key.

-u user   The login name used to log into the primary and replicate data servers.

-U primary_user

> The login name used to log into the primary data server. Use this option and the -u option when different login names are required for the primary and replicate data servers.

-p passwd   The password to use with the user login name and, if supplied, the *primary_user* login name.

-P primary_passwd

> The password to use with the *primary_user* login name.

-B primary_init_batch

> The command batch to be executed when initially connecting to the primary database. The batch is run after **rs_subcmp** logs into the primary database.

-b replicate_init_batch

> The command batch to be executed when initially connecting to the replicate database. The batch is run after **rs_subcmp** logs into the replicate database.

-n num_iterations

> The number of times that **rs_subcmp** examines the inconsistent rows that it locates. The default is 10 iterations.

-w wait_interval

> The number of seconds **rs_subcmp** waits before beginning another iteration. The default is 5 seconds.

-e float_precision

> The number of decimal places for floating point values. Defaults to the maximum precision supported by the platform.

-E real_precision

> The number of decimal places for real values. Defaults to the maximum precision supported by the platform.

-k primary_key_column

> The column names that constitute the primary key for the table. The primary key column cannot be a text or image column. Use the –k option for each column in the primary key. If the primary and replicate column names are different, the name specified here is the replicate column name.

-i identity_column

> The name of the identity column in the replicate table.

-l text_image_column_name

> Turns off logging of updates to a replicate text or image column. By default, text and image column updates are logged.

-N text_image_column_name

> Indicates that a null value is allowed in the text or image column of the replicate table. By default, the replicate table does not allow null values for text or image columns.

-Z language   The name of the language in which **rs_subcmp** generates error and informational messages. Defaults to the "default" locale entry for the platform.

-o sort_order The name of the sort order used in your replication system. The **rs_subcmp** program uses this information when comparing column names.

-J rs_subcmp_charset

The name of the character set used by **rs_subcmp** error and informational messages and in all configuration parameters and command line options. Defaults to the "default" locale entry for your platform.

-j rep_charset

The name of the character set used by the replicate data server. Defaults to the *rs_subcmp_charset* character set.

-a replicate_column_name primary_column_name

Specifies the primary column name associated with a replicate column. Use this option if a replicate column name is different from that of the primary column.

rs_subcmp –r –f$SYBASE/etc/rs_sub_cmp.cfg –tCUSTOMERS

-c"select * from CUSTOMERS order by last_name, first_name"

-klast_name –kfirst_name

with a configuration file of:

PDS = PLN_MKT

RDS = PNY_MKT

PDB = SALES_DB

RDB = SALES_DB

PUSER = sa

RUSER = sa

PPWD = sa_pw

RPWD = sa_pw

Configuration file parameters are shown in table E.1.

Configuration Parameter	Command Line Option	Value
PDS	-S	Primary data server name.
RDS	-s	Replicate data server name.
PDB	-D	Primary database name.
RDB	-d	Replicate database name.
PTABLE	-T	Primary table name.
RTABLE	-t	Replicate table name.
PUSER	-U	Primary user name.
RUSER	-u	Replicate user name.
PPWD	-P	Primary password.
RPWD	-p	Replicate password.
KEY	-k	Primary key column in replicate table.
PINITBATCH	-B	Primary database connection initialization batch.
RINITBATCH	-b	Replicate database connection initialization batch.
PSELECT	-C	Primary select command.
RSELECT	-c	Replicate select command.
RECONCILE	-r	Reconcile differences (Y or N).
RECONCILE_CHECK	-R	Reconcile differences with primary verification (Y or N).
TRACE	-z	Enable trace.
FPRECISION	-e	Expected floating point precision.
RPRECISION	-E	Expected real precision.
WAIT	-w	Seconds between comparisons.
NUM_TRIES	-n	Number of comparisons.
VISUAL	-V	Print results (Y or N).
IDENTITY	-I	Identity column name in replicate table.
NO_LOG	-l	Do not log updates for this replicate text or image column.

NULLABLE	-N	The text or image column in the replicate table accepts null values.
LANGUAGE	-Z	Language of error and informational messages.
SORT_ORDER	-o	Name of the sort order used in your replication system.
SCHARSET	-J	Character set.
RCHARSET	-j	Character set of the replicate data server.
REP_PRI_COLNAME	-a	Replicate-Primary column name pair.

Table E.1: rs_subcmp configuration file parameters

Configuration file entries have the format:

parameter_name = value

If a parameter can span multiple lines the newline characters are preceded by a backslash "\". Up to 1024 characters per line with a maximum of 64K characters.

If both a command line option and a configuration file parameter are quoted, the command line option takes precedence.

The **select** commands must return the same column names and datatypes from both databases.

Index